BLOOMSBURY AESTHETICS AND THE NOVELS OF FORSTER AND WOOLF

By the same author

NOVELISTS ON NOVELISTS

BLOOMSBURY AESTHETICS AND THE NOVELS OF FORSTER AND WOOLF

David Dowling

St. Martin's Press   New York

© David Dowling 1985

All rights reserved. For information, write:
St. Martin's Press, Inc., 175 Fifth Avenue, New York, NY 10010
Printed in Hong Kong
Published in the United Kingdom by The Macmillan Press Ltd
First published in the United States of America in 1985

ISBN 0–312–08517–6

Library of Congress Cataloging in Publication Data

Dowling, David
  Bloomsbury aesthetics and the novels of Forster and
Woolf.

  Bibliography: p.
  Includes index.
  1. English fiction – 20th century – History and criticism.
2. Forster, E. M. (Edward Morgan), 1879–1970 – Criticism
and interpretation.   3. Woolf, Virginia, 1882–1941 –
Criticism   and   interpretation.   4. Bloomsbury   group.
5. Aesthetics, British.   6. Art and literature – England –
London.   I. Title.
<u>PR881.D68   1985</u>   823'.912   83–40124

ISBN 0–312–08517–6

To Shawna

How difficult criticism is! Not a single word has the same meaning for two people.

Virginia Woolf, *Letters*, III, p. 20

If we wheel up an aesthetic theory – the best attainable, and there are some excellent ones – if we wheel it up and apply it with its measuring rods and pliers and forceps, its calipers and catheters . . . we are visited at once by a sense of the grotesque. It doesn't work. . . .There is no spiritual parity.

E. M. Forster, 'The *Raison d'Être* of Criticism in the Arts', in *Two Cheers for Democracy*

Contents

List of Plates

Plates 1, 2, 10, 11, 13–18, 20–22 and 24 are reproduced by kind permission of Mrs Angelica Garnett; Plate 3 is reproduced by kind permission of Islington Libraries; Plates 4, 6 and 19 are reproduced by kind permission of Mrs Pamela Diamond; Plate 5 is reproduced courtesy of the Provost and Fellows of King's College Cambridge; Plate 12 is reproduced courtesy of the Imperial War Museum; and Plate 23 is reproduced courtesy of the Tate Gallery.

Acknowledgements

The section on *Jacob's Room* in Chapter 7 first appeared as 'Virginia Woolf's Own *Jacob's Room*' in *Southern Review*, vol. 15, no. 1 (March 1982) pp. 60–72, and Chapter 6, 'Woolf and Painting', first appeared, in substantially the same form, as 'The Aesthetic Education of Virginia Woolf' in *The Journal of Aesthetic Education*, vol. 17, no.2 (1983) pp. 71–82. The author should like to thank the editors of these journals for permission to reprint this material.

The author and publishers wish to thank the following who have kindly given permission for the use of copyright material:

The Hogarth Press Ltd and the Literary Estate of Virginia Woolf, and Harcourt Brace Jovanovich Inc., for the extracts from *Night and Day*, *To the Lighthouse*, *The Waves*, *Between the Acts* and *A Writer's Diary* by Virginia Woolf; copyright 1920 by George H. Doran Co.; copyright 1927, 1931, 1941 by Harcourt Brace Jovanovich Inc.; copyright 1948, 1953, 1954, 1955, 1959, 1969 by Leonard Woolf; copyright 1981, 1982 by Quentin Bell and Angelica Garnett.

Editions Cited

Page references are to the following editions.

E. M. FORSTER

Where Angels Fear to Tread, in *Collected Forster* (London: Heinemann/Octopus, 1978).
A Room with a View, ibid.
The Longest Journey, ibid.
Maurice (Toronto: Macmillan, 1971).
Howards End, Abinger edn (London: Edward Arnold, 1973).
A Passage to India (London: Edward Arnold, 1947).

VIRGINIA WOOLF

The Voyage Out (Harmondsworth: Penguin, 1970).
Night and Day (London: Hogarth, 1919).
Jacob's Room (Harmondsworth: Penguin, 1965).
Mrs Dalloway (Harmondsworth: Penguin, 1964).
To the Lighthouse (St Albans: Triad/Panther, 1977).
Orlando (Harmondsworth: Penguin, 1942).
The Waves (Harmondsworth: Penguin, 1964).
The Years (London: Hogarth, 1937).
Between the Acts (Harmondsworth: Penguin, 1972).

Introduction: Painting and Writing

Yes, gentlemen of letters, you are not capable of criticising a work of art, or even a book.[1]

Jeffrey Meyers begins his book *Painting and the Novel* with a quotation from Baudelaire: 'A characteristic symptom of the spiritual condition of our century is that all the arts tend, if not to act as a substitute for each other, at least to supplement each other, by lending each other new strength and new resources.'[2] That statement might be clarified by stipulating that it deals with artists rather than with art consumers, for the latter have enjoyed the various arts for centuries by appropriating from one the terms of enjoyment for another.

The 'locus classicus' is, of course, Horace's *ut pictura poesis*. The original context, the complaint that some poems can be exhausted at one glance, has greater relevance to the contemporary state of critical affairs than the usual way that phrase is understood to signify a simple, two-way analogy. That idea is more clearly stated in a remark attributed by Plutarch to Simonides of Ceos: 'painting is mute poetry and poetry a speaking picture'.

It was left to two German aestheticians to tease out the implications of these fragments, and particularly the meaning and import of that elusive middle term, speech or silence. In 1766 Lessing's *Laocöon* took up the matter, beginning, 'The first who likened painting and poetry to each other must have been a man of delicate perception. . . .' Lessing observes that in some senses the perceiver of a poem may receive the impression not of a succession of actions but of a whole; but he goes on to elucidate the real differences in form between painting and poetry. His example is the shield of Achilles, which, although it is essentially a painting, becomes in Homer's hands 'a thing in process . . . turning the co-existing of his design into a consecutive'.[3] Literature, Lessing

1

implies, is experienced in a temporal dimension as fine art is not

Schiller, in his letters on the aesthetic education of man, elucidated Horace's aphorism in terms of the observer, suggesting that the idea of the kinship of the arts has to do not with form (which Lessing showed to be a false idea anyway) but with the final aesthetic effect of great art on the consumer:

> It is an inevitable and natural consequence of their approach to perfection that the various arts, without any displacement of their objective frontiers, tend to become ever more like each other in their effect upon the psyche. . . . Poetry, when most fully developed, must grip us powerfully as music does, but at the same time, like the plastic arts, surround us with a serene clarity. This, precisely, is the mark of a perfect style in each and every art: that it is able to remove the specific limitations of the art in question without thereby destroying its specific qualities, and through a wise use of its individual peculiarities, is able to confer upon it a more general character.[4]

Schiller's is an extremely sophisticated argument, carrying with it as it does the difficult ideas of form and experience. Here poetry is capable of moving us with the rhythmic, temporal development of music, and at the same time pleases us by its sense of spatial shape.

The fine art of the Modern period – the art which Bloomsbury followed, popularised and contributed to – had often little to do with 'serene clarity'. In 1874 Jules Laforgue wrote 'The Impressionist Eye', which 'should know only luminous vibration'; which

> sees the real living lines built not in geometric forms but in a thousand irregular strokes, which, at a distance, establish life . . . perspective established by a thousand trivial touches of tone and brush, by the varieties of atmospheric states induced by moving planes.[5]

For Picasso, the nail was the undoer of painting; his canvases had a life of their own sustained by contact with viewers, not an abstract form to be put away and admired from time to time. Expressionist or Impressionist, what painting of the Modern period has in common (to simplify rather crudely) is a sense of the living canvas, implying a sense of the living viewer living with the painting. This development thus brought painting closer to the temporal world of literature in a way undreamt of by Horace or indeed Lessing.

It is instructive to see how two of the greatest contemporary aestheticians, Arnheim and Gombrich, deal with modern art. Both critics begin from a phenomenological study of perception, since that element has become crucial in the creation and consumption of modern art. Arnheim talks about 'the activity of perceptual forces' and, from a consideration of seeing as an active process of reading the message before one, infers that 'seeing is the perception of action'.[6] From this angle he can give a purely aesthetic account of such challenging formal works of art as Cubist paintings or film montages, for here the individual units 'must refute one another's solidity . . . only a delicate balancing of the innumerable forces meeting one another at innumerable angles can provide a semblance of unity'.[7] Arnheim is able to incorporate with ease into his aesthetic the temporal literary notion of narrative, treating what he calls the 'path of disclosure' as simply a formal element, and equating literature and painting as the spatialisation of intelligible facts into a harmonious balance; for instance,

> Just as the young Michelangelo's *Pièta* in St Peter's shows a mother holding her child and at the same time a man leaving his mother behind, so does the story of the Gospel, like every great narrative, contain its end in its beginning and its beginning in its end.[8]

Gombrich is not as sure as Arnheim about the intelligibility of form or the regularity of the perceptual process. In his essay 'How to Read a Painting' he asserts,

> Critics like to tell us how the artist 'leads the eye' along the main lines of his composition. But our roving eyes will not be thus led. The critic's phrase should have become obsolete when eye movements could be filmed and fixation points plotted on pictures. These records confirm what Escher made us suspect: Reading a picture is a piecemeal affair that starts with random shots and these are followed by a search for a coherent whole.[9]

By focusing on Escher, Gombrich reminds us that the willingness of the eye to arrange and order a painting in recognisable dimensions of space and time is precisely what limits our aesthetic development. Modern artists deliberately challenge those habitual patterns of appreciation in order to free us for pure aesthetic contemplation:

> At all times, of course, the aesthetics of picture-making had more to do with composition than with illusion. Artists have always been poets, striving to achieve a fine balance of shapes and colours and to devise a beautiful pattern to fill the painting surface in a pleasing way. But these efforts could easily be destroyed by the reading mind that rearranged these shapes in an imaginary depth. [10]

Although Gombrich stresses the aesthetic element of painting, he is able (because of his emphasis on perception) to make the leap to metaphysics more easily than Arnheim:

> The true miracle of the language of art is not that it enables the artist to create the illusion of reality. It is that under the hands of a great master the image becomes translucent. In teaching us to see the visible world afresh, he gives the illusion of looking into the invisible realms of the mind. [11]

It is possible, then, to make analogies between these two critics and Roger Fry and Clive Bell. Like Gombrich, Fry was alive to the two-dimensional picture and to the third dimension, and referred to the 'intractable material' which the artist is illuminating for us. Bell on the other hand, for all his easy equation of art with ethics and religion, saw art as essentially detached from life, illuminating it if at all only through the rather obvious narrative content of Arnheim's example. Ortega y Gasset, thinking of the appreciation of art as looking at a garden through a window, said, 'To see the garden and to see the windowpane are two incompatible operations which exclude one another because they require different adjustments.' [12] Bell preferred the windowpane, as Solomon Fishman observes: 'He is really voicing an innate preference for architectonic form. Bell's temperament inclined him towards what Heinrich Wölfflin distinguished as static as against dynamic form.' [13] Fry preferred the garden, rendered as form.

When painting reached such a sophisticated point of concentration on the painter's own processes of perception and those of his audience, art could really no longer be discussed in such crude terms as windowpane and garden, terms which assumed a distinction between observed and observer which was no longer valid. The possibilities for aesthetic creation were boundless. Kandinsky, for all his talk of art being like religion, 'showing new perspectives in a blinding light',[14] suggested this limitless freedom for self-expression independent of the shared physical world when he wrote, 'Painting is a thunderous collision of different worlds, intended to create a new world in, and from, the struggle with one another, a new world which is the work of art. . . . The creation of a work of art is the creation of the world.'[15] This suggests the conflicts, tensions and energies balanced into unity of Arnheim's artistic form. But Cézanne, whom Fry admired above all other painters, attempted to take his form from nature:

> He began with nature, looking at it with scrutiny and recognising its inherent individuality. He exploited its particular characteristics to develop a style which, he felt, corresponded as closely as possible to his aesthetic perception of nature, however much in a nonnaturalistic manner.[16]

This is part of a convincing essay divorcing Cézanne from Cubism; and, while the argument might seem peripheral, it brings us to a crucial point when we make the move from painting to literature.

I began by observing that the context of Horace's *ut pictura poesis* was a complaint about poems which could be too quickly grasped and exhausted. The assumption there was that painting is an immediate experience; but the attempt in modern art to render the life of the world or the life of the artist in the canvas itself has challenged that assumption. Gauguin in 1890 wrote, 'Like literature, the art of painting tells us whatever it wants, with the advantage of letting the reader immediately know the prelude, the direction, and the dénouement. Literature and music ask for an effort of memory to appreciate the whole.'[17] But in the painting of Cézanne, the element of time does come in. The objects themselves 'move' between the worlds of windowpane and garden, and the observer's pleasure comes from experiencing both dimensions in the same canvas, remembering one while experiencing the other. Fry puts it this way: 'Objects retain their abstract intelligibility, their amenity to the human mind, and regain that reality of actual things which is absent from all abstractions.'[18] And the idea of the possible temporality of painting is more exhaustively put by the philosopher Merleau-Ponty, again talking about Cézanne:

> Lived perspective, that which we actually perceive, is not a geometric or a photographic one. . . . It is Cézanne's genius that when the overall composition of the picture is seen globally, perspectival distortions are no longer visible in their own right, but rather contribute, as they do in natural vision, to the impression of an emerging order, of an object in the act of appearing, organizing itself before our very eyes.[19]

Here the idea of 'life' in painting is applied in a complex way, not to the interaction of elements on the canvas, or their referents, but to the interaction of canvas and viewer; it is the most sophisticated development of the emphasis on perception in aesthetics.

Painting can appear in the temporal form of the novel, which is my main concern here, in the obvious sense of a reference to a painting as part of the narrative. We shall find many instances of this in the novels of Woolf and Forster (especially the latter), and most often the writer's point is to tell us something about the viewer's state of mind. These references to paintings are in time and refer to development of character in time. Even painterly visions, as Edith Wharton observed, should in a novel refer to history: 'The impression produced by a landscape, a street or a house, should always, to the novelist, be an event in the history of a soul.'[20]

There is another sense in which a fiction can be related to a painting, in the sense of a piece of abstract art. This has been mainly a recent development, post-Joycean, such as in the works of Donald Barthelme (himself an art curator) where the literary object is a new creation to be added to the objects already in the world (or the gallery). But as a critic of Barthelme observes, the idea of the art object as object 'has never really caught on in fiction-writing',[21] because the medium of words always points elsewhere, to a real world outside the object. Sound and pigment can more easily be divorced from the 'ordinary' world than can words.

The third sense in which literature and painting can be related is the crucial one for this book: the sense that a novel should be *appreciated* in the same way as a painting is. The attempt to create literature which is immediately apprehensible in the way that paintings are (often mistakenly) assumed to be is also a modern phenomenon. In 1915 a movement called 'Simultanism' proclaimed, 'In literature the idea is expressed by the polyphony of simultaneous voices which say different things. Of course, printing is not an adequate medium, for succession in this medium is unavoidable and a phonograph is more suitable.'[22] One still cringes at the result of such an enterprise! But a more flexible analogy between painting and writing has long been a staple of literary critics and creators; its most eloquent exponents and explorers were Henry James and Marcel Proust.

James argued that literature, while it plucked its material from the garden of life, transformed it into an intelligible shape, 'life being all inclusion and confusion, and art being all discrimination and selection'. James used painterly terms such as 'foreshortening' but usually in a straightforward sense of the proportions within the work – the dominant characters, subordinate plots, and so on. Of paramount importance to a novel was its 'felt life' and the line of its plot since 'the soul of a novel is its action'. Aesthetics were predicated on human meaning:

> James disapproved of the Goncourts' attempt to 'poach' on the art of painting and was always severely critical of writers merely interested in pictorial descriptions and local colour. 'Picture' is not enough. Every good story is of course both a picture and an idea, and the more they are interfused the better the problem is solved.[23]

In *The Portrait of a Lady*, for example, Isabel Archer actually *becomes* a portrait – the term is not simply descriptive of the form of the novel. *The Ambassadors* has the celebrated hourglass form, but again that form serves to underline the progress of the characters in the novel. While James's use of painterly imagery in his prefaces did much to remind later writers that novel-writing was an art, he was limited in his own development of the implications of the analogy by his adherence to realism and to the simple unities of tone and story.

The French critic Georges Poulet has described Flaubert's style as 'a representation of life brought out of the past up to the present', so that even each periodic sentence echoes this synthesis into a unified present – 'time become a question of style'. [24] Proust, in *Time Regained,* reflects that 'a writer's style, and also a painter's, are matters not of technique but of vision'. [25] The perception that a writer's style may reveal or embody his world view is not a new one, but what Proust contributed to the idea of the novelist as painter or stylist was the dimension of human time or memory. 'Unlike the painter,' says Proust, 'the writer observes and abstracts the general truth beneath appearances.' Here again, Proust is working with a limited conception of painting, one which does not embrace the complexities of a Cézanne. But his point about the novelist can be reiterated in terms of time; that is, the novelist not only records the present moment but also unites it to reflections which draw upon the past to construct a system, a vision of life.

The artist's memory becomes the melting-pot where the continually changing present meets with the past to produce the artist's consciousness. As Roger Shattuck points out, the principle of Proust's great novel, like his principle of human psychology, is a 'stereoscopic' one, looking at the same material from two different perspectives. It

> selects a few images or impressions sufficiently different from one another not to give the effect of continuous motion, and sufficiently related to be linked in a discernible pattern. This stereoscopic principle allows our binocular (or multiocular) vision of mind to hold contradictory aspects of things in the steady perspective of recognition, of relief in time. [26]

The achievement is similar to that of Cézanne's paintings, where we recognise the pattern in space (the apples, say) but also appreciate the disparate elements making up the composition. Proust's novel is a temporal or linear demonstration of the same principle at work. As readers, and as viewers, we have to work at two operations at once, encountering the new and recognising the old. Proust's style, like Cézanne's, *is* vision.

The philosophical underpinning for Proust is of course provided by Bergson, a philosopher whose concept of *durée* or duration has also been freely applied to the characteristic style of stream of consciousness in Woolf. Bergson's exploration of memory is a counterpart to the modern aesthetician's exploration of perception, and it is particularly applicable to the kind of novel written by Forster and Woolf. Not yet completely experimental in form (some of Woolf's novels may be exempted here), these novels deal with the traditional central element of the novel, the Jamesian character. What gives a character a unity or significant form is memory, for, as Bergson observed, 'Every perception is already memory. Practically we perceive only the past.'[27] Memory is a way of linking time and space, the past with the present dramatic moment, just as for modern artists 'significant form' is a way of uniting time and space in the visual medium – things in space given a meaning in time. Duration, says Bergson, is 'a multiplicity of moments bound to one another by a unity which runs through them like a thread'.[28] That unity, which in James and the Victorian novelists was largely assumed, in the modern novel becomes problematic, and the novelist/painter focuses on the succession of moments.

These ideas will be developed fully in relation to the novels of Forster and Woolf; but, before proceeding to their specific aesthetics, I must observe that Bergson's psychological theories, like those of his aesthetic counterparts, can be applied to the actual processes of *reading* as much as to the development of the characters within the novel. The phenomenological analysis of the reading-process considers the reader as he proceeds through a novel, perceiving the text as the characters perceive the world, relying very much upon memory to create and recreate patterns. One of the leading researchers in this field, Wolfgang Iser, has described the reading-process in terms which could very easily be transferred to the criticism of modern painting:

> The written text imposes certain limits on its unwritten implications in order to prevent these from becoming too blurred and hazy, but at the same time these implications, worked out by the reader's imagination, set the given situation against the background which endows it with far greater significance than it might have seemed to possess on its own. . . . We look forward, we look back, we decide, we change our decisions, we form expectations, we are shocked by their non-fulfilment, we question, we muse, we accept, we reject; this is the dynamic process of recreation.[29]

If one adds to this the terms in which Bergson describes our mental operations in daily life – 'the picture of our past life . . . juxtaposing recollections . . . planes of memory . . . we must place ourselves on the two extreme planes of consciousness', etc. – one realises just how far the language of modern literary criticism and psychology is itself endebted to the criticism of painting. The wheel appears to have come full circle. Now, instead of learning how to read a painting, we are learning how to paint a reading.

1 Bloomsbury Aesthetics

What quality is shared by all objects that provoke our aesthetic emotions? . . . Only one answer seems possible – significant form. [1]

The history of the Bloomsbury Group, with a special emphasis on its involvements in art and literature, has been well told and often. [2] It is not my intention to retread this ground here, but rather to tease out and assemble certain aspects of this history which are relevant to an approach to the novels of Forster and Woolf. I have written this book not from inferences derived from historical fact, indeed, but from a critical consideration of the novels themselves. I have arrived at the conclusion that an appreciation of Forster and Woolf from the point of view of fine-art aesthetics is not only revealing but also entirely appropriate. Bloomsbury aesthetics, come at from this way round, seem to me not simply relevant but essential to an understanding of the achievement of these two novelists.

In 1917, Roger Fry contemplated painting a great historical portrait of the Bloomsbury Group. The members would include Virginia Woolf, Clive and Vanessa Bell, himself and Duncan Grant – but not E. M. Forster. He did not complete his project, but Vanessa Bell did paint *The Memoir Club* in 1943, including Forster. Forster was always on the fringes of Bloomsbury, but even that metaphor assumes that the group could be set apart and labelled, which was never the case. Certainly in 1929 Forster looked at the group from a rather critical distance, labelling them 'essentially *gentlefolks*. . . . Academic background, independent income, Continental enthusiasms, sex-talk and all.' [3] But as S. P. Rosenbaum points out, Forster was friendly with and admired many of its members, not least Roger Fry, 'whose lectures Forster attended in the late Nineties – lectures in which Forster says he detected the essential Bloomsbury undertone that maintained it was not the subject but the treatment that mattered in art'. [4] In terms of the evolution of this book, then, Forster's inclusion need

11

not be argued on historical grounds; nevertheless, there are such grounds as well.

To present the aesthetic ideas of Roger Fry and Clive Bell in this chapter is no easy task, and considerations of space alone would preclude any comprehensive discussion of their practice. I shall, instead, concentrate on the theoretical bases for their aesthetic theories, and on those points where either they applied their theories directly to literature or those theories might profitably be extended from the fine arts.

In 1910 Clive Bell met Roger Fry on the train from Cambridge to London; they began talking about art, and as a result they planned the first Post-Impressionist exhibition, held in London the following year. In 1913 Bell published *Art*, part of *The New Renaissance*, an expression of the glorious optimism shared by many thinking people in those few heady years before the Great War. Although Fry was undoubtedly the greater and more influential critic, and had been practising criticism for many years by this time, it is helpful to start this account with Bell's *Art*. The book puts forward in a relatively simple, exuberant way the premises which underlie Fry's thought. In his preface, Bell is the first to admit this:

> For some years Mr Fry and I have been arguing, more or less amicably, about the principles of aesthetics. We still disagree profoundly . . . and it is certain that some of my historical generalizations have been modified, and even demolished, by Mr Fry.[5]

In 'The Aesthetic Hypothesis' Bell argues,

> For a discussion of aesthetics, it need be agreed only that forms arranged and combined according to certain unknown and mysterious laws do move us in a particular way, and that it is the business of the artist so to combine and arrange them that they shall move us. These moving combinations and arrangements I have called, for the sake of convenience and for a reason that will appear later, 'Significant Form'.[6]

The theory is ahistorical and anti-content except in terms of the elements of design; thus, 'to appreciate a work of art we need bring with us nothing but a sense of form and colour and a knowledge of three-dimensional space'.[7] In a subsequent essay, 'The Metaphysical Hypothesis', Bell addresses squarely the implications of the word 'significant'. It has to do with right relations, hence with 'right' emotions, hence with the artist's conception of the world about him. But, Bell admits, 'we cannot know exactly what the artist feels. We only know what he creates'. Nevertheless, Bell reaches out into the unknowable on the evidence of his own sensations during aesthetic ecstasy, and infers that the artist, like himself, has seen beyond the concerns of life to a metaphysical pattern:

> Call it what name you will, the thing that I am talking about is that which lies behind the appearance of all things – that which gives to all things their individual significance, the thing in itself, the ultimate reality.[8]

Bell's conviction of the metaphysical basis of aesthetics is shown in his essay on Cézanne, where he argues that Cézanne was involved in a personal quest towards 'a complete revelation of the significance of form'[9] and, unusually, depended on a life model as a point of departure. The paintings themselves, says Bell, were discarded once completed 'to be stumbling-blocks for a future race of luckless critics'.

As a result of his outspoken claims for fine art, Bell suggests implicitly in *Art* a range of responses. At the lowest level there is the recognition in the viewer of a representational scene. Then, as he describes vividly when he listens to a musical concert, one may use art as a means to the emotions of life, reading human elements into austere musical forms.[10] There is the appreciation of poetry, which because of the verbal medium is never purely formal: 'poetry, though it has its raptures, does not transport us to that remote aesthetic beatitude in which, freed from humanity, we are upstayed by musical and pure visual form'.[11] Then there is the appreciation of significant form, which, if perfect, will elevate the viewer into the metaphysical heights of religious ecstasy, for 'art and religion are means to similar states of mind'.[12]

Roger Fry, in entitling his 1920 collection of essays *Vision and Design*, was signifying his intention to expand and clarify Bell's notions of 'significant' and 'form'. His 'Essay on Aesthetics' from 1909 calmly pursues the difference of artistic appreciation from the rest of life. It has no moral dimension but frees the imagination to pure contemplation. It is pleased by such elements as order, unity and variety. But Fry adheres closer than Bell to the natural world, asking the artist to 'adequately discover the emotional elements in natural form',[13] and asserting that those emotional states which the viewer experiences on looking at a painting are 'based upon the fundamental necessities of our physical and physiological nature'. Perhaps because Fry was a working critic and painter himself, he retained this reference to the natural world and emphasised it in the same way in which Bell more cavalierly asserted the metaphysical 'reality' of significant forms. This led Fry to praise negro sculpture for its 'logical comprehension of plastic form', to dwell on the elements of a painting – the texture, volumes, planes, relationships of tones, etc. – in other words to value the form, as it were, as much as its significance. So in his retrospective essay Fry disagreed with Bell in *Art* for saying that representation was irrelevant to significant form: 'This last view seemed to me always to go too far since any, even the slightest suggestion, of the third dimension in a picture must be due to some element of representation.'[14] What Bell in fact said was this:

> If the representation of three-dimensional space is to be called 'representation', then I agree that there is one kind of representation which is not irrelevant. Also, I agree that along with our feeling for line and colour we must bring with us our knowledge of space if we are to make the most of every kind of form.[15]

Nevertheless, Fry's misreading indicates an important shift in emphasis in Fry's aesthetic, and the difference between Bell and Fry will become even more important when we come to apply their ideas to literature. There was always the tendency in Bell towards an appreciation of the abstract art of Picasso, and in Fry a similar penchant for the representational works of other Post-Impressionists such as Cézanne and Manet.

A similar division of attitude can be seen in the final pages of Fry's book, where he takes up Bell's question about the nature of significant form:

> I think we are all agreed that we mean by significant form something other than agreeable arrangements of form,

harmonious patterns, and the like. We feel that a work which possesses it is the outcome of an endeavour to express an idea rather than to create a pleasing object. Personally, at least, I always feel that it implies the effort on the part of the artist to bend to our emotional understanding by means of his passionate conviction some intractable material which is alien to our spirit. [16]

Significantly, Fry goes on to refer to the novelist Flaubert's concept of 'the idea', before stopping at the edges of the gulf of mysticism. Whatever Fry's last sentence means, it seems to involve a struggle for the artist to mediate between us and the physical predicament rather than, in Bell's terms, to escape the immediate for the 'real'. The art critic, too, must continue to struggle to interpret increasingly difficult works of art to the public. There is, as a result, an unexpected reversal in the spirit of the works of these two critics. Bell, beginning with a flourish of statements about man's soul, goes on in books such as *Civilisation* to suggest that the appreciation of works of art is either achieved or not achieved by the civilised person: 'Works of art being direct means to aesthetic ecstasy are direct means to good.' Bell has much of worth to say about exposing children and the masses to fine art, but he has increasingly little to say about the arduous task of learning how to appreciate a painting. Fry, on the other hand, while he begins from an apparently modest, dry, academic standpoint, persists in his task with greater and greater penetration and profundity.

Fry's greatest work of criticism was *Cézanne* (1927), a book on the French artist he discovered for England and whom he admired devoutly. Throughout that book he stresses life – the life of the painting, and the life of the observer: 'In spite of the austerity of the forms, all is vibration and movement. The apparent continuity of the contour is illusory, for it changes in quality throughout each particle of its length.' [17] Of a landscape Fry writes, 'the perpetual slight movements of the surface, the vibrating intensity and shimmer of the colour . . . gives to this austere design the thrill of life'. Always the simplicity of the design is stressed, and the complexity and life of the vision. Because of these paradoxical qualities, Cézanne's paintings give us life and art at once: objects 'retain their abstract intelligibility, their amenity to the human mind, and regain that reality of actual things which is absent from all abstractions'.

The observer is caught up in this life, his mind 'held in a kind of thrilled suspense by the unsuspected correspondences of all these related elements'. The movement is at an interface, with the canvas itself seething with life and the spectator resolving it, as did the artist, into a simple, grand harmony:

> The more one looks the more do these dispersed indications begin to play together, to compose rhythmic phrases which articulate the apparent confusion, till at last all seems to come together to the eye into an austere and impressive architectural construction, which is all the more moving in that it emerges from this apparent chaos.[18]

The 'intractable material' or chaos upon which Cézanne's genius worked is the clutter of life itself, from apples to card-players. It is not simply a physical disarray but something corresponding to spiritual patterns. This is an idea Fry was groping towards in his 1924 essay *The Artist and Psychoanalysis*. There he talks of something in addition to an architectural balance, of an 'emotional tone'; art 'seems to derive an emotional energy from the very conditions of our existence by its revelation of an emotional significance in time and space'.[19]

The following year, conversations with the Frenchman Charles Mauron provided Fry with the label he needed: *psychological volumes*. He wanted to connect shape with emotion in a more precise, scientific way than Bell had in his rather mystical assertion of 'significant form'. The psychological volume, like many other terms, was an attempt to bridge the gap between craft and meaning, design and vision.

Another element in Cézanne, as I said, was the idea of effort on the spectator's part. A great work of art had an immediately comprehensible form, but its significance might reside in the fact that it can never be 'completed', the relationships and rhythms endlessly expanding for the attentive observer. This combination of simplicity and complexity became an increasingly important concept for Fry:

> What we desire in a work of art is the feeling of an inexhaustible wealth of significant relations which lie ready to hand for our investigation. We feel at once that a work of art has an

idea that is intelligible, and that it is infinite in its possibilities.[20]

It may be that a 'psychological volume' too shared these qualities – at once a comprehensible volume, and a potential variety of manifestations, as in a personality or psyche. At any rate, these two trends in Fry's thought – towards the psychological content and inexhaustibility of fine art – led him also to a reassessment of literary art, and brought him closer and closer to the writers of Bloomsbury.

The literary metaphor was never far from Fry in his aesthetic writings. In *Cézanne* he talked about the artist's 'handwriting' and saw still lifes as 'dramas deprived of all dramatic incident'. Watteau he described in this way: 'In his feeling for psychological values he was a great poet, but he was none the less intensely an artist with an artist's specific sense of visual values.'[21] But one can trace more clearly in his letters his initial distaste and gradual fascination for literature, especially poetry.

In 1902 Fry read *Moll Flanders* and objected that it needed more 'artistic sense' in the telling of the story and far less of what is normally thrown into a 'novel', for his taste.[22] In 1913 he asserted, 'Literature is usually very little to do with art; I mean, it's so much mixed with intellectual curiosity.'[23] But by 1915, in keeping with the new developments of Modernism, he recognised that besides the 'conspicuously impure art' of literature there was 'a pure or nearly pure art of words'.[24] Around this time, of course, he was reading and translating Mallarmé; in his early introduction to his translation he described his poetry as if it were word painting. Fry compared Mallarmé to the Cubist painters, but at the same time he referred back to his old quarrel with Bell about the degree of representation in art, when he admitted, 'It may be that the greatest art is not the purest, that the richest forms only emerge from a certain richness of content, however unimportant that content may be in the final result.'[25]

As we have seen, the term 'psychological volume' was indicative of Fry's attempt in the twenties to restore content to painting and to include literature as an appropriate object of aesthetic study. So he wrote to Charles Mauron, 'One must admit the possibility of psychological volumes in the visual arts. . . . The art I call illustration is rather a branch of literature and paintings concerned with psychological volumes are cases of mixed arts like songs and opera.'[26] In 1928, indeed, Fry was proposing in a lecture to divide paintings into the symphonic, containing pure significant form, and the operatic, where content counted for part of the aesthetic impact.

Fry found he was able to apply his fine-arts assumptions to literature with results. Picking an obvious candidate, he boasted that he could 'almost draw James's psychological patterns'[27] in 1926; but in 1921 Chekhov's play *Uncle Vanya* seemed in performance 'much more coherent as design, though I still find it too vague and blurred in outline. It's really a very impressionist idea of art.'[28] His most illuminating comments were made to and about Virginia Woolf, of course, and these will be examined in a later chapter.

Apart from the Mallarmé poems, Fry's consideration of literature and admiration for it is most clearly shown in two occasions, one theoretical, one practical.

At the beginning of *Transformations*, Fry considers the differences between art and ordinary life, particularly concerning 'the special cases of literature and representative painting':[29]

> With regard to literature, much misunderstanding is likely to arise owing to the absence of any proper classification and nomenclature of the very various purposes which are covered by the term. . . . It is a medium which admits the mixture of aesthetic and non-aesthetic treatment to an almost unlimited extent. Even in the novel, which as a rule has pretensions to being a work of art, the structure may be so loose, the aesthetic effects may be produced by so vast an accumulation of items that the temptation for the artist to turn aside from his purpose and interpolate criticisms of life, of manners or morals, is very strong. Comparatively few novelists have ever conceived of the novel as a single perfectly organic aesthetic whole.

Fry contrasts I. A. Richards with the admirable aesthetic astringency of A. C. Bradley, from whose 1901 lecture 'Poetry for Poetry's Sake' he took his key idea of 'significant form'.[30] Fry concludes that 'The purpose of literature is the creation of structures which have for us the feeling of reality, and that these structures are self-contained, self-sufficing, and not to be valued by their references to what lies outside.'

In the realm of painting, Fry singles out caricature (a sub-category of representational painting) as the clearest example of Mauron's 'psychological volumes', where aesthetic shape can be made out of what is virtually content rather than out of the plasticity of form and colour. Fry was particularly interested in this form of painting because it provided a test case for Mauron's concepts. His conclusion regarding Hogarth appears to be that he did not capitalise on the aesthetic possibilities in caricature. With an appreciation of Fry's distinction between aesthetic and non-aesthetic effects, he implies, 'He might have learnt that it was possible to do a comedy of life and at the same time create a beautiful and consistent design.'[31]

Although Fry's appreciation of literature had been extended and sharpened by his experience in translating Mallarmé, these theoretical discussions display a mind remarkably well attuned to the main issues of literary criticism, and a mind ready to allow a mixture of qualities in, above all, prose fiction, including the all-important aesthetic quality.

A practical example of Fry's concern with literature came to him in the form of a collection of travel essays called *A Sampler of Castile*, which the Woolfs published in 1923. In May of that year Fry had praised Woolf's own account 'To Spain': 'You really needn't want to paint when you can do a landscape like that. . . . In fact I'm not sure whether words as you use them don't give me more of what the Germans call *stimmung* . . . than painting can ever do.'[32] Woolf returned the compliment when she read his essays: 'You have found a genuine and most successful way of giving shape to all sorts of things which normally run off in talk or thinking to oneself.'[33] And, in reply, Fry confessed himself 'elated' by her praise and ready to 'pull the construction together a little more'.[34]

A Sampler of Castile is in the form of eighteen short episodes, some as short as a page, documenting Fry's travels around Spain and his comments on the people and places. Aesthetic appreciation is mingled with human observation:

If you have an air-cushion like the chance-met friend I was with for the time being, it is best to go outside the motor bus, as the inside is filled with peasant women returning from Segovia market. These are doubtless sympathetic, but they obscure the view and condense the atmosphere.[35]

In his introduction, Fry claimed the book

> was written so that I might let some or all those variegated,
> vivid, and odd impressions run themselves clear on to paper
> before they became part of the vague mist of blurred images
> which move like ghosts in the dim world of the past. It has been
> botched together from scraps written . . . whenever or
> wherever, in short, the chance of crystallizing some of these
> haunting images in words presented itself to a capricious and
> unmethodical mind.[36]

The emphasis of both Fry and his 'editor' was on the structure of
the book ('shape', 'construction'), which has no mathematical
balance but follows spontaneously the weight of each moment. It
is reminiscent of Sterne's *Sentimental Journey*, which Woolf was
quoting from two years earlier in *Jacob's Room* and whose creator
Fry and Woolf enjoyed together.[37] The difference is in the personality of the observer. Here, the 'psychological volume' which
is Fry himself is a continual balance of detached appraisal (of art
and architecture) and involved sharer in the moment. Most of the
episodes, taking the traveller to certain spots because of an
aesthetic interest, dissolve also into an appreciation of the life that
goes on there. After talking briefly about the architecture of
Calatayud, for instance, Fry ends the chapter,

> Here, watercourse and wide avenues and cooling shade attract
> the whole population of the town towards evening; and for
> hours the people walk up and down, see and are seen and
> gossip and idle and laugh till it is quite dark and the feeble elec-
> tric lights shimmer through the foliage.[38]

The passage could be from Woolf herself, with its emphasis on
sound and light. Although 'botched together', *A Sampler* has a
uniquely literary 'significant form' which is a matter of a relationship between the observed and the observer, and a pace or
rhythm of experience. The book mixes scene-painting with what
Fry, not disparagingly, called 'intellectual curiosity', without
disturbing a balance between the two.

It would seem that, in theory and practice, Fry carried Bell's
idea of significant form to greater levels of sophistication and
relevance to literature than he might have imagined. Certainly

iterature figures little in *Art* or *Civilisation*; but in his later writing
Bell proved himself as adept as Fry at applying the language and
principles of fine-art criticism to literature. In 1928, during a
discussion of the French artist Constantin Guys, for example, Bell
made specific analogies with modern literature:

> Without Constantin Guys that essentially modern reaction to
> contemporary life, that passionate but impartial preoccupation
> with the actual and evanescent, could hardly have been
> rendered in line. . . . Not only painters, but novelists and
> intelligent lookers-on, Jean Cocteau and Aldous Huxley, Paul
> Morand and Virginia Woolf, all the bright and disinterested
> amateurs of evening parties and port-side cafés, all owe him
> something.[39]

While Woolf might not have been flattered by the company, the
visual analogy is illuminating for Woolf's work. In 1928 Bell
wrote equally vividly on Proust, describing his effects in visual
terms:

> It is in states, not action, that he deals. The movement is that of
> an expanding flower or insect . . . the fact remains suspended
> while we watch it gradually changing its shape, its colour, its
> consistency . . . .
>
> Proust brings the past into the present and creating a shape not
> in space but in time . . . situations unfold themselves not like
> flowers even but like tunes.[40]

The musical analogy was the more likely one to be used by Bell,
perhaps because of his 'purer' aesthetic tastes. One of his
favourite descriptive terms was 'rhythm', while for Fry
plasticity' with its spatial references was more important.

In their appreciation of the two Bloomsbury painters Vanessa
Bell and Duncan Grant, these predilections of Bell and Fry are
also manifest. Bell was an early advocate of Grant's genius:

> Duncan Grant is the hope of patriotic amateurs; blessed with
> adorable gifts and a powerful intellect, he should, if he has the
> strength to realize his conceptions and the courage to disdain

popularity, become what we have been awaiting so long, an English painter in the front rank of European art. [41]

Six years later, in 1923, Roger Fry was more guarded, praising Grant for his simplicity and gaiety, recommending him as a decorative designer more at home on flat surfaces than with 'constructions in a logically coherent space', but by implication barring him from the domain of the great painters. 'The very idea of invention in painting implies a literary or representational element', Fry argues, and Grant is the lesser artist for failing to develop this inventive faculty. [42]

As for Vanessa Bell, Fry's relationship with her was lengthy and intimate. In 1911 he wrote to her while on holiday in France with Clive Bell (her husband) and Duncan Grant, 'I don't think I forget you for a single moment of the day, and always it makes the country a little better and the colours purer and the sky gayer to think that you are there always in the background of my consciousness.' [43] But this intimacy was a product rather than a cause of Fry's profound affinity with and admiration for her work. He would agree with Raymond Mortimer when he distinguished Grant's work from Vanessa Bell's:

> Careful comparison suggests moreover that, though they share many tastes, they are quite unlike in temperament. Vanessa Bell is, I think, by nature a realist. (Unlike Grant she has a great gift for catching a likeness.) She is altogether a graver, less exuberant artist. Their virtues seems to me markedly different in character, and each paints best when painting least like the other. The tempo natural to her is *andante*, while his is *allegro*. [44]

Again the difference in taste between Bell and Fry is illustrated by Fry's 1922 review of a Vanessa Bell exhibition, when he praises her for having a 'handwriting' less elegant than Grant's, but more profound in that it is always trying to 'express an idea'. [45] [Plate 1] She is praised as a colourist of honesty and purity, conveying feelings of 'grave, untroubled serenity and happiness'. Indeed, Grant is referred to only as a rather bad influence in that he encouraged her to divorce design from vision: 'I suspect it is in this question of design rather than elsewhere that the influence of Duncan Grant's more playful and flexible spirit shows itself.' In his opinion, however, Bell feels that Grant's influence on his wife's painting is all to the good. He senses in her work 'a large simplicity of style' and 'something oddly sympathetic';[46] for Bell, sympathy and human dimensions in art were odd, not invigorating and sublime as they were and remained for Fry.

Vanessa Bell once complained to Fry, 'It's all this awful question of the content of a work of art',[47] and certainly Fry insisted on the primacy of design in painting, leaving the vexed question of 'content' often to manifest itself in the terms he used to describe the form, such as 'serene', 'humane' or 'humble'. In his own paintings, and those of Cézanne and Vanessa Bell, the ostensible subject matter is generally domestic and tranquil, which might in itself suggest the subconscious preferences of Fry for pacific, modest matter. Fry began from the perception that, 'with their essentially literary bias, the English have never understood plastic art'.[48] He set about teaching them [Plate 3], and worked his way back from design to vision so that in his later years especially he spent much time developing his ideas about inter-relationships between the arts, particularly the painterliness of literature and the literariness of painting. He was not above confessing, for example, that 'painting often does inadequately what language does well' – that is, exhaust the background and meaning of a dramatic moment.[49] The solution was not for each art to limit its focus, but to draw on the principles of each discipline to extend its own. Fry referred to the common pursuit of painter and writer often in his letters to Virginia Woolf. Comments such as this abound: 'I know quite well that this queer business of writing is quite as odd and peculiar as ours of putting paint on.'[50]

It was another member of Bloomsbury, Vanessa's son Julian, who most accurately analysed the late trends in Fry's aesthetic thinking in an essay written in China in 1936, shortly before his tragic death in Spain. Bell admired Fry greatly, and his sympathetic analysis brings out the unifying impetus in Fry's thought, the attempt to bridge the gap – or rather close it – between form and content, design and vision: 'His intelligence always asked the satisfaction of design, coherence, the play and harmony of relations: his sensuality appreciated the direct satisfaction from the elements of the construction.'[51] Here again we see an awareness of Fry's relish for both the immediate, broad structural impact, and the more leisurely, time-consuming analysis of intimate correlations within the design. It was this desire to luxuriate in paintings, to read them deeply and repeatedly, which drew Fry also to literature and an analogous contemplation. As Bell perceived, the critical stance in each case was the same:

> the attitude of mind that results from habitually treating figures of Christ as 'important masses' and looking through the ordinary purposes of life for formal relations and the beauty that results from them. In literature, it is the attitude that can be at once completely sensitive to human emotion, yet can find its highest pleasure in the movement and relations of the construction in which these emotions play. It is the habit of mind, in creator, critic, and contemplator, that does not want to act, but to understand. [52]

We may come at the differences in the aesthetics of Fry and Bell, and at Fry's developing interest in the aesthetics of literature, in this way: by considering the attitude of the *artist* towards his work. Bell explored the 'habit of mind' of the creator most deeply in the chapter on 'The Metaphysical Hypothesis' in *Art*. There he considers the notion that what makes the aesthetic emotion so important for the contemplator is also what made it so for the artist in the first place: it is a feeling that one is 'seizing reality (generally behind pure form)'. [53] Bell is uneasy with metaphysical claims, and at once appears to retract: 'But many people, though they feel the tremendous significance of form, feel also a cautious dislike for big words; and "reality" is a very big one. These prefer to say that what the artist surprises behind form, or seizes by sheer force of imagination, is the all-pervading rhythm that informs all things; and I have said that I will never quarrel with that blessed word "rhythm".' [54] Nor does Fry quarrel with that word, of course, and Forster takes it over gratefully into the criticism of fiction when he entitles Chapter 8 of his *Aspects of the Novel* 'Pattern and Rhythm'. But for all Bell's disclaimers, the word has a powerful metaphysical sense, most notable in the pantheism of the English Romantic poets. Bell admits as much at the end of his essay when he describes the detachment of the artistic point of view, that contemplation which allows a grasp of the whole: 'Instead of recognising its accidental and conditioned importance, we become aware of its essential reality, of the God in everything, of the universal in the particular, of the all-pervading rhythm.'[55] Bell clearly believes in his hypothesis, in art as the perception, communication and contemplation of 'some more ultimate harmony'.

When Fry was driven inexorably to the same metaphysical gulf at the end of *Vision and Design*, he stopped. However, he did say that the aesthetic emotion had to do with 'an idea', a 'peculiar quality of reality'.[56] He described 'the effort on the part of the artist to bend to our emotional understanding by means of his passionate conviction some intractable material which is alien to our spirit'.[57] While this definition places rather more emphasis on the struggle involved than does Joyce's Stephen Dedalus with his definition ('art is the human disposition of sensible or intelligible matter for an aesthetic end'), Fry would agree with the fictional theorist's famous conception of the artist as, finally, detached from his handiwork, 'paring his fingernails'. In his 1924 essay on *The Artist and Psychoanalysis*, Fry confronted the Freudians head on, and denied that art had anything to do with the expression of dreams or fulfilment of wishes. Interestingly, he takes his examples from literature:

> They [novels] depend on the contrary for their effect upon a peculiar detachment from the instinctive life. Instead of manipulating reality so as to conform to the libido, they note the inexorable sequence in life of cause and effect, they mark the total indifference of fate to all human desires, and they endeavour to derive precisely from that inexorability of fate an altogether different kind of pleasure – the pleasure which consists in the recognition of *inevitable sequences*; a pleasure which you see corresponds to the pleasure which we found in marking the inevitable sequence of the notes in a tune; in fact again a pleasure derived from the contemplation of the relations and correspondences of form. To give you instances – no one who hoped to get an ideal wishfulfilment would go to *Mme. Bovary* or *Anna Karenina* or even *Vanity Fair*.[58]

It is important to understand that the artist's detachment, especially in literature, does not necessarily imply the long view or an attitude to life. Woolf praised the James Joyce of *A Portrait of the Artist as a Young Man* for 'recording the atoms as they fall upon the mind. . . . Let us not take it for granted that life exists more fully in what is commonly thought big than in what is commonly thought small.'[59] When Fry considered the intensely psychological art of the modern novel, he adapted his aesthetic to fit this highly specific experience. In the best fiction, relations were to be perceived between the various atoms of the minds, not necessarily as the reflection of some larger 'rhythm' of life but perhaps as a reminder of archetypal human patterns of behaviour and experience. This is how he struggled to put it at the end of his essay on Freud:

> It is not a mere recognition of order and inter-relation; every part, as well as the whole, becomes suffused with an emotional tone. Now, from our definition of this pure beauty, the emotional tone is not due to any recognizable reminiscence or suggestion of the emotional experiences of life; but I sometimes wonder if it nevertheless does not get its force from arousing some very deep, very vague, and immensely generalized reminiscences. It looks as though art had got access to the substratum of all the emotional colours of life.[60]

For Fry, then, the literary artist in his detachment may explore, not the 'ultimate harmonies' of the universe, but rhythmic patterns in the ebb and flow of the stream of consciousness itself. The question of the perspective of the literary artist or reader becomes an extremely complex one. Fry was fascinated by the early cinema, and referred to it at least twice: once in the essay on Freud, when he complained of our readiness to identify with the hero in his amazing adventures;[61] and once in *Transformations*, when he recounted the experience of watching the film of a maritime disaster, and concluded that what made tragic drama valuable was not emotional intensity but the shape of the events, 'the curve of crescendo and diminuendo which their sequence describes, together with all the myriad subsidiary evocations which, at each point, poetic language can bring in to give fullness and density to the whole organic unity'.[62] If we can think of film as a kind of midpoint between the stasis of fine art and the temporal experience of narrative, Fry's reactions are significant. The language of fiction can add 'density' (Woolf's 'atoms' of the mind), and shape or pattern. The writer must be at once inside and beyond his fiction, as must the reader, so that the issue of perspective in literature is highly complex and sophisticated. Unlike the filmgoer, who is either detached or totally involved, a reader must be both, at the same time.

When reading the art criticism of Bell and Fry, one is aware of an occasional yearning for these literary complexities. Fry could not resist deducing an attitude to humanity in the work of Walter Sickert, in a 1911 review:

> Something of an attitude to life, a very unconscious and little defined one it is true, comes through the impassive mask of Mr. Sickert's imperturbable manner; an odd refusal to have any dealings with the material of romance, a persistent devotion to the banal and trivial situations of ordinary life, at times even an attraction for what is squalid.[63]

Then, aware that he has gone too far, perhaps, he quickly recants: 'All this seems to belong to his supreme and splendid indifference to anything that does not concern the artistic vision in its most limited sense.' In Bell, too, one can find a literary analogy slipping in; in this case, ironically, it is a review of Duncan Grant in 1920 – a painter who, according to Fry, did not use his faculty of 'literary invention' enough: 'In Duncan Grant there is, I agree, something that reminds one unmistakably of the Elizabethan poets, something fantastic and whimsical and at the same time intensely lyrical. . . . But though they may be lyrical or fantastic or witty, these pictures never tell a story or point a moral.'[64] Again, the hasty recantation.

What is clear is that Roger Fry's regard for literature increased during the years when he was associated with the Bloomsbury Group (and, I suspect, began to read Virginia Woolf's novels). Bell's anecdote of him reciting 'gibberish which did possess recognisable similarity of sound with the *Ode on the Nativity*'[65] and claiming that his creation had as much worth as Milton's, must surely belong to the very early years. He was soon to lose what Bell called his 'puritanical' conception of poetry as a system of sounds which could be reduced to 'clean, dry bones'. In his review of *Art* in 1914, Fry pointed the way:

> I wish he had extended his theory, and taken literature (in so far as it is an art) into fuller consideration, for I feel confident that great poetry arouses aesthetic emotions of a similar kind to painting and architecture. And to make his theory complete, it would have been Mr. Bell's task to show that the human emotions of *King Lear* and *The Wild Duck* were also accessory, and not the fundamental and essential qualities of these works.[66]

And by 1926 he was writing of poetry, 'There is, of course, the pleasure of rhythmic utterance, but this is already concerned with relations, and even this is, I believe, accessory to the emotion aroused by rhythmic changes of states of mind due to the meanings of the words.'[67]

We are clearly approaching a literary aesthetic here. I believe that aspects of the ideas of Bell and Fry – significant form, psychological volume, rhythm, the aesthetic emotion – inform, in different ways, the novels of Woolf and Forster. In succeeding chapters I shall document more fully the relationships, both biographical and theoretical, between them. Not only does this approach open up new avenues of interpretation and criticism for these authors, but it suggests (without perhaps confusing, like some of the hermeneutical jargons of structuralism and deconstructionism) new ways of approaching a wide range of modern novelists.

2   Two Connections

CHARLES MAURON

Where then is literary beauty?[1]

The French aesthetician and translator Charles Mauron provides a convenient personal and theoretical locus for the literary theories of Fry, Forster and Woolf. [Plate 4] The practical contribution of Mauron, whom one critic called 'Bloomsbury's Gallic representative',[2] can be seen by considering his translations – all of Forster's novels (excluding *Maurice*) between 1927 and 1954, 'Le Temps Passé' from *To the Lighthouse* in 1926, *Orlando* in 1931 and *Flush* in 1935 – and his two works published by the Hogarth Press: *The Nature of Beauty in Art and Literature* in 1926, and *Aesthetics and Psychology* in 1935. His importance lay in his encouraging Roger Fry, and through him the two novelists, to apply the aesthetics of fine arts to literature.

Fry met the Maurons during his travels in France in 1919, but his most important contact with them came in 1925, when Charles Mauron's theories were fully developed. Forster, at Fry's suggestion, had also just met and stayed with the Maurons, exclaiming in May 1925 that Charles was 'a great find'. Fry himself, writes Frances Spalding, 'never tired of discussing literature and aesthetics with this intellectual';[3] and Woolf quotes a letter of Fry: 'Charles Mauron is so terribly good at analysis that it sometimes seems impossible to make any positive construction that will resist his acids.'[4] In the summer of 1925 Fry joined his intellect with Mauron's at the Décades de Pontigny, an annual seminar of ideas, and he described the results delightedly in a letter:

> Saturday was the day when at last Mauron and I had our innings and brought things down from the abstract. I elaborated a good deal on my empiricism. . . . Then Mauron

29

read an essay on literary beauty which was by far the most creative and masterly contribution. . . . It was beautifully written, transparently clear, and perfectly developed and full of the most original ideas. . . . We two brought the thing out into daylight.[5]

Fry's reaction to Mauron's paper, which presumably became the substance of his first Hogarth essay, is recorded in more detail during a conversation he had with Prince Mirsky:

He suggested that just as the artist models visual volumes, the writer models 'psychological volumes'. That isn't to say that he was being a psychologist, but that the subject-matter of psychological science – the successive états d'âme of which our psychological existence consists – is also the stuff in which the literary artist works – modelling (as he expresses it) psychological volumes. These may be so small as, in the case of a short lyric, to consist of a single état d'âme, but generally – as in a novel – the volumes the writer builds for us are extremely complex and intricate, implying innumerable états d'âme . . . .

Naturally I felt sympathetic to Mauron's hypothesis because it fits in so clearly with my own conjectures about the aesthetic of the visual arts.[6]

Let us compare this now with Mauron's own formulation in his Hogarth essay of the following year:

What analogue in literature shall we give to volume? It suffices to transfer it from the domain of space to that of the spirit; and as the notion of volume admits of all spatial possibilities, the corresponding literary notion ought to admit of all spiritual possibilities. The psychological reality, the psychological complex – there is the material which the writer should work upon. Notice that in both domains our aesthetic sensibility rejects realities that are too simple, geometric volumes in one and pure ideas in the other. In spatial world [*sic*] there remains the vast crowd of complex volumes: in the spiritual there remain the everyday realities of our soul, all the forms of our inner life.

'As the painter creates a spatial being, the writer creates a psychological being.' Such, I think, is the hypothesis that we might admit as the basis of all literary criticism.[7]

Mauron goes on to argue that literary art is a complex made up from certain pure types or elements, which are characters, relations between facts (or 'situations'), and 'moments of the spirit' which comprise 'a single whole'. Although this part of the essay is the most crude and unsatisfactory, it is clear that Mauron is trying to avoid temporal notions of story, and 'real' notions of moral or psychological development. Instead, he wishes to describe literature in static, spatial terms. His later analogy of a statue is more illuminating, when he describes the literary text as the 'surface which delimits the volume',[8] a 'good' work of art being one where this surface or skin stretches perfectly over the particular volume. Involved with this idea is the other original contribution of the essay concerning the medium of the word, which, even in prose narrative, must be part of an interconnecting web – again like the surface of a sculpture, or the texture of a painting. Each word, says Mauron, is 'in touch with the rest of the discourse'.

In his collection of essays *Transformations* (1926), Fry refers to Mauron's 'brilliant suggestion': 'It may be no more than an analogy, but it enables us for the first time dimly to grasp what it is of which the relations are felt by us when we apprehend aesthetically a work of literature.'[9] Although the context of Fry's reference is a discussion of the ideas of I. A. Richards, Fry does not develop his ideas about literature further here, being more interested in using Mauron's concept of 'psychological volumes' to explore those kinds of visual art which approximate to literature. In his essay he goes on to discuss caricature: 'Here clearly we are dealing primarily with "psychological volumes." Provided that surprising, vivid and consistent suggestions of a peculiar psychological entity are given to us we need not clamour for significant plasticity.'[10] I shall return to Fry's notion of 'mixed arts' in the next chapter when I discuss the aesthetic ideas of Forster. For the moment it should be noted that *Aspects of the Novel* was published a year after Mauron's essay, and was dedicated to him.

It may also be appropriate at this point to outline Woolf's relationship with Mauron. Her contact with him was limited, and the effect of his ideas upon her was at second hand: through conversation with Fry, or through supervising the publication of his Hogarth essays. Her first contact with him, indeed, was inauspicious. In 1926 Mauron, at Fry's suggestion, seized upon

the central section of *To the Lighthouse* for translation, resulting
Woolf wrote angrily, in a 'hopeless mess'.[11] In 1929 she referred
in a letter to 'that rather obese and almost blind Frenchman'[12]
and described a discussion with him in unflattering terms
'Mauron and Roger last night confuted Leonard and Oliver and
proved beyond a doubt the non-existence of everything but Idea.
So there.'[13] When she was researching for her biography of Fry,
Woolf came into contact with him again, and either her opinion of
him had mellowed or perhaps since Fry's death her feelings of
jealousy for his friendship had abated. At any rate she wrote, 'I
liked him very much. He's a real humorous, vigorous little man,
and we talked about Roger.'[14]

Mauron's second essay, *Aesthetics and Psychology* (translated by
Fry and Katherine John), was a corrective to what Mauron felt
was Fry's tendency to make art seem like 'a purely intellectual
pastime'.[15] He set out to show that art is both good for the mind
and good for one's subsequent appreciation of real life. The work
of art, by this account, is like a sophisticated puzzle, complex but
containing certain analogies which, once discovered by the
intellect, give not only pleasure but a feeling that the world, too,
has a shape and meaning. For the artist, Mauron warns, 'must
pretend, while composing his work, to copy nature'[16]
– presumably, for the novel, those everyday forms of our inner
life which he talked of in his first essay. Analogies are essential,
for without them 'there can be no rhythm, nor order, nor unity of
any kind'.

The essay may be seen as an attempt to elucidate what may be
'significant' or worth caring about in the 'form' or psychological
volume expressed in literature. Mauron is careful to insist on the
artist's control of his medium, so that the sculpted form which the
writer clothes in words is itself beautiful, harmonious and balanced. Mauron and Fry had an opportunity to give a practical
demonstration of their literary method when Mallarmé's *Poems*
were published in 1936 – edited by Mauron and Julian Bell but
with translations by Fry which he had begun before 1920. In his
early introduction to the volume Fry wrote,

> Every word carries with it an image or an idea surrounded by a
> vague aura of associations. . . . When a word is apprehended,
> then, this aura takes shape in the mind, and when a second
> word is joined up to the first . . . this changes the aura of the

first word, expanding, contracting or colouring it as the case may be.[17]

Each word, like each of a painter's brush strokes, has its unique shape and colour, but the artist must also be mindful of resemblances and harmonies which govern the overall work of art.

In 1938 Mauron's continued friendship with Forster came under close examination when both men found themselves contributing to a memorial volume on Julian Bell. Mauron praised Bell for being not at all like the aristocrat Forster would describe him as, but a Viking warrior. 'The world', says Mauron, 'can appear to us either as a conflict of forces or as a source of feelings'; the one results in an aristocratic life of action, the other in a democratic life of art. People like Forster, he says, 'cannot get out of the circle, because the will to power is foreign to them, nor yet remain happy therein, because they feel the danger and unreality of such a refuge. They are logically despairing liberals.'[18] The world of art is the only world wherein the conflict can be, in a sense, resolved, for there the artist wields his power over a world of feelings, shaping it into art: 'The discipline of the classical artist, like intelligent military discipline, is a matter of containing violent emotion with a view to effective action.'[19] Whether all this constitutes an attack on Forster is unclear. Mauron does seem to side, implicitly, with Julian Bell, who, in a letter quoted in the volume, challenged Forster to 'acquire the military virtues' as a way of surviving in the twentieth century without compromising one's views. Perhaps Mauron is suggesting to Forster, by way of Bell, that his longstanding disillusionment with creative writing is unjustified, and that there are still battles to be won through fiction. Perhaps he feels that Forster's fiction never did fight enough with psychological realities to create complex and challenging volumes.

Whatever Mauron's intentions, Forster continued to care deeply for his French comrade during the Second World War. According to Forster's biographer, 'The fate of Charles Mauron took on a symbolic importance for him. . . . He would re-read the letters of his "loved and lost Charles", copying portions out into his Commonplace Book.'[20]

Mauron survived the war and continued to translate Forster. Both his life and thought were intricately intertwined with Fry

and Forster for many years, and his efforts to bridge the ga
between fine art and literary criticism were a significant factor i
the direction of evolution of the critical work of Forster and th
creative work of Woolf.

'GOLDIE'

A connection between Fry and Forster, of biographical but als
critical importance, was Goldsworthy Lowes Dickinson, whon
they both met at Cambridge. Declarations of the close persona
friendships are not hard to find. Dickinson wrote of Fry, 'All ou
life we have been friends and I have a kind of married feelin
towards him.'[21] Woolf quotes Fry's response to 'Goldie's' deatl
in 1932:

> He had been all through my youth my greatest and mos
> intimate friend. . . . I owe such an immense amount to hi
> influence and his extraordinary sympathy. I begin to see wha
> a tremendously big place he had in shaping all that counts i
> our world.[22]

And Forster, in the preface to his 1934 biography, writes, 'I knev
him for thirty-five years, and knew him well for twenty.'[23]

Forster in that book gives a portrait of Dickinson before refer
ring to the frontispiece, Fry's painterly portrait [Plate 5]:

> There was a beauty about him which cannot be given tha
> patronising label 'spiritual', a beauty which, though it hac
> nothing to do with handsomeness, did belong to the physical
> so that his presence was appropriate amid gorgeous scenery o
> exquisite flowers.[24]

Forster ends his biography by throwing up his hands and pro
testing that no literature could hope to capture this 'indescribabl
rare being', but perhaps only music. Woolf, looking from a
distance and one unsullied by the homosexual attractions which
partly inspired both Fry and Forster, saw Dickinson's 'other
worldliness' in a rather different light. She describes the Apostles
Society at Cambridge through which Fry was introduced tc
Dickinson:

Art was for them the art of literature; and literature was half prophecy. Shelley and Walt Whitman were to be read for their message rather than for their music. Perhaps then, when Mr Benson talks of the pallor of the Apostles, he hints at something eyeless, abstract and austere in their doctrines.[25]

It was against this Platonic austerity that Fry worked out his aesthetic theories, and Forster his literary preferences. Dickinson insisted to Fry in 1891 that he must have 'form' in painting and not simply colour and tone; such insistence helped Fry towards his concept of significant form. With Forster the reconciling of the influence was not quite so simple. He refers to Dickinson in *Aspects of the Novel*, praising *The Magic Flute* as an 'exquisite' example of fantasy.[26] In his consideration of Dickinson's works in the biography, he stresses and admires the formal control of the various points of view, epitomised in Dickinson's favourite form of the Socratic exchange:

> He had not the novelist's eccentricity, which permits a sudden swerve from the main course. . . . His own method, working from within, allowed no vagaries, not even the development of a character under the stress of talk. His business was the argument, human and humanly held, but not allowing irresponsive interludes.[27]

Forster concludes, 'Dickinson always needs a form which will allow him to express the views of others without judging them by his own',[28] and sees that this distancing and control reach their apotheosis in *The International Anarchy* (1926):

> He refuses to show his readers how much he suffers, in case they are diverted from the facts and discount the argument. And so, paradoxically enough, 'The International Anarchy' ranks high as a work of art. It is supported by an intense emotion which is never allowed to ruffle the surface. It is the quality which, working through another temperament and in another medium, has produced Bach's fugues.[29]

One could predict from this that Dickinson's response to Forster's fiction was guarded until *A Passage to India*, where, he wrote to Forster, his characteristic 'double vision' stopped squinting and became whole.[30] The connecting of the real and the ideal necessarily involves an intrusion of the author's personality, but the location of India brings the two worlds naturally much closer together, and the author can remain more detached.

Indeed, *A Passage to India* can be seen as the perfect novelistic extension of Dickinson's notions of Socratic dialogue, as noticed by Forster. The dialogue of Aziz and Fielding at the end is unresolved, but the reader, observing the whole, apprehends the unity of diversity, the many psychological volumes which make up the vision of that novel. Forster's characters, whether they realise it or not, are up against 'last things' in that novel, chiefly death, a notion which Forster expressed in a letter to Dickinson during the novel's creation:

> If you can pretend you can get inside one character, why not pretend it about all the characters? I see why. The illusion of life may vanish, and the creator degenerate into the showman. Yet some change of the sort must be made. The studied ignorance of novelists grows wearisome. They must drop it. Also they must recapture their interest in death. . . .[31]

But one need not think that this multiplicity of viewpoints must tend to muddle instead of mystery. Forster would agree with Dickinson about the necessity of form, arising not simply from the tripartite division of the text, but from the subject matter itself. When Dickinson quizzed Forster about the central episode of the novel and what happened in the cave, he replied that he refused to find out – 'This isn't a philosophy of aesthetics. It's a particular trick I felt justified in trying because my theme was India.'[32] Forster's aesthetics remain, but his patterning surrounds and embraces a core of confusion. After this extreme triumph of aesthetic unity over multiplicity, it is difficult to imagine an artist retreating to the simpler unities of more tangible human verities. Yet, even in Forster's last novel, there is an overarching dialogue between writer and reader, and that constant debate carries on throughout Forster's subsequent journalism.

3 Forster and the Arts

The arts were to be enriched by taking in one another's washing. [1]

Lionel Trilling, in his book on Forster, recalls Lessing's *Laocöon* when he concludes, 'He raises the shield of Achilles, which is the moral intelligence of art.' [2] Trilling is correct to align Forster with Lessing's poet who capitalises on the unique virtues of his medium: the cause and effect, the accumulation of plot; and the elucidation of the motives and aspirations of real men in real predicaments. But at the same time Forster had an admiration for the arts which manifested itself particularly in his love of architecture, music and opera. Besides the love of earnest moral truth there was a constant inclination to the pure, apparently trivial, delights of what one might call 'incidental' art. Forster reveals this in his introduction to a translation of the *Aeneid*:

> [Virgil] loves most the things that profess to matter least – a simile rather than the action that it illustrates, a city full of apple-trees rather than the soldiers who march out of it, the absent friends of a dying man rather than the dying man. . . . He illuminates objects that are often isolated and sometimes contradictory. [3]

Forster admires Virgil for loving the shield as well as the stories engraved upon it, and for making his epic not quite coherent. The same love of the incidental and spontaneous gives Forster's own novels their distinctive, elusive shape.

Roger Fry, not given to whimsicality, maintained an uneasy friendship with Forster. [Plate 6] His reservations about him as a writer began upon his reading the short stories. He wrote to Woolf in 1920, 'I like Morgan's *Siren* well enough . . . but it's always the same theme; I wish he could get something new and more solidly constructed. He exploits too much his fancy.' [4] Although he persuaded Charles Mauron to translate *A Passage to*

India because of its 'marvellous texture', Fry was disappointed
that here too the construction failed: 'The design [after the acquit
tal of Aziz] gets wobbly and indistinct because he has too many
themes to work in. The fact is that he is an artist but he despises
his art and thinks he must be something more.'[5] Fry's point was
that meanings and significances must come unconsciously into
the design rather than being consciously sought, as he felt Forster
was seeking them. Forster's attitude to the aesthetic emotion was
quantitative rather than qualitative; beauty was beautiful, but life
demanded something more. He hurt Fry with his 'terrible phrase'
describing Fry's own paintings – 'Why so many pictures?'[6]

Despite this antagonism, Forster respected Fry's achievement
and in his obituary notice concluded, 'He believed in reason . .
rejected authority, mistrusted intuition. . . . He is a terrible
loss.'[7] What he admired most about Fry was his personal energy
and excitement. In his appreciation at least, if not in his own
work, he was able to give the impression that art mattered
supremely. 'If the cultured person', Forster wrote in 1940, 'like
the late Roger Fry is obviously having a good time, those who
come across him will be tempted to share it and to find out how.'[8]

Forster tried to find out how, and his efforts under Fry's
tutelage are documented in the essay 'Not Looking at Pictures':

> I am bad at looking at pictures myself, and the late Roger Fry
> enjoyed going to a gallery with me now and then, for this very
> reason. He found it an amusing change to be with someone
> who scarcely ever saw what the painter had painted. 'Tell me
> why do you like this, why do you prefer it to that?' he would
> ask, and listen agape for the ridiculous answer. . . . I liked the
> mountain-back because it reminded me of a peacock, he
> because it had some structural significance, though not as
> much as the sack of potatoes in the foreground.[9]

Forster goes on to explain how he learnt about composition and
colour from Fry and from Mauron, and concludes that it is indeed
more rewarding to see paintings aesthetically than as catalysts for
personal reflection.

Nevertheless, there is always in Forster's comments about
painting a tone of amusement, as if he is describing an activity
which is a pleasant escape from life, but an escape none the less.
His opinion of art critics can be sensed in a 1920 review of a book

about Macao, when he exclaims 'O beautiful book!' while reminding us that the art critics 'have the gift of words and can state
with precision which of your pages are Illustrations and which
Significant Forms'.[10] For all its mockery of the aesthetic
discipline, this does at least show that Forster was listening attent-
ively to the developing theories of Fry and Bell.

In 1937 Forster wrote on Van Gogh, who 'sees the colour
"blue", observes that the colour "yellow" always occurs in it,
and writes this preposterous postulate up upon the white walls.
He has a home beyond comfort and common sense, with the
saints, and perhaps he sees God'.[11] This apparent praise is
modified by a later observation: 'When a great artist like Van
Gogh does see [fields] blue, I am thankful to look for a moment
through his eyes.'[12] Painting is used here as part of an argument
against Nazism, but only in so far as it celebrates the individual
vision, not the possible common sensation of aesthetic ecstasy;
Van Gogh may see God, but we shall not see him in his paintings.
Forster's essays of this time confirm his attitude towards painting
as mildly belittling and damning with faint praise. 'Art', he writes
in 'Art for Art's Sake', 'is a self-contained harmony . . . it has to
do with order, and creates little worlds of its own, possessing
internal harmony, in the bosom of this disordered planet.'[13] The
work of art 'stands up by itself, and nothing else does';[14] artists
recreate the world in their special world, 'temporarily sheltered
from the pitiless blasts and the fog'.[15]

Forster, then, can only praise fine art in so far as it escapes
from rather than illuminates the real world of telegrams and
anger. This attitude surfaces again and again in various contexts.
In his guidebook to Alexandria, for example, Forster takes the
visitor to the Graeco-Roman museum, but warns him not to visit
the collection 'until he has learned or imagined something about
the ancient city'.[16] Called upon to review a book called *Indian
Painting for the British*, he concludes, 'Though the book can present
little of aesthetic value, it is a delightful record socially.'[17] And in
an essay called 'Art Treasures of Cambridge' he confesses his
coldness before exquisite china – 'I prefer things that are plain
and have dents in them to things that seem to have other things
stuck on to them' – and goes on to profess far more interest in the
apparatus of Rutherford and Chadwick for identifying neutrons:
'These quiet exhibits lie in the midst of the College Feasts and the
pretty pictures . . . of the civilised world. They have come to stay

with us and to expand.'[18]

Forster's real love amongst the non-literary arts was music. Benjamin Britten calls him 'our most musical novelist'[19] and attempts to analyse his novels in musical terms. The idea is attractive, for, as Forster himself observed, 'The more the arts develop the more they depend on each other for definition.'[20] But Britten does not get very far by using the genre terms of music. He compares the construction of Forster's novels to classical opera with alternating recitative and arias, but then goes on to argue that Forster prefers 'striking themes, dramatic happenings, and strong immediate moods, rather than classical control and balance. . . . He prefers the Romantic to the Classical.'[21] Forster himself, wisely, is far more reticent when he comes to suggest why music is so important; but important it is:

It seems to be more 'real' than anything, and to survive when the rest of civilization decays. In these days I am always thinking of it with relief. It can never be ruined or nationalized. . . . There's an insistence in music – expressed largely through rhythm; there's a sense that it is trying to push across at us something which is neither an aesthetic pattern nor a sermon.[22]

It is perhaps Forster's cynically realistic, reductive attitude towards both aesthetics and religion that forbids him to use either as an analogy to express his emotion upon listening to music. In the last analysis one wonders if it can be different to what Bell describes as the aesthetic ecstasy.

The difference between Bell's and Forster's aesthetics lies in the different emphases placed on space and time. For Bell, beauty is spatial and exists out of time; for Forster it is intimately connected with time. This is why in *Aspects of the Novel* he depends so heavily on the word 'rhythm', preferring it to 'pattern' because it carries with it an essential temporal dimension. Even pattern is harnessed firmly to the reins of Cronos: 'it springs mainly from the plot, accompanies it like a light in the clouds, and remains visible after it has departed'.[23] The great novels, such as *War and Peace*, have a rhythm which is not the simple beauty of pattern, 'the shape of the book, the book as a whole, the unity'. In his efforts to describe the effect of this rhythm, Forster resorts to music, and it is ironic to note that the spatial metaphor creeps back in:

That is the idea the novelist must cling to. Not completion. Not rounding off but opening out. When the symphony is over we feel that the notes and tunes composing it have been liberated, they have found in the rhythm of the whole their individual freedom. Cannot the novel be like that? Is not there something of it in *War and Peace*? . . . do not great chords begin to sound behind us, and when we have finished does not every item – even the catalogue of strategies – lead a larger existence than was possible at the time?[24]

The 'opening out', 'liberation', 'larger existence', all refer to a widening sense of space; but it is not the space enclosed by the frame of a Cézanne. Rather, it is an explosion of the frame and an engulfment of the reader and the reader's world by the work of art.

But it is also something that happens after the novel is finished – a movement away from the work of art which is left 'behind'. It happens inside the reader as part of his spiritual journey. This is why Forster places so much emphasis on the ends of novels, and complains in *Aspects* that too many novels 'go off at the end'.[25] One 'aesthetic' solution is the prophet's song: writers such as Lawrence and Melville 'irradiating nature from within, so that every colour has a glow and every form a distinctness which could not otherwise be obtained'.[26]

Even prophecy, although it receives close attention in *Aspects*, has its inadequacies, since it tends to rely on the author's exertions and essentially detracts from the 'reality' of what is presented. And Forster will never abandon that reality. One might think of Fry's planes when recalling Forster's famous distinction between round, living characters and flat ones – 'little luminous discs of a prearranged size, pushed . . . like counters across the void'.[27] While Forster makes a gallant attempt to use the language of aesthetic criticism – calling characters at one point 'word-masses' – his whole argument is against abstraction. 'If [humanity] is exorcized or even purified the novel wilts, little is left but a bunch of words. . . . The novel that would express values only becomes unintelligible.'[28] For Forster, James's *Ambassadors* is an example of a 'bunch' of words, its characters maimed and castrated. These sexual images, the novel wilting or castrated, suggest his extreme antagonism to aestheticism and his devotion to organic, ongoing life.

Wilfred Stone says of Forster's literary criticism, 'He is trying to do for the novel what Fry tried to do for the plastic arts, and his aesthetics are largely a restatement of Fry's general principles. His aesthetics begin, one might say, at the point where Fry and Mauron link "plastic values" with literature.'[29] I have been suggesting that this is untrue, and that Forster's ideas of round characters and of rhythm in the novel have little to do with Fry's painted surface or the rhythm of the artist's line. Forster insisted that literature was a 'man-to-man business', and the focus was on the reader's response to the writer's arrangement of real life. Certainly his talk of large chords suggests that what is shared in a great work of literature is a Jungian pattern of archetypes, recognised at play in a real world. Forster, that is, begins with mysticism, and Stone is right to argue that 'the aesthetic unity he cherishes . . . is a vision of ontological completion . . . idealism indeed . . . and had Forster really practised what he preached, his books could not have existed except in ideal'.[30] Only this last part is misleading: for Forster the ideal always had to be glimpsed through the fabric of quotidian reality. But the difference between him and Fry is clear – Fry introduced mysticism, tentatively and with reservations, only at the end of his book *Vision and Design*. Design could take Fry a long way down the path to vision, while for Forster it was either debilitating (Stein and James) or the crude mechanism for a rhythm which might carry the reader on past the work of art, as it were, on another plane.

Forster's insistence on the reading-process suggests an intriguing extrinsic connection between the stuff of his novels and their intention:

> His novels imply but never categorically assert a connection between the transfiguring acts of consciousness enjoyed by some of the characters as they struggle to harmonise the disparate elements of their experience, and the unifying process of the literary imagination.[31]

Woolf, as we shall see, followed Fry more closely than Forster did, claiming for art the difficult but more attainable virtues of insight, understanding and beauty. Woolf's characters occasionally aspire to moments of vision, but these are embedded in the larger design and come and go. Forster's characters also experience moments of vision, but they are permanent transfiguraions – 'eternal moments', in fact. Analogously, Forster claimed for the greatest novels an illuminating effect upon the reader which would last long beyond the final pages of the novel. Great literature, like great music, does 'try to push across at us something which is neither an aesthetic pattern nor a sermon'. Just how Forster attempted to do this in his novels, the place of character, plot, authorial voice and design, will be the subject of the following chapter.

4 Forster's Novels

WHERE ANGELS FEAR TO TREAD (1905)

> ·That is why Baedeker gives the place a star.   (p. 63)

In his first novel Forster sets up an opposition between north and
south, England and Italy, and a plot which encourages (on the
surface) ideas of symmetry. One critic sees 'a thesis–
antithesis–synthesis progression':

> In these early novels Forster's combination of the relatively
> rigid pattern and fluid, 'easy' rhythms serves the purpose of
> exposing unconscious psychological processes while creating a
> sense of aesthetic wholeness.[1]

But a close examination of the novel will reveal that these symmetries are apparent only, and that Forster may use the paintings
of Italy and images of the aesthetic viewpoint, but only to develop
a story which unravels into the muddle of failed aesthetes rather
than into the mystery of consummation.

The novel resolves into two halves rather than into three sections. The first five chapters concern Lilia's marriage to Gino and
her death in childbirth, ending with Mrs Herriton's decision to
send Philip a second time to Italy to rescue the baby. The second
five chapters centre on Philip and Caroline coming to terms with
Italy, specifically with Gino. Instead of the unthinking sexuality
of Lilia, we have the knowing sensuality of both these principals,
the one aesthetic and the other motherly. The strikingly
ambivalent conclusion reveals that neither Caroline nor Philip
has been able to connect English prose with Italian passion; but
the failure of their own friendship will not be repeated in the form
of such a bleak ending until *A Passage to India*.

Forster establishes the opposition between Italy and England as
much through architecture, art and the physical landscape, as

through national character traits. Mrs Herriton reads out her Baedeker description of Monteriano with its one star for the church of Santa Deodata, and its prophetic comment, 'The inhabitants are still noted for their agreeable manners' (p. 20). Philip later tries to re-establish this sense of hermetically sealed distance by reading from Baedeker on his return to Italy (p. 69); but Forster wastes little time in turning our attention to the question of how one relates to the physical setting. Philip's conception of Italy is dangerously romantic:

> False teeth and laughing gas and the tilting chair at a place which knew the Etruscan League, the Pax Romana, Alaric himself, and the Countess Matilda, and the Middle Ages, all fighting and holiness, and the Renaissance, all fighting and beauty! He thought of Lilia no longer. He was anxious for himself: he feared that Romance might die. (p. 25)

So important is this theme of the right conception of Italy's formal beauty that Forster intrudes at this early stage to tell us that Philip was indeed losing this sense of the romantic, and that the sooner it goes the better.

If one reads the above quotation carefully one sees the typical Forsterian stance in the description of Italian history: religion and beauty there were, certainly, but above all there was fighting. This refusal to ignore the paramount human foibles extends to Forster's description of Ghirlandaio's fresco of Santa Deodata. [Plate 7] Here he scorns the art historians ('Giotto came – that is to say, he did not come') and aestheticians in favour of the evidence of human folly epitomised in the saint: 'She was only fifteen when she died, which shows how much is within the reach of any schoolgirl', and wars were won and lost in her name. So throughout the novel we find that Forster's extolling of Italy is always in human terms: 'your tower' outside Philip's window, which reminds you of the time in 1338 when 'your friend' was killed (p. 70), or Gino and his house, intimately described. When Forster plays at Baedeker the tour guide, he takes us not to churches and art works but to the house in which the domestic drama will be played out (p. 32). More important even than the buildings is the natural landscape – the light which wakens the soul of Italy 'when the tourists have left her' (p. 59) or the wood with its flowers which no artist would dare to reproduce (p. 24).

In his excellent article on the way the paintings of Ghirlandaio and Giotto 'suggest the symbols, reveal the characters and emphasise the themes'[2] of this and Forster's other Italian novel, *A Room with a View*, Jeffrey Meyers notes that in the legend of Santa Deodata the board on which she died became covered with white violets. Forster fills his novels with violets when the 'good' moments happen, again suggesting that for him the miracle of Nature was far more important and beautiful than the miracle of the child saint. Forster's evaluation of aesthetic appreciation is thus assured, but the novel traces his characters as they learn, falteringly, how not to look at pictures.

Philip lags behind his narrator but becomes educated to his point of view. Although he begins the novel insisting that Lilia not 'go with that awful tourist idea that Italy's only a museum of antiquities and art' (p. 13), he must himself, like the women, learn the truth of that statement in his own experience; romance is just as unreal and unhelpful to human affairs as the aesthetic outlook. Forster's portrait of Philip comes, significantly, after the chapters describing Gino's marriage, in which Gino's point of view regarding Lilia is sympathetically put forward: 'Nor should she shake her fist at you when she leaves the room' (p. 46). True, Forster had earlier noted frankly that Italy is no place for women (pp. 35–6), but coming after this torrid relationship the portrait of Philip seems particularly anaemic:

> At all events he had got a sense of beauty and a sense of humour, two most desirable gifts. . . . At twenty-two he went to Italy with some cousins, and there he absorbed into one aesthetic whole olive-trees, blue sky, frescoes, country inns, saints, peasants, mosaics, statues, beggars . . . .
>
> In a short time it was over. . . . He concluded that nothing could happen, not knowing that human love and love of truth sometimes conquer where love of beauty fails.
>
> A little disenchanted, a little tired, but aesthetically intact. . . . (p. 47)

Philip has cultivated the artist's detachment. This has given him 'a general view of the muddle' (p. 88) but in regarding life as a spectacle he has starved his own soul. He has remained, in Forster's devastating anatomical sneer, 'aesthetically intact'.

From Gino's first push, with its homosexual overtones, Philip

egins to learn to respond to human beings. At the opera he is
etter able than the women to join in and appreciate the Italian
ay when he is hauled from one box to another to meet Gino and
is friends. It is typical of Forster that he should set this climactic
moment at the Italian opera, where the extreme stylisation of
uman drama is, for the Italian audience, only a pretext for spon-
neous outbursts of love which extend to the singers themselves.
ven Philip's brutal beating after he announces the death of
ino's baby is, in a sense, enjoyed by Philip as a process of
uman interaction. But his sense of detachment remains to the
nd. He can judge Sawston and his mother 'but he could not
ebel' (p. 56). He is the type of the English character about which
orster wrote an essay in 1920: 'There is plenty of emotion
urther down, but it never gets used.'³

Miss Abbott, the second angel of the novel (in contrast to the
ol Lilia who rushed in), begins her conversion at the opera.
here she rekindles the spirit 'bathed in beauty within and
ithout' (p. 75) in which she promoted the relationship between
Lilia and Gino. For Forster beauty is definitely within, in the soul
f the beholder. He tells us explicitly that the Italian opera
observes beauty, and chooses to pass it by' (p. 72), yet on the
ext page we read that Caroline Abbott 'rejoiced in the existence
f beauty' (p. 73). Philip sees that there is the potential for
nchantment in Italy (p. 61), but it is the Snow White Miss
Abbott who falls under its spell. Her attempts to see the baby as a
rinciple and Gino as a posing artist's model (pp. 78–9) collapse
efore the throbbing reality of his domesticity.

Miss Abbott has attempted to live the life of a Santa Deodata,
ut her salvation comes in renouncing such religiosity. When
Philip comes upon her holding the baby, after she and Gino have
athed him, he sees the composition as 'Virgin and Child, with
Donor' by Bellini, Signorelli or Lorenzo di Credi. The irony is
hat the attraction between Gino and Caroline is earthly and sensual, as is her attraction for the baby, and this irony is
underscored by the fact that, as Meyers observes, the three of
them form a composition very like the one in the Ghirlandaio
fresco.⁴ The warning has been clear to us all through the novel
never to confuse art with life, and it should be clear to Philip also.
But Philip has replaced the romance of Italian history with the
romance of Italian painting, a disastrous progression which is
most fully seen after his fight with Gino when he watches him

collapse 'with a piercing cry of woe' and cling to Caroline like child:

> Philip looked away, as he sometimes looked away from grea
> pictures where visible forms suddenly became inadequate fo
> the things they have shown to us. He was happy; he wa
> assured that there was greatness in the world. There came t
> him an earnest desire to be good through the example of thi
> good woman. He would try henceforward to be worthy of th
> things she had revealed. Quietly, without hysterical prayers o
> banging of drums, he underwent conversion. He was saved
> (p. 101)

Philip's religious ecstasy is exactly like the kind of experienc which the Ghirlandaio fresco was intended to inspire, and represents in its otherworldly religiosity everything which Forste abhorred.

That Philip has failed dreadfully in his spiritual journey is con firmed by the last pages, where a remarkable series of image gives us Caroline's point of view on the world, Philip's, and thei relationship to each other. While Caroline confesses that she ha been possessed, 'wrapped round' by Gino and what he stands for Philip congratulates himself for having once more obtained ar objective viewpoint: 'And to see round it he was standing at ar immense distance' (p. 106). At first he sees Caroline as Pasiphae and Gino by implication as a bull (p. 105) – an interpretation which says much about Philip's concealed homosexual tenden cies, Gino's potent heterosexuality and Philip's deep sense o betrayal and jealousy. At the end, however, he casts Caroline as Endymion, a reference to one of the most etherealised Greek myths, as idealised as a Renaissance painting on the subject of the myth itself. Philip 'had reached love by the spiritual path' (p. 102) and here attempts to glorify it.

There is an overwhelming sadness about this last scene, however. Caroline, the frustrated spinster, has run away from the challenge of physical fulfilment, and Philip will not challenge her again. What kind of apotheosis is it for Philip when he regards this woman of such potential human warmth as an ethereal god dess and feels, 'For all the wonderful things had happened'? Both characters are condemned to a future of sterility and memories. Above all, they have both lost their sense of humour. As they rush ff to protect Harriet's vision from the train's smuts, we wonder whose vision is the more blinkered.

In this first novel Forster used a simple, dialectical framework to tell a simple parable. The life force of Gino and the baby is contrasted with the English boy and the English girl, both attracted sexually to his promise of life and both, having refused the challenge, unable to recognise the need even in each other. Forster uses motifs of Italian art and architecture to argue against the aesthetic view of life in favour of the muddle of human relationships. Nevertheless the simplicity of this tragedy gives *Where Angels Fear to Tread* a beauty comparable to the aesthetic balance of Santa Deodata and St Gregory. Only the messages are opposite.

A ROOM WITH A VIEW (1908)

> *It was something to have retained a View, and secure in it and in their love as long as they have one another to love, George and Lucy await the third World War. . . .* [5]

The first book of *A Room with a View*, the first seven chapters set in Italy, were written very early in Forster's career. The last thirteen chapters were written after he had published two other novels, *Where Angels Fear to Tread* and *The Longest Journey*.[6] We are reminded of this sequence when, in chapter 15, Minnie, 'rushing in where Cecil feared to tread' (p. 400), offers to play tennis. Cecil belongs with Philip and the aesthetes, but Forster is on the side of the Italians, Emersons, and fools.

While there are the remnants of an aesthetic shape to the book – George's kisses in chapters 4, 7 and 15, or the turn of the tide in chapter 10 (halfway through), when Cecil invites the Emersons into his cottage – the story element is clearly dominant. Lucy's education should be seen as all of a piece, and the recurring images from landscape and painting, as in the earlier other Italian novel, are simply clues to the morality which the narrator endorses and which Lucy must learn to recognise. The whimsical chapter-headings, such as those to chapter 4 ('Fourth Chapter') and chapter 6 ('The Reverend Arthur Beebe, the Reverend Cuthbert Eager . . . Drive out in Carriages to See a View; Italians Drive Them'), reinforce this impression that Forster tried to make the form of this novel as innocuous and unobtrusive as possible.

Frederick Crews, dismayed perhaps that the heroine of the novel is a young girl, and one what is more who ends happy, argues that Forster is concerned here with morals rather than with metaphysics.[7] But even the title of the novel suggests that how one sees one's neighbour is intimately bound up with how one sees the world. Again the arts come in for a beating, but landscapes and landscape-painting are exempt from the general censure, because they have much to do with one's moods and responses to others. Views are extremely important to rooms.

Cecil, for example, is an aesthete who sees Lucy as a desirable painting:

> She was like a woman of Leonardo da Vinci's, whom we love not so much for herself as for the things that she will not tell us. The things are assuredly not of this life; no woman of Leonardo's could have anything so vulgar as a 'story' . . . at his words she had turned and stood between him and the light with immeasurable plains behind her.   (p. 357)

He is as interested in her setting as in her, and he is interested only in her surface and her suggestiveness, never her reality. In the following chapter, 'Lucy as a Work of Art', he allows her a modicum of life, but only because Leonardo had before him:

> It was as if one should see the Leonardo on the ceiling of the Sistine. He longed to hint to her that not here lay her vocation, that a woman's power and charm reside in mystery, not in muscular rant. But possibly rant is a sign of vitality: it mars the beautiful creature, but shows that she is alive.   (p. 364)

Forster extends this anti-aesthetic attitude through morality to metaphysics, introducing Cecil as the mediaeval man, ascetic like a Gothic statue (p. 356). The historical analogy has already been made in the crucial chapter 4, where the murder takes place, and Forster writes an essay on the mediaeval woman. This is no haphazard social history, nor is it simply a moral plea for the equality of the sexes. Like Virginia Woolf, Forster saw that how the sexes regard each other has a direct bearing on their metaphysical orientation towards the universe. Hence we learn that 'the only relationship which Cecil conceived was feudal: that of protector and protected. He had no glimpse of the comradeship after which the girl's soul yearned' (p. 399). But not only this: we learn that Italy offers a metaphysical challenge to this apparently trivial social arrangement:

> Nor did he realise a more important point – that if she was too great for this society, she was too great for all society, and had reached the stage where personal intercourse would alone satisfy her. . . . Italy was offering her the most priceless of all possessions – her own soul.   (p. 372)

Cecil cannot cope with life in the raw, as passion and flux; Forster loses no opportunity to tell us this, but always it is done in terms of perception. For example, when he warns Beebe not to sit in a chair in which Honeychurch has left a bone, Forster comments, 'he did not realise that, taken together, they kindled the room into the life that he desired' (p. 358). Italy tolerates the tourist with his Baedeker, but the more spiritual landscape of Greece makes too personal a challenge, which is why Cecil agrees with Beebe not to go there; it is 'not for our little lot' (p. 415).

Beebe, initially a sympathetic character, is perhaps even more of an evil aesthete than Cecil, since his desire for Lucy to remain a sterile portrait originates in a profound misogyny. This life-denying yearning for virginity unites Beebe with one of the other clergymen who seem to swarm through this novel – the Reverend Cuthbert Eager. They would replace the call of the Greek boy Phaeton, 'courage and love' (pp. 345–6), with 'courage and faith'; they would admire Santa Deodata.

With at least three unlikable aesthetes in the novel, art would seem to be under attack, and indeed it is. Lucy's home life is present to her 'bright and distinct, but pathetic as the pictures in a gallery to which, after much experience, a traveller returns' (p. 337). Miss Bartlett, working to destroy Lucy's soul forever after George's assault, 'works like a great artist' (p. 352); the 'tactile values of Giotto' (p. 311) are mocked by Forster and by Emerson; Lucy (the satire only partly rebounds upon her) buys photographs of Fra Angelico, Giotto and 'some Della Robbia babies' (p. 327) but 'the gates of liberty seemed still unopened'. Giotto's *Ascension of St John the Evangelist* in Santa Croce [Plate 8] is important not for what the people get from looking it, or for who looks at it at all, but for the image it suggests of man transcending the everyday reality through a spiritual insight. As Meyers observes, Lucy's own pilgrimage is habitually seen as one of ascension, and even Beebe draws her as a kite on the end of a string which is about to be let go.

The Emersons, of course, replace the Berensons and the Frys as Forster's ideal art critics. They go to Italy to appreciate art, but they can do so equally well in the National Gallery, and always life comes first. At the start of the novel they offer up their room with a view, because they want to *share* that view. Nature is not only to look at but also to be immersed in, so they fill the same room with those Italian violets which are such a prominant leit-motif in the novel (p. 374). Under the Emersons' tutelage, Lucy learns how Nature transcends and incorporates art. In the carriage Mr Emerson tells her that the young lovers in front are Spring incarnate, and shortly afterwards she kisses George amongst the violets in a landscape as lush as a Renoir: 'He saw radiant joy in her face, he saw the flowers beat against her dress in blue waves. The bushes above them closed. He stepped quickly forward and kissed her' (p. 345).

Landscape-painting, that art most in touch with the real world, is the one art to escape censure in the novel. In Mr Emerson's transcendental theory aesthetics leaps into metaphysics, because he regards all landscapes as copies of the ideal landscape which is the limitless perfection of the sky (p. 402). In their admiration for views the Emersons are at one with their narrator, for Forster sets all his epiphanic scenes in the most sumptuous natural settings: not only the glorious swimming-scene, but even the scene in the Piazza Signoria, when Lucy confronts life and death, and art is relegated to bloodstained photographs which young Emerson throws into the Arno:

> The Piazza Signoria is too stony to be brilliant. It has no grass, no flowers, no frescoes, no glittering walls of marble or com-forting patches of ruddy brick. By an odd chance – unless we believe in a presiding genius of place – the statues that relieve its severity suggest, not the innocence of childhood, nor the glorious bewilderment of youth, but the conscious achievements of maturity. Perseus and Judith, Hercules and Thusnelda, they have done or suffered something, and though they are immortal, immortality has come to them after experience, not before. Here, not only in the solitude of

Nature, might a hero meet a goddess, or a heroine a god. (p. 338)

This landscape, Forster is at pains to explain to us after the event, has to do with life and not with art.

The question, not so much moral as metaphysical, is, as Lucy tells Cecil, how to *use* beauty (p. 411). At the beginning of the novel we see Lucy using a Beethoven sonata to explore her own feelings of triumph (p. 320), and later Forster reminds us even more clearly of the disjunction between art and life when he has her playing Schumann in her dejection: 'It broke; it was resumed broken, not marching once from the cradle to the grave. The sadness of the incomplete – the sadness that is often Life, but should never be Art' (p. 379). To impute emotions to art, especially to music, is a very dangerous thing to do, Forster suggests. Whereas when Lucy sings her lament she almost reconciles herself to Windy Corners and a life of resignation (p. 423), the true song is 'not distinguishable from the comic song' (p. 388).

Forster's novel, likewise, is a comedy. It transcends such emotional works as those of Miss Lavish. Indeed there is a wonderful passage where Forster describes the warm Italian sun rising upon a deserted world and shining on a book lying on the ground. The book has a red cover and purports to be Miss Lavish's embodiment of Italy, but we are told that it is bloodless and sentimental. Even Mr Beebe's *Santa Conversazione*, 'in which people who care for one another are painted chatting together about noble things' (p. 422) – surely the quintessential Bloomsbury experience – is inadequate, at least as a conception. The novel even transcends Cecil's reference to Meredith's theory of comedy, which he expounds as he hires his house out to the man who is going to break down his fences, blow a fresh breath of wind into Windy Corners, and steal away his love. The instrument of Forster's transcendence is old Emerson, who declares, 'Italy is only an euphuism for Fate' (p. 418). His teaching is identical with Forster's: 'passion is truth' says the narrator (p. 413); 'passion is sanity' echoes old Emerson (p. 428). 'To see the whole of everything at once' (p. 433) is not to achieve the painter's aesthetic detachment but to surrender to the holiness of the heart's affections and direct desire, even if that surrender encourages, as with the Emersons it does, a bit of muscular rant. Just as Lucy finally learns to leap 'across the rubbish that cumbers the world' (p. 387) so Forster attempts in this novel to transcend the very unaesthetic, realistic substance of the fiction. Instead of moulding the novel into a work of art, he tries to insert a work of art (a fateful story with a comic resolution) into the 'rubbish' of a realistic narrative. Art as aesthetic balance loses out all through the novel and also when considering the novel as a whole, but artifice, the artist as magician, can be seen to return as a matter of rhetorical persuasion. The only Fate really operating in this novel, Forster wants to convince the reader, is neither the narrator nor Emerson, but the individual human spirit (Lucy's) in quest of fulfilment. Perhaps Forster chose Giotto's *Ascension* not for any aesthetic reason but because it is an artist's rendition of a human impossibility, as St John rises through the air towards salvation. At any event, it is certainly not the experience of significant form in Italian painting which liberates Lucy. Meyers is quite wrong to argue that 'Italy and its art work some marvel in Lucy: they make her aware of her craving for sympathy and love, and manifest their power to evoke passion and bring it to fulfilment.'[8] For it is the Emersons themselves, who are as opposed to aesthetic criticism as they are to Baedeker, who change her life.

Forster ends his novel with his lovers back in Italy, but an Italy full of the spirit of Nature: 'they heard the river, bearing down the snows of winter into the Mediterranean'. So resolute is the author's stand against aesthetic completion, that fifty years later he was prepared to destroy even that fateful shaping of plot in the novel. In his 'Anniverary Postscript' Forster described what happened to all the characters in his novel, even claiming to have met Cecil in Alexandria in 1914.[9] The room with a view, he said, is gone now, but George and Lucy are still inspired by its memory. It is not the memory of Giotto which inspires aesthetic contemplation, but the memory of a honeymoon hotel room which inspires human love.

THE LONGEST JOURNEY (1907)

> *Though I can think about the new world I cannot put it into fiction.*[10]

The Longest Journey is the first of Forster's novels to reveal a clear skeletal structure. If one assigns *A Room with a View* to a date

before this novel (as indeed half of it was composed previously)
one can say that the last four novels of Forster have such a structure of major movements.

While the titles of the divisions are geographical –
'Cambridge', 'Sawston', 'Wiltshire' – *The Longest Journey*, as
S. P. Rosenbaum has persuasively argued, had its origin in a
philosophical debate which

> involved converting the refutation of epistemological Idealism
> into an ethical conclusion about accepting the objective reality
> of other people, of other loves, of other societies, of nature, and
> finally of time. From Moore's interest in arguments against the
> existence of objective reality Forster develops his own novelistic
> interest in the objective and subjective assumptions that his
> characters act upon in their lives.[11]

This philosophical approach to the novel can be very rewarding,
but if the novel is considered as a work of art it is a frustrating,
disappointing affair. The reason is that Forster here faces in
artistic terms the dilemma about idealism and realism which his
characters discuss in the novel, but finds no satisfactory solution
or reconciliation.

The first section, set in Cambridge, occupies just over half the
novel, and, because his characters are relating and maturing
through the discussion of ideas, Forster succeeds in creating a
convincing world where the split between daily life and art is not
yet apparent. Ansell's historically justified example of the cow in
the quad will reverberate quite 'naturally' later in the novel when
the scene moves to the bucolic countryside. Even the pervasive
light imagery is supported by the actual philosophical examples of
Ansell's match or Plato's parable of the cave. Agnes, with her
golden earrings, bursts into the room making the students (except
Ansell) 'fly like mists before the sun' (p. 115). Mr Pembroke
observes that 'life without an ideal would be like the sky without
the sun' (p. 122), and Rickie recalls Agnes's entrance to Ansell,
when someone was playing Wagner's *Rheingold*

'. . . and he'd just got to the part where they sing

Rheingold!
Rheingold!

and the sun strikes into the waters, and the music, which up to
then has so often been in E flat – '
'Goes into D sharp . . . .'   (p. 122)

We go along with this pattern of imagery because much of it is
inherited or wilfully invented by the students themselves. Rickie,
for example, after the talk about ideals, suddenly sees in the night
sky 'gods and heroes, virgins and brides, to whom the Greeks
have given their names'. Later on Rickie describes love to Ansell
as 'a light suddenly held behind the world' (p. 165).

Gradually this fabricated imagery is challenged and replaced
by a more natural imagery. Agnes proves not to be a source of
illumination to the dying Gerald, who complains that he cannot
see her. And in the later sections Stephen becomes the bearer of
light, in a far more complicated and elusive way. He seems to
exist in the darkness rather than the light, yet despite the trivial
illumination of his pipe he does spread a spiritual light wherever
he goes.

It would be appropriate if this light-imagery were typical of a
larger movement in the novel from the theoretical, imposed
imagery of Cambridge to the testings of the real world of Sawston
and the survival of the true values in Wiltshire. Unfortunately,
what should be a real world in the second half of the novel is clut-
tered with novelistic fabrications in the form of imagery and symbolic plot. The style of *The Longest Journey*, in other words, parts
company from the thematic drift, and, even as Rickie learns to
accept the real and participate in it, the reader is being asked to
erect his fate and Stephen's victory into an abstract symbolic
structure.

The countryside of Wiltshire is impressive for its barrenness,
which Rickie appreciates during his first ride with Stephen
(p. 183). Earlier Agnes complained of Turner's landscapes
because he always 'introduces a man like a bolster into the
foreground' (p. 157); but Forster the novelist, unsympathetic to
Agnes's form of idealism, paints the Cadover landscape for us
and gives us Rickie, 'that anxious little speck', dwarfed upon it.
He goes on to tell us of 'nature's one joke' in Wiltshire, which is
to impose tiny pockets of civilisation on such an uninviting
terrain.

Such description carries over the concerns of the Cambridge
section and transforms the imagery into the appropriate imagery

of the real world. But as a novelist Forster is uneasy with barrenness, and contrives to populate these sections with Greek
goddesses, as if he were unsure of himself out of the conveniently
allusive environs of an Italian city, or a Greek ruin. Gerald looks
like a Greek but has none of the spirit; Agnes is like a goddess
imported to Greece from elsewhere (pp. 142–3); and Ansell, after
his interview, sees Stephen as one of those primitive Greeks 'to
whom', says Forster sheepishly, 'we continually return' (p. 148).
Ansell's classical allusions may be justifiable, as when he is
reminded by Rickie's situation of the Greek drama, 'where the
actors know so little and the spectators so much' (p. 251). Forster
reminds us shortly afterwards that all the world is a stage and that
Ansell has his part to play; nevertheless, his novel is given those
'inevitable' features of a Greek drama such as the elimination of
the maimed and the curse of the fathers, and as an audience the
reader may well protest that he knows too much.

These fatal patterns are reinforced not just by Greek similes,
but also by a clutter of Greek objects. Stephen has a painting of
Demeter which hangs and twirls in his room 'like a joint of meat'
(p. 188). (One can almost feel Forster's unease here, as he
attempts to animate such a heavy piece of imagery.) As in
Maurice, Forster is determined to get us into the British Museum
to make a classical point, so Widdrington and Ansell talk near the
Parthenon frieze, which depicts a festival procession in honour of
the patroness of Athens. The chapter ends by reminding us,
through Ansell, of the less sociable and communal deities:

He left the Parthenon to pass by the monuments of our more
reticent beliefs – the temple of the Ephesian Artemis, the statue
of the Cnidian Demeter. Honest, he knew that here were
powers he could not cope with, nor, as yet, understand.
(p. 228)

In this portentous passage Forster, the guide, talks through Ansell
to the humble reader. Sure enough, the parallels with Demeter
are later spelled out in Stephen's life. As Demeter roamed the
world in search of her daughter, lighting the way with torches, so
Stephen briefly illuminates the way to others and finds his
daughter.

The Hermes of Praxiteles, that god of revels with winged feet,
is another obvious and recurrent motif. Agnes dusts the bust effi-

ciently while it stands in the Pembroke house, but Stephen smashes it with a brick on his return. This episode in turn relates to Rickie's knowledge that 'the artist is not a bricklayer at all, but a horseman, whose business it is to catch Pegasus at once' (p. 121). But more is needed than these neat verbal connections to make a unified work of art. Indeed, Rickie's own stories are rejected by his editor because they 'do not convince as a whole' (p. 204), and, while Forster may have in mind his own early stories of Pan, he might also consider this very novel. The theoretical answer, at any rate, comes in Mr Failing's essay 'Gaps', which Ansell reads:

> Solitude, star-crowned, pacing the fields of England, has a dialogue with Seclusion. He, poor little man, lives in the choicest scenery – among rocks, forests, emerald lawns, azure lakes. To keep people out he has built round his domain a high wall, on which is graven his motto – 'Procul este profani.' But he cannot enjoy himself. . . .   (p. 245)

Only when the Profane are allowed in, can Seclusion glimpse the heart of Nature. The essay is Forster's crude gloss on the earlier comment by the aesthete in Rickie's own dell, '*Procul este, profani!*' In life, as in art, one must somehow connect the real and the ideal, and let insight emerge from friction between the two. But, if Rickie's stories do not fulfil this prescription, does Forster's novel?

The conflict between realism and pattern is ubiquitous in Forster's approach to novel-writing, but in *The Longest Journey* it is also the theme. In theory it would seem quite a straightforward task to proceed from the theorising of Cambridge to the working-out of the themes in the activity of the last sections, to show, with Mr Jackson, that Demeter and Aphrodite, 'poetry, not prose, lies at the core' (p. 223). But the poetry in *The Longest Journey*, with its roots so vibrantly in the Cambridge of Ansell, Forster's own youth and the Shelley who gave Forster the title for his novel, wells up from that homosexual attachment which Forster felt himself forbidden to explore. In his heyday with Ansell Rickie yearns for 'a kind of friendship office, where the marriage of true minds could be registered' (p. 153), but Forster denies his characters that sort of office in the second half of his novel. Instead, his story becomes an imposed cautionary parable, its negations pointing in a vague way to a centre which is never stated and never filled. Forster gives us a kind of dell, but one whose meaning is conveyed through plot rather than through passion.

The narrator goes out of his way to take charge and, trying to forsake the realism which he knows is not the heart of his message, he sets himself up as the chronicler of an old parable. At the beginning of Rickie's story he says, 'The reader who has no book will be obliged to listen to it' (p. 126), and he steps forth again to judge Rickie and Agnes and reveal their destinies:

> Henceforward he deteriorates. Let those who censure him suggest what he should do. He has lost the work that he loved, his friends, and his child. He remained conscientious and decent, but the spiritual part of him proceeded towards ruin. (p. 235)

> For Agnes also has her tragedy. She belonged to the type – not necessarily an elevated one – that loves once and once only. . . .
>   She is not conscious of her tragedy, and therefore only the gods need weep at it. But it is fair to remember that hitherto she moves as one from whom the inner life has been withdrawn. (p. 239)

By imposing his own authorial pattern, Forster is conscious that he has muddied his original philosophical debate between realism and idealism. The confusion is evident in the passage in which Forster attributes the division of the novel into three parts to Rickie himself:

> He would compare Cambridge with Sawston, and either with a third type of existence, to which, for want of a better name, he gave the name of 'Wiltshire'.
>   It must not be thought that he is going to waste his time. These contrasts and comparisons never took him long, and he never indulged in them until the serious business of the day was over. And, as time passed, he never indulged in them at all. (p. 211)

A more mature novelist, or someone, such as Virginia Woolf, more highly conscious of the novel as an artefact with its own fictional reverberations, might have capitalised on this confusion by playing off shape and content, or making the central character more consciously a writer (like Bernard or Miss La Trobe). But Forster's pattern remains imposed from without (as Duncan Grant's circular pattern is imposed on his screen [Plate 2]), just as Rickie's lameness destines him to non-issue and the stage-managed death by having the offending limbs crushed by a train.

In *Maurice* Forster would be able to create real people in a real countryside, but in *The Longest Journey* he gives us the vague symbolism of the Figsbury Rings and a gesture towards a rosy domestic future. The ending of this novel, so similar to the end of *Howards End* with the establishment of a contingent heir full of promise, has a similar air of artifice about it. But within the novel art has been so denigrated in favour of life that we do not believe in it. The Ansells have 'a complete absence of taste' (p. 131); Rickie's father collects art objects but never had 'thought one single thing that had the slightest beauty or value' (p. 127); the Pembroke house is filled with 'decent water-colours' and 'Madonnas of acknowledged merit' (p. 133). Yet a novel which is intended to refute idealism turns out to be one of Forster's most patently fabricated creations.

HOWARDS END (1910)

> *Elaboration, skill, wisdom, penetration, beauty – they are all there, but they lack fusion. . . .* [12]

Forster's own estimation of *Howards End* is echoed in Woolf's bewilderment at why it does not quite succeed. He called it 'my best novel and approaching a good novel. Very elaborate and all-pervading plot that is seldom tiresome or forced, range of characters, social sense, wit, wisdom, colour.' [13] The plot certainly does dominate the novel as in none of Forster's other works, since it is the outcome of the plot – who gets Howards End – which totally comprises the theme. Because of this, Forster was unable to shorten the manuscript at his publisher's request. [14] That infamously casual opening – 'One may as well begin with . . . ' – belies this plot framework of steel, yet Forster's instinct to work against the portentous, allegorical shape was correct. Woolf

attributed the failure of the novel to just this largeness of conception, the lyrical passages saying too much too grandly:

> Instead of flowering naturally – as in Proust, for instance –
> from an overflow of interest and beauty in the object itself, we
> feel that they have been called into existence by some irritation,
> are the effort of a mind outraged by ugliness to supplement it
> with a beauty which, because it originates in protest, has
> something a little febrile about it. [15]

R. N. Parkinson argues that 'Forster's novel seems to offer two
kinds of completeness: the completeness of a carefully meditated
symbolic pattern and the completeness of a comprehensive picture of human nature'. [16] But whatever that last phrase might
mean it is just this feeling that the novelist has *not* accounted for
the 'whole' of English society that keeps the reader from acceding
to Forster's eventual, evolutionary solution to the whole social
problem. Leonard Bast is the most obvious example of a
simplified conception of social unrest, and this, coupled with the
incredibility of Margaret's attraction to Henry Wilcox, renders
the allegorical shape 'febrile' indeed when it is considered *in vacuo*.
What gives the novel its power, despite this, is the way the powers
of human beings, through love but especially through the creation
of works of art, are steadily eroded in favour of the impersonal
powers of nature, and finally, of Howards End itself.
Howards End is full of movement and trains. We begin in
London with the set piece about the railway termini, 'gates to the
glorious and the unknown' (p. 9). The main impulse of the novel
is centrifugal from London, a city decaying under the developers'
sledgehammers into a characterless sludge of housing-estates.
Margaret almost escapes with Mrs Wilcox, but is held up on the
very platform. It is Leonard Bast who makes the first foray into
the real England, and his account of his nocturnal pilgrimage is
both inspiring and pathetic, building as it does to Helen's question, ' "But was the dawn wonderful?" . . . With unforgettable
sincerity he replied: "No" ' (p. 117).
   The Schlegel house is itself demolished, caught up in the
transformation of the city into a 'tract of quivering grey' (p. 106),
but Margaret's salvation begins when she walks out into the
shires of southern England. The opening of chapter 19 recalls to
us Forster's fondness for travel guides in its birds-eye view of

England as it is pointed out to Frau Liesecke: 'the imagination swells, spreads and deepens, until it becomes geographic and encircles England' (p. 165). Here the metaphoric landscape is identified with the physical one, an appropriate resolution of the engagement – just announced – between Margaret and Henry, the one seeing life steadily, the other seeing it whole. Forster reinforces the identification of an attitude of soul and an attitude towards landscape when Frieda comments, 'One is certain of nothing but the truth of one's own emotions':

> It was, however illogically, the good, the beautiful, the true, as opposed to the respectable, the pretty, the adequate. It was a landscape of Böcklin's beside a landscape of Leader's, strident and ill-considered, but quivering into supernatural life. It sharpened idealism, stirred the soul. (p. 167)

Forster is as careful as Roger Fry in a lecture on landscape-painting to remind his audience that the pathetic fallacy is indeed a fallacy – when Margaret confesses to Helen that she does not actually love Henry, she does so with 'her eyes shifting over the view, as if this county or that could reveal the secret of her own heart' (p. 170) – but he ends the chapter with a rhetorical flourish, looking again at the whole of southern England and celebrating a particular attitude not towards landscape but towards the land:

> Frome was forced inward towards Dorchester, Stour against Wimborne, Avon towards Salisbury, and over the immense displacement the sun presided, leading it to triumph ere he sank to rest. England was alive, throbbing through all her estuaries, crying for joy through the mouths of all her gulls, and the north wind, with contrary motion, blew stronger against her rising seas. What did it mean? For what end are her fair complexities, her changes of soil, her sinuous coast? Does she belong to those who have moulded her and made her feared by other lands, or to those who have added nothing to her power, but have somehow seen her, seen the whole island at once, lying as a jewel in a silver sea, sailing as a ship of souls, with all the brave world's fleet accompanying her towards eternity? (p. 172)

This is just one of many paeans of praise which Forster offers to
the English countryside. His nature worship takes him from the
green and pleasant land of Bunyan and Blake to the imagery of
D. H. Lawrence:

> Margaret greeted her lord with peculiar tenderness on the mor-
> row. Mature as he was, she might yet be able to help him to the
> building of the rainbow bridge that should connect the prose in
> us with the passion. Without it we are meaningless fragments,
> half monks, half beasts, unconnected arches that have never
> joined into a man. With it love is born, and alights on the
> highest curve, glowing against the grey, sober against the fire.
> Happy the man who sees from either aspect the glory of these
> outspread wings. The roads of his soul lie clear, and he and his
> friends shall find easy-going.   (p. 183)

His characters are defined by the way they view the land: Henry
cannot see the 'illimitable views' (p. 184); Helen, praising her
sister for being spiritual, is accused of 'closing' vistas rather too
quickly (p. 192). Even Leonard is vouchsafed a vision of both
realms, prose and passion, as he travels through the landscape of
Hertfordshire on his fatal visit: 'powdered in between, were the
villas of businessmen, who saw life more steadily, though with the
steadiness of the half-closed eye. Over all the sun was streaming,
all the birds were singing' (p. 320). This, finally, is Forster's
rather disappointingly simple answer to the problem of vision:
one must look at the real landscape, but with 'half-closed' eyes.

If Forster is unsure of his own affirmative stance towards
nature, it may be because in *Howards End* he refuses to resort to
the nymphs and Dryads of earlier novels and stories. His
pastoralism is now no longer a matter of primitive identification,
but a more mature husbanding of nature's bounty, and the image
he invents for the purpose is the wych elm growing up beside
Howards End. It is an effort to evoke a more complex truth than
in the earlier stories, and as an image it is more successful than
the equally difficult attempt to marry opposites in the marriage of
Henry and Margaret.

One thing Forster is clear about is the place of aesthetics in his
brave new world. In the famous chapter 5 Forster dramatises the
responses to Beethoven that he later described in his essay 'On
Not Listening to Music'. Forster confesses himself to be like

Helen, letting the music suggest goblins walking over the universe, and their final rout: 'But the goblins were there. They could return. He had said so bravely, and that is why one can trust Beethoven when he says other things' (p. 32). If those 'other things' have to do with beauty, they have credibility only because they have their roots in reality. Of course, the danger with 'meaning' is that one may lose sight of the form altogether. Both Margaret and Forster observe that Monet can become Debussy, that 'the arts can take in each other's washing'. But, when Margaret explains to Leonard that 'music is different to pictures' (p. 36), the poor young man, converted to Fryean aestheticism, rushes off to digest Ruskin, that man 'who had never been dirty or hungry, and had not guessed successfully what dirt and hunger are' (p. 47). There is the beauty of nature and fine art on the one hand, and there is Jacky and a sordid London flat on the other. Ruskin is inadequate because, unlike Beethoven, he did not perceive this tension and look in art for an expression of it. Instead, or so Forster ends chapter 6, 'It occurred to him, as he glided over the whispering lagoons, that the power of Nature could not be shortened by the folly, nor her beauty altogether saddened by the misery, of such as Leonard' (p. 53). Nowhere in Forster's work is his aesthetic as clearly stated as in these two chapters. Forster's anguish at the inevitable selectivity of art extends to satirising his own novel, since he begins chapter 6 alarmingly, 'We are not concerned with the very poor. They are unthinkable . . . .' This is part of the honesty which Woolf complained of, which however true and poignant totally undermines the overall attempt of the novel to say something conclusive about England as a whole.

The extremity of Forster's antagonism to art shown in these chapters is repeated throughout the novel in the way he rejects painting in favour of the land (compare Fry's uneasy abstracting of pastoral landscape in 'The Barn' [Plate 9]). While Helen discounts the aesthetic, formal element in a work of art, and Leonard gives it too much value, Margaret is seen for a time as the balancing rainbow arch. She explains, 'Of course Böcklin strains because he wants something – beauty and all the other intangible gifts that are floating about the world. So his landscapes don't come off, and Leader's do' (p. 73). But for Forster there is something suspect in the subjectivity of the German painter, just as the romanticism of the Schlegel sisters must be tempered with

Anglo-Saxon utilitarianism. Forster is in fact unsure of Margaret's aesthetic tastes, as is evidenced in his changing one of her paintings from a Blake in manuscript to a Ricketts (p. 37). I suspect that Forster wanted to deny *all* art, even Blake's (which among English art must come close to Forster's ideal of a spirituality rooted in nature), from satisfying Margaret's yearning for wholeness, which must come only from Howards End.

For romanticism itself can be an artificial taste, replacing personal development. If, as we are told by the narrator, the essence of life is 'romantic beauty' (pp. 104–5), we must be careful to clarify what we mean by that. Leonard's mistake is to take his romance with a capital R from books and paintings and music, rather than from life. To him the Schlegel girls 'were denizens of Romance, who must keep to the corner he had assigned them, pictures that must not walk out of their frames' (p. 120). But, as Forster sarcastically observes of the London 'scene', 'It was doubtless a pity not to keep up with Wedekind or John, but some closing of the gates is inevitable after thirty, if the mind itself is to become a creative power' (p. 259).

Forster always sees art from the point of view of the consumer, and its effect on personal development. Total devotees are doomed to Leonard's fate if they are lower-class, or to become colossal egotists like Pierpont Morgan (p. 232) if they are successful. Art, for Forster, is to be taken if at all in small doses, to be seen as providing clues to one's personal pilgrimage. Wickham Place, it is true, 'had not mistaken culture for an end' (p. 254) – one can see in such a statement the vast distance between Forster and Clive Bell – but it is only a terminus on the route out into nature towards Howards End, which replaces all works of art in the novel and speaks to those who are attuned, like Margaret, to 'hope on this side of the grave' (p. 203). At Howards End the only art is fugitive or minor: the hedge in spring; 'a half-painted picture which would be finished in a few days' (p. 266); Margaret's love for Henry 'stamped with his image like the cameos we rescue out of dreams' (p. 329). The only romance is an intensely human, temporal sense of history and tradition – the memory of Mrs Wilcox, the promise of a new child and inheritor.

Forster's answer in *Howards End* is embedded in the healing-process of time. Unlike *To the Lighthouse*, where a similar matronly presiding spirit guides an artist to her vision and the novel completes a clear tripartite pattern, *Howards End* ends with a literal

vision – 'We've seen to the very end' – which directs us, literally
to the English fields and to the cycles of the crops. The
incredibilities of Helen's and Margaret's courtships are there
solely to manoeuvre the evolutionary pattern into position and to
set the frozen vision of Mrs Wilcox, a wisp of straw in her hair
into motion again. Unlike *Wuthering Heights*, where a similar
evolutionary conclusion is balanced by the overwhelming reality
of the central passion, the whole meaning of *Howards End* lies in
its plotted conclusion. But, with neither the convincing reality of
its principal perpetrators, nor the apparent endorsement of pattern as artistic vision, Forster has cut away all possible support for
his climactic vision.

Yet, as usual in a Forster novel, a close examination shows that
art has not been repudiated with the vehemence at first apparent.
There are the specific instances where Forster relies heavily on
artists such as Böcklin and Beethoven to convey his vision, or
where he resorts to Drayton to repopulate the shires with real
nymphs instead of motor cars (p. 195). But there is also an overall
pattern to the all-important plot. The central scene is the proposal
scene between Henry and Margaret; it also falls at the centre of
the novel. Though improbable, it is prepared for very carefully
and is bathed in a 'central radiance' which then radiates out to
touch both ends of the novel. The scene ends with Mrs Wilcox,
'ever a welcome ghost; surveying the scene, thought Margaret,
without one hint of bitterness' (p. 163). The unfulfilled promise
of Ruth's friendship with Margaret so firmly established at the
beginning of the novel hovers over the rest of it, and the book is
structured around those moments when Margaret comes closest
to her spirit once more. Mrs Wilcox dies at the end of the first
quarter of the novel and Margaret enters Howards End in the
third quarter – once when she is mistaken for Mrs Wilcox
(pp. 198–204), and once after the Oniton interlude when she
enters the house, again alone, and Mrs Avery insists that she and
her furniture belong there (p. 264). The last quarter is then
centred on Howards End, as Forster turns over the plot devices in
order to establish a Schlegel–Wilcox dynasty in the house.

Although Forster does not divide *Howards End* into books or
even into numbered or titled chapters, then, the novel still has
four large movements based on the friendship of Margaret and
Ruth. It is the resonance and satisfactory completion of *this* shape
which gives the novel any conviction that it has. As passion is

ncomplete without prose, so the goblins set loose in the English
countryside are composed not simply by a genetic pattern, but by
the pattern of art.

MAURICE

> *I was trying to connect up and use all the fragments I was born
> with.* [17]

Written in 1913–14 and published in 1971, *Maurice* shows more
clearly than any other Forster novel his apparent disregard for art
in favour of human happiness. In the opening scene, Mr Ducie
the schoolmaster draws sexual diagrams in the sand for Maurice,
then rushes back to delete them before they are seen by others.
Maurice's reaction to this – 'Liar, coward' (p. 9) – is symbolic of
Forster's own special stand for art in this novel. Morality should
not be a matter of concealment, and neither should art attempt to
conceal figures in carpets. Art is 'this man-to-man business' and
in *Maurice* that image has a quite explicit reference to the bold,
frank openness of love between two men. [Plate 10]

The courtship of Maurice and his first lover, Clive Durham, is
conducted very much in the terms of an aesthetic inquiry. Early
on, Clive reads Dante's *Paradiso* (p. 41) to prove that the poet
believed in the Trinity, symbolised by the three intersecting rain-
bows. Maurice's imagination stirs at the idea of the face seen at
their junction, because it reminds him not of a holy Beatrice but
of a secular male lover. Later, Clive reveals that his own aesthetic
theory would see Maurice's subjective response to Dante as
valid – indeed, as the only really vivid aesthetic response. He is
explaining to Maurice that the beauty he once saw in a male nude
of Michelangelo he now responds to in him:

> Look at that picture, for instance. I love it because, like the
> painter himself, I love the subject. I don't judge it with the eyes
> of a normal man. There seem two roads for arriving at
> Beauty – one is in common, and all the world has reached
> Michelangelo by it, but the other is private to me and a few
> more.   (p. 83)

Through the banter, Clive – and Forster, one feels – is making a very serious case here for what he calls the 'influence of Desire upon our aesthetic judgements'. He goes on to consider the 'Aesthetic Philosophy of the Decalogue', suggesting the inevitability of a relative aesthetics because each person's graven image of God will appeal to his own particular desires. God, Clive suggests, is simply ill informed; and society is equally ill informed, Forster is saying, when it insists on impartial, absolute aesthetic standards. The only 'safe' subject for aesthetic debate is landscape.

This radical attack on aesthetics is admittedly part of an excited banter of courtship, but Forster clearly endorses Clive's stance. Not only does Maurice, looking at the Michelangelo, say flippantly, 'I can give points to a picture, I dare say' (p. 82), but just after this debate Forster the narrator sums up their homosexual passion for each other:

> a passion that few English minds have admitted, and so created untrammelled. Something of exquisite beauty arose in the mind of each at least, something unforgettable and eternal, but built of the humblest scraps of speech and from the simplest emotions.   (p. 84)

Unlike a Bloomsbury conversation, which Woolf would picture as a glorious yet ephemeral construction of elegant phrases and pointed, protracted arguments, the love of these two boys is, Forster insists, a work of art which is composed from real life, its scraps, orts and fragments.

For Forster the countries of the Mediterranean – especially Greece and Italy – serve to shock his English heroes and heroines out of their frigidity and complacency. Here he distinguishes between the living culture of Italy and the dead one of Greece. Maurice has no use for Greece, 'a heap of old stones without any paint on' (pp. 100–1), and when Clive gets there he too is awakened to new truths. Those Greek stories of homosexual love between characters such as Harmodius and Aristogeiton are replaced by the barrenness of the theatre of Dionysus, which does not simply remind Clive of the larger issues of death, procreation and offspring. It has become for him a negative lesson too, its barrenness a symbol of homosexual love, the antagonism of Dionysus to the homosexual love rumoured to be practised by the musician

Orpheus a reminder of the real antagonism between the two ways of love. In *Maurice* Greece is no storehouse of art but simply a reminder of last things, and the appropriate place for Clive to 'become normal' (p. 106).

Forster takes care to show that art is of little help to these young men who are trying to clarify the nature of their sexual desires. Clive sees a film which is 'unbearable artistically' (p. 108) but which testifies to the acceptability of normal heterosexual love. In the penultimate scene we find ourselves, as in so many Bloomsbury writings, in the British Museum. There Mr Ducie, spokesman of art and culture, speaks vaguely about the value of aesthetics: 'a stimulating place – it raised questions even in the minds of boys – which one answered – no doubt inadequately' (p. 209). In the ensuing muddle Maurice finds himself protesting his love for Alec, while the 'rows of old statues tottered' (p. 209) like a line of horror-struck gentlemen. Indeed, Forster sums up the attitude of the novel towards art when he laments over the 'poor B. M., solemn and chaste' (p. 202).

There is one work of art which inspires Maurice, and that is Tchaikovsky's *Symphonie Pathétique*. Clive played it to him at Trinity and he hears it again in London. But Forster chooses it because it is a work inspired by the homosexual love of the composer for his nephew and a symbol of his 'spiritual and musical resurrection' (p. 149). For Forster, a mere musical resurrection would not be enough. Indeed, we are told that the biography of the composer which Maurice then reads is 'the one literary work that had ever helped him' (p. 149). This is one of Forster's most outspoken attacks on the aesthetics of literature, and it is appropriate that it should come in a novel which is itself trying to change the novel's tendency to ignore the vital questions.

The irony is that as a novel *Maurice* still retains many formal elements which give an extra resonance to the apparently single thrust of Maurice's pilgrimage. The novel can be pictured as a wedge-shaped descent and resurrection, recollecting perhaps Dante's *Divine Comedy*, which forms a motif throughout. Maurice is said at the outset to be 'descending the Valley of the Shadow of Life' (p. 14), and at the end he leaves a pile of petals of the evening primrose with Clive and reunites with Alec at the Penge boathouse after a sunset with 'a gorgeous horizon' (p. 224). Other repetitions reinforce the mirror effect, such as the appearances of Mr Ducie and Clive at the beginning and end, and Forster's own pairings: 'Risley's room had its counterpart in the wild rose and the evening primroses of yesterday, the side-car dash through the fens foreshadowed his innings at cricket' (p. 191).

There is of course the main opposition between Clive and Alec, and the climactic scenes with each are full of resonances. Compare 'his heart leapt alive and shook him to pieces' on a night 'drizzly with faint stars' (p. 57) with 'he seemed to crackle and burn' on a night where 'mist covered the grass of the park' (p. 178). Even the central episode with Dickie has these resonances: 'This episode burst Maurice's life to pieces . . . the fires died down as quickly as they had risen' (p. 138).

These climactic scenes also divide the novel into four distinct and equal books. Book One takes us up to Maurice's appearance to Clive at his window; Book Two shifts our attention to Clive and documents his evolution towards heterosexuality; Book Three, after Maurice's painful, futile efforts to cure himself, ends with his ecstatic union with Alec (also involving appearances at windows); and the final book works out their lasting union. The first half of the book descends to the nadir of Maurice's fortunes when Forster comments, characteristically drawing attention to the novel's fictionality, 'One cannot write those words too often: Maurice's loneliness' (p. 130). The second half of the novel replays the first but with more sophistication and with an upward rather than a downward movement. Instead of Mr Ducie we have Doctor Lasker Jones; instead of Clive, Alec.

For all Forster's protestations within the novel, then, that life should come first, that the connection of Maurice with an object worthy of his love was the paramount motivation behind writing the novel, we clearly see artifice at work. The notes which surround the text of *Maurice* point insistently to the story element, the arbitrariness of the design and its subordination to moral, almost political, themes. The introduction quotes a letter to Dickinson where Forster confessed to 'the overwhelming temptation to grant to one's creations a happiness actual life does not supply' (p. vii), and in his 'Terminal Note' Forster explained the changes made to the last part of the novel to make it more explicit. But, while Forster and his characters mocked the elegant impartiality of aesthetic shape, he continued to structure his fictions and reinforce his themes through forms as significant, in their way, as the ideas so tentatively put forward within them.

A PASSAGE TO INDIA (1924)

> *It doesn't do to think. To follow the promptings of the eye and the imagination is quite complicated enough.* [18]

Forster's last and greatest novel has continually teased critics into endless debate about its completeness as a work of art. Virginia Woolf was clearly unimpressed by the 'wholeness' of it when, after praising its observations and social satire, she rather archly commented, 'Mr Forster has almost achieved the great feat of animating this dense, compact body of observation with a spiritual light.'[19] 'Clear and triumphant. beauty', she said, existed only in chapters. Wilfred Stone has been far more affirmative, calling it 'perhaps the greatest English novel of this century as an aesthetic accomplishment'.[20] His ensuing discussion toys with the principle of rhythm as the 'incarnation of the book's meaning'[21] but finally settles on the spatial metaphor of the mandala. The practice of applying Forster's critical principle of rhythm to *A Passage to India* was begun, of course, by E. K. Brown in his *Rhythm in the Novel*, where he praised the tripartite, symphonic structure of the novel in those terms which Forster used to describe *War and Peace*. So convinced is Elizabeth Heine that there is indeed an order in the novel, whether rhythmic or spatial, that she attributes an order to the metaphysical meaning of the novel as well:

> Thus this final development of Forster's consistent 'structure' in *A Passage to India*, where the characters' mental experiences are shaped in mysterious ways beyond the knowledge of psychology, indicates Forster's aesthetic faith in an order beyond 'humanism'. The paradoxical fact that he has created the ultimate order of the novel does not change the reader's conviction that the structure as created reflects a non-human absolute. [22]

This plethora of observations about the unity of the novel is a testimony to the deceptive confidence of Forster's habitual tone and of the three sections of the novel. But a genuine effort to explicate the unity and harmony inevitably lead one back to Woolf's reservation, though not, perhaps, with her overtone of censure.

When Forster revisited India in 1921, he recorded some revealing responses. Those responses were so strong that they inhibited his working on the novel while he was there; 'the gap between India remembered and India experienced was too wide'.[23] This gap between the organised memory and the chaotic experience was never resolved; indeed, it became itself the new centre of the completed novel. Forster recorded while he was in Dewas, 'I could never describe the muddle in this place. It is wheel within wheel.'[24] Of the festival of Gokul Ashtami he wrote, 'The noise the noise the noise which sucks one into a whirlpool . . . music has never existed.'[25] And in a letter to Dickinson he confessed that he found the Hindu character 'unaesthetic'.[26]

Such comments clearly explain why Forster could not write in India. He found the country inimical to the artistic endeavour itself, at least as it is conceived in the West as an effort towards balance, harmony, and a form which must have significance. This does not mean that Forster was antipathetic to Indian society, however. He found the life as congenial as ever, responding fully to the affection which he felt 'quivered through everything'.[27]

Analysing Forster's response to India over the years in his writings, G. K. Das concludes that, while Forster responded warmly to Islam, he was also drawn towards elements of Hinduism: not the obliterating pantheism of the 'Temple' section, but the paradoxical affirmation of the individual. In 1953 Forster recalled a Hindu temple:

> There often exists inside its complexity a tiny cavity, a central cell, where the individual may be alone with his god. . . . It is only a cell where the worshipper can for a moment face what he believes. He worships at the heart of the world-mountain, inside the exterior complexity. And he is alone. Hinduism, unlike Christianity and Buddhism and Islam, does not invite him to meet his god congregationally; and this commends it to me.[28]

Forster's attraction to Hinduism, this religion which, as he said in 1915, says 'I am different from everybody else' *and* 'I am the same as everybody else',[29] is at the heart of the meaning and technique of *A Passage to India*. The division of the novel into three sections – 'Mosque', 'Caves', 'Temple' – suggests such a religious patterning or debate. Where the novel differs from such other tripartite novels as *To the Lighthouse*, *The Longest Journey* and *Howards End* is in the disproportions of each section here. The quantitative relationship of 3:4:1 belies the emotional and symbolic importance given to the final section, 'Temple', which is only one-eighth of the novel's bulk.

The explanation of this feature goes a long way towards reconciling the various responses to the novel here summarised. The fact is that we cannot argue for the 'ultimate order of the novel' from the point of view of themes any more than we can from the point of view of three balanced sections. John Beer suggests we can read the novel 'in three quite differing ways'[30] according as we see the central character as Fielding, Mrs Moore or Adela. But what about Aziz, Godbole, or even Ronnie? Benita Parry also seizes on the number three, which Forster has so teasingly dangled before us, to argue that the novel presents 'three major Indian philosophical–religious systems'.[31] But can the Moslem religion be said to dominate the first section, and what about Christianity? Such attempts to impose a neat thematic order on the novel are not only reductive but also ignore the constant ambiguities and bewildering multiplicity of perspectives which is the experience of reading *A Passage to India*.

Nevertheless, Parry is closest to the central issues of the novel by focusing on the issue of how to be, or how to see. She writes,

> The novel offers this triad as the form of paradoxical differences contained within the unbroken whole: incorporated in the enclosing frame is the gracious culture of Islam in India, a society where personal relations amongst Moslems do flourish; the unpeopled Jain caves, place of the ascetic renunciation of the world; and the buoyant religious community of the Hindus, internally divided and internally cohesive. The approach to the component meanings of these systems is, however, profoundly ambiguous, moving between responsiveness and rejection, making the myth and subverting it.[32]

This is a clear case of trying to have one's three-tiered cake and eating it, too. The insistence on an 'unbroken whole' and differences which are not differences is founded on the unnecessary assumption that novels, particularly this one with its three sections, should be watertight conceptual tanks. Again, it ignores the reading-experience, which focuses not on systems but on individuals, and which ends with two men on horseback alone in the wilderness.

It should be agreed, then, that *A Passage to India looks* like a novel of ideas. Indeed, as Edwin Thumboo puts it, 'The metaphysics . . . at key moments moves from background to middleground and foreground.'[33] Life does seem to be examined against the backdrop of the eternal verities – 'a continual recurrence, surge, or movement of man between the poles of being and nothing, between the primary and tertiary levels of experience and between birth and death.'[34] Even the habitual movement of the prose is from assertion to negation[35] or from language to silence.[36] But still, *A Passage to India* is not a religious meditation or a sociological tract, it is a novel. From first to last, from the meeting of Aziz with Mrs Moore to the ride of Aziz and Fielding, it is 'this man-to-man business' of human relations, and we must not lose sight of that fact in the seductive lure of the politics of Chandrapore or the metaphysics of Godbole.

The novel is essentially a love story – not that of Aziz and Mrs Moore, or Ronnie and Adela, or even Mrs Moore and India, but that of Aziz and Fielding. The question is whether friendship, that cardinal Moorean virtue, can flourish between individuals of different backgrounds and beliefs. For such a friendship to occur, the participants must stand apart from their communities, alone, confronting the nothingness of non-being itself, like the Hindu in the innermost cell of the temple or the tourist in the Marabar Caves. The only value that will sustain him in that extreme situation is the friendship itself. Luring him back from friendship is the comforting security of the group: the Anglo-Indian community, the circle of Moslem friends around the hookah, the swarming Hindu mass. If we restore individuals to their central place on Forster's canvas, we can see that the supposed philosophical dialectic between being and nothingness resolves itself into a debate between belonging to the group and belonging to the individual.

Forster's earlier novels had translated this issue into the conventions of the love story (*A Room with a View*) or the symbolic counters of an evolutionary parable (*The Longest Journey, Howards End*). In *A Passage to India* he was able to return more directly to the issue which concerned him in *Maurice*, but without feeling limited by the sexual debate within the mores of one restrictive society. The word 'homosexual' thus becomes ludicrously limiting, unless one can apply the word equally to the impulses underlying Forster's declarations in 'What I Believe': 'I believe in personal relationships. . . . If I had to choose between betraying my country and betraying my friend, I hope I should have the guts to betray my country.' Of course, the relationship of Aziz and Fielding is affected by their attitudes towards women and wives – indeed, this becomes the crisis at the end of the 'Caves' section and persists in 'Temple'. But marriage itself should be seen here as an aspect of a society's communal force – at least in the ways Aziz and Fielding regard their particular wives – and not as a demand on their spiritual resources equal to that of friendship.

A comparison with Lawrence's *Women in Love* will clarify this difference. Both novels end in a similar way, with the unfulfilled urge towards a homosexual friendship. Lawrence, however, gives us a drama hermetically sealed around four characters. Their response to the Austrian snow (so similar in many ways to Forster's placing his characters in the alien environment of the Marabar Caves) is in terms of pre-existing relationships being challenged. Forster's novel is far more tentative, theoretical almost. Fielding's friendship with Aziz is not welded and distorted in the heat of battle, as it were, but rather contemplated as a possibility, weighed up against the other possible strategies of returning to England, getting married, and so forth. This is why *A Passage to India* seems like a novel of ideas: the crucial point is that it is the ideas of Forster's characters, not of Forster, which are being formulated and challenged.

The proportional imbalance of the three sections, then, is a function of the rhythms involved in Fielding's inner debate and in our reading-experience. We shall appreciate the aesthetic shape of the novel only if we follow the fortunes of its characters through step by step.

The opening chapter takes us on a brilliant, bird's-eye view of Chandrapore, from the muddy Ganges to the Marabar Caves in the distance. Arranged like various strata are the quarters of the various races. The progression is not only hierarchical but also metaphysical, from the undifferentiated mass of the Hindu river-dwellers – 'like some low but indestructible form of life' – through the exclusive civil station to the individual's confrontation with self in the caves. Between these poles, social and philosophical, the story will play itself out. The movement of the novel from overview to intense personal drama is illustrated in the way this opening chapter contrasts with the beginning of 'Caves', which is an intimate description of the interior of the caves towards which the characters are hastening, and the beginning of 'Temple', which does not set the physical scene but concentrates on Godbole and the activities of the mass of celebrants.

The first scene of the Moslems gathered round their hookah defines the virtues and vices of that community. There is the congenial friendship, the beautiful poetry which reminds them of departed greatness, and 'for the time India seemed one and their own' (p. 17); but there is also the antagonism towards the British, and what we should now call the male chauvinism in their attitude towards women. All these will be important elements in Aziz's friendship with Fielding.

Alone in the mosque, which 'alone signified' (p. 21) to Aziz, in the sense of making sense of the world of human affections through a work of art, Aziz stumbles upon Mrs Moore. It is important to note that Aziz approaches her initially only because he thinks she is a younger woman. The sexual possibilities however are soon replaced by warm friendship, partly because Mrs Moore is no longer sexually active and so Aziz sees no possible threat to his affections. That affection, the Forsterian narrator clearly states, is worth more than aesthetic satisfaction – 'the flame that not even beauty can nourish' (p. 25). This idea is supported later when Adela laments that, unlike Mrs Moore, she will see India only as a frieze (p. 50) and not as a living spirit.

The 'Indian problem' is beautifully and succinctly revealed in the bridge party, a term which itself betrays the ignorance of the British in supposing that the two societies are somehow on an equal level. Forster surrounds the episode with clues as to the real nature of reality as an indivisible whole, from the debate with the missionaries about where to draw the line concerning admission into Heaven (p. 41) to the narrator's own reminder that the physical setting is an infinite regression of spheres (p. 42). After the bridge party, however, we do see one momentary, casual example of a true communion, when Aziz plays polo with an unidentified subaltern on the Maidan. The two men, through physical exertion and concentration on the ball, achieve a warm fellowship. The scene prefigures the final scene in the novel, and also prefigures the limitations to Aziz's own abilities to bridge the ap between one individual and another.

The narrator's approval of Fielding is evident from his first
ntroduction:

> The feeling grew that Mr Fielding was a disruptive force, and
> rightly, for ideas are fatal to caste, and he used ideas by that
> most potent method – interchange. Neither a missionary nor a
> student, he was happiest in the give-and-take of a private con-
> versation. The world, he believed, was a globe of men who are
> trying to reach one another and can best do so by the help of
> good will plus culture and intelligence . . . .   (p. 65)

But the eventual doom of Fielding's friendship with Aziz is also
specified in this description, when Forster says, 'He had
discovered that it is possible to keep in with Indians and
Englishmen, but he who would also keep in with Englishwomen
must drop the Indians' (p. 66). Indeed, despite the porten-
tousness of Fielding's first words to Aziz – 'Make yourself at
home' – we see Aziz, by tearing out his collar stud and offering it,
almost repeating the same gesture of misplaced kindness which
destroyed the bridge party. In keeping with the novel's general
anti-art attitude, too, Aziz's mention of Post-Impressionism also
leads to a confusion of meaning between the two men.

Once introduced, however, the relationship between Aziz and
Fielding is left to simmer in the background, while we concentrate
on Ronnie and Adela in their attempts to cope with the muddle
which is India. Unable to face Godbole's haunting 'Come,
come', which remains unanswered as a refrain throughout the
novel (India itself is seen as singing the same words – p. 143), the
couple reaffirm their engagement as if cowering from the unidentified beast which attacked their car. Adela, who becomes the
focus for the central third of the novel, fails the first challenge of
the spirit of India.

When we return to Aziz and Fielding, it is to learn about their
relationships with their own communities. Aziz is ill and so is surrounded by his Moslem friends, while Fielding is seen more than
once as the spectator of the play of his English colleagues (p. 81).
This detachment from his own society makes him able to
approach Aziz but at the same time unable to appreciate some of
the values of community which Aziz holds. Aziz observes that his
friend is 'truly warm-hearted and unconventional, but not what

can be called wise' (p. 127), while the narrator warns us, 'Experience can do much, and all that he had learnt in England and Europe was an assistance to him, and helped him towards clarity, but clarity prevented him from experiencing something else' (p. 123).

Because the great stumbling-block to the friendship of the two men is the sexual impulse, Forster deliberately focuses on the two women, Mrs Moore and Adela, and takes them through the caves as a kind of harrowing of hell, a sort of unholy experiment to see what will happen to that impulse. He emulates Fielding's namesake Henry Fielding when he introduces one chapter with the observation that much of our lives is an emptiness of non-sensation, when 'a perfectly adjusted organism would be silent' (p. 139). This is why, Forster implies, I as author have been silent about the two women, who have nevertheless been continuing their spiritual pilgrimage since we last left them with Godbole's song. It is crucial in the lead-up to the caves that we see Adela and Mrs Moore engaged in a steady modification of their ideas by their confrontation with India.

Mrs Moore, being beyond the sexual impulse, is further on the road to 'enlightenment' than Adela, since she is in harmony with the nothingness of the caves and the landscape leading to it (the non-event of the sunrise, for example) by reflecting that relations between people are unimportant – 'in particular too much fuss has been made over marriage' (p. 141). Unlike the tradition of Forsterian mother figures (and even Mrs Ramsay), Mrs Moore here departs from the model of matchmaker, perceiving the sexual impulse to be something which actually militates against friendship. Discussing the Moslem heroes, Aziz and Adela cover the same ground theoretically. Aziz admires Babur because he never betrayed a friend (p. 150) and Adela searches for universal brotherhood.

Mrs Moore, then, is more ready for the experience of the caves and more ready to submit to the horror of it – 'the universe . . . offered no repose to her soul' (p. 157) – while Adela, theorising only, and a young girl, turns the conversation to sex and marriage even as she enters the fateful cave. All her biological instincts are pointing her towards Ronnie. Although she already has her doubts, when this basic impulse is questioned or rather exposed in the cave for the animal motivation which it is she panics, and in just those sexual terms. Even Forster's later comments on the

icident are sexual; the caves were to 'engender an event like an
gg'.

The result of this event, which comes at the exact centre of the
ovel, is to align the social groups along battle lines even as it has
he opposite effect of breaking up the received ideas of the more
nlightened principal characters. 'The Europeans', says Forster,
were putting aside their normal personalities and sinking
hemselves in their community' (p. 173). Nowhere is his hatred of
he mob more pronounced. Fielding is rejected by the Club – 'you
an't run with the hare and hunt with the hounds' – and the
xperience is akin to that of the women in the caves: 'After forty
rears' experience, he had learnt to manage his life and make the
nest of it on advanced European lines . . . but as the moment
nassed, he felt he ought to have been working at something else
he whole time' (p. 199). Fielding, unlike Aziz, has not cultivated
a small circle of friends.

The considered reactions of the two women are now examined,
und these too emerge as a reorientation of their attitudes towards
nersonal relationships. Adela confesses, 'I'm not fit for personal
relationships' (p. 205); Mrs Moore angrily rejects 'all this marriage, marriage' (p. 210). The same qualities which made Mrs
Moore more accessible to the truth of the caves make her
defenceless to its repercussions. She has no community and no
friends, and she leaves the stage in a confusion of sentiments. One
cannot even justifiably erect her death into a kind of noble
suicide – it just happens. Adela, on the other hand, is young and
resilient. Ironically, her turning-point towards the truth and
towards a more genuine life comes in the courtroom when she sees
the punkah wallah working the fan. This Indian, 'almost naked
and splendidly formed' (p. 226), seems to her like a 'male fate, a
winnower of souls'. The epiphany is, ironically, heavily sexual in
origin, but its effect is to convince Adela that if life is to be lived at
all it must be lived with dignity.

So she tells the truth and becomes an outcast, too, flung in the
way of Fielding. This is the masterstroke of Forster's design,
because the symbolic issue represented by Adela, which had
pushed Aziz and Fielding towards each other, now becomes an
actual, human issue which divides them again. Adela comes
across Fielding's path at the moment when he is learning, by taking his stand for Aziz, the value of friendship, of involvement in
personal relationships: 'He lost his usual sane view of human

intercourse, and felt that we exist not in ourselves, but in terms o
each other's minds' (p. 259). It is Fielding's answer to Ansell's
problem of the cow in the quad, and it leads him to contemplate
Mrs Moore's immortality as well as to try to reconcile Adela and
Aziz. With Adela he finds he is able to approach the kinds of truth
presented by the caves without breaking into violence or insanity
simply because he reaches them in the companionship of another
human being, and Adela finds this too:

> A friendliness, as of dwarfs shaking hands, was in the air. Both
> man and woman were at the height of their powers – sensible,
> honest, even subtle. They spoke the same language, and held
> the same opinions, and the variety of age and sex did not divide
> them.   (p. 274)

It is one of the rare moments of genuine friendship in the novel,
notwithstanding Forster's rather brutal placing of them in
perspective as 'dwarfs'. It is not insignificant that they can actually speak to each other, something which rarely happens in this
novel.

But, while Fielding is moving towards Adela, he is moving
away from Aziz. The prophecy of the beginning of the book is
starting to come true, not because Fielding is inciting Aziz's
jealousy, but because he is revealing the presumptions of his
society in its attitude towards women. In no aspect is a society
more distinctive than in its attitude towards women, a fact Aziz
has always been acutely aware of. His own Islamic attitude was
one which we would now call male chauvinism:

> It enraged him that he had been accused by a woman who had
> no personal beauty; sexually, he was a snob. This had puzzled
> and worried Fielding. Sensuality, as long as it is straightfor-
> ward, did not repel him, but this derived sensuality – the sort
> that classes a mistress among motor-cars if she is beautiful, and
> among eye-flies if she isn't – was alien to his own emotions,
> and he felt a barrier between himself and Aziz whenever it
> arose.   (p. 251)

Fielding is caught. Forster reminds us that it is 'essential in
friendship' (p. 265) to respect the other's every opinion, but
Fielding cannot go along with Aziz regarding Adela as a mindless

creature. Aziz, in effect, wants Fielding to become 'a sort of Mohammed Latif': 'When they argued so about it something racial intruded – not bitterly, but inevitably, like the colour of their skins: coffee-colour versus pinko-grey' (p. 271).

Fielding recoils from this impasse to the familiar forms – and here Forster neatly conflates the significant form of works of art and the social forms of custom and sexual mores – of Italy:

> He had forgotton the beauty of form among idol temples and lumpy hills; indeed, without form, how can there be beauty? Form stammered here and there in a mosque, became rigid through nervousness even, but oh these Italian churches! . . . something more precious than mosaics and marbles was offered to him now: the harmony between the works of man and the earth that upholds them, the civilization that has escaped muddle, the spirit in a reasonable form, with flesh and blood subsisting. (p. 293)

When he returns to India, it is to the Hindu festival, which Forster describes as 'this approaching triumph of India . . . a muddle (as we call it), a frustration of reason and form' (p. 297). Once the muddle is cleared up over Fielding's wife, we might expect the two friends to come together again. Aziz has a kind of marriage, and Stella is 'after something' (p. 331) which she finds partly in the Hindu ceremony. The reader is left asking if the rocks and temples which deny their friendship are any more than Forster the narrator refusing the happy ending.

The ending does indeed seem perverse if one sees the novel as an abstract, allegorical structure. But I have suggested that it really tells the quite specific story of Aziz and Fielding, with the caves providing the metaphysical background and the experiences of the two women providing the plot complication which finally separates the two men into their two cultures. From Aziz's first contact with Mrs Moore, the question of the place of women has loomed as the central issue between the two men. The final section has little to say on the metaphysical level. It simply serves as the setting for the meeting of the two men again, and for the neatly symbolic collision of the boats when Stella is thrown into Aziz's lap. Fielding speaks of his wife as being ahead of him in the spiritual quest, something which the Moslem Aziz would never say of his woman. It reminds him of the very bitter row over

Adela which began to kill their friendship two years earlier. As result of that row, Aziz's poetry has become more and mor nationalistic. Earlier, the Moslem poem had voiced 'our nee for the Friend who never comes yet is not entirely dis proved' (p. 111). Now, under the invitation of the Hindu M Bhattacharya, Aziz's poems look forward and salvation will com through the motherland of India (p. 279). In fact most recently h has become a 'feminist': 'His poems were all on on topic – Oriental womanhood. "The purdah must go," was thei burden, "otherwise we shall never be free" ' (p. 305). It is as i Aziz (in theory anyway) were looking to his own women as counter to such Englishwomen as Adela and a substitute for th friendship offered by such as Fielding. But one suspects that it i only theory, and that for someone such as Aziz the fact would b very hard to stomach. Still, the whole complex o nationalism–feminism is what turns his horse away from Fielding's at the end. It is not a historically accurate symboli conclusion, but was never intended to be. It is the natural conclu sion of this particular muddle.

That we must read *A Passage to India* in this specific, contingent way is suggested also by the references to art in the novel. I have said that it is essentially an anti-art novel. This is not simply because it is set in India, a country inimical to the significant forms of art: 'Men yearn for poetry though they may not confess it; they desire that joy shall be graceful and sorrow august and infinity have a form, and India fails to accommodate them' (p. 219). But everywhere the confident assumptions of art are attacked. During Mrs Moore's disillusionment Forster observes, 'All heroic endeavour, and all that is known as art, assumes that there is such a background' (p. 216); at the moment of their communion Adela says to Fielding, 'I used to feel death selected people, it is a notion one gets from novels' (p. 274); and of the Hindu festival Forster writes, 'Did it succeed? Books written afterwards say "Yes." But how, if there is such an event, can it be remembered afterwards? How can it be expressed in anything but itself?' (p. 300). Forster even goes so far as to challenge the serious framework of his own novel, when he attempts to describe Mrs Moore's vision: 'Visions are supposed to entail profundity, but – Wait till you get one, dear reader!' (p. 217). Such an eruption into the fabric of the novel makes one wonder if Forster really means to say, 'Novels are supposed to entail profundity.'

This anti-art stance, then, underlines the idea that the meaning of the novel will not be got from standing back and toting up motifs and symbols, and balancing the three unbalanceable sections. The ending of the novel is far more like the ending of Forster's first novel, *Where Angels Fear to Tread* – equivocal and particular – than like the large symbolic tableaux at the end of his other novels. Thirteen years and one Great War after *Howards End*, Forster is no longer writing neat parables about the condition of India, England or the liberal soul. He is following through faithfully the tangled relationship between one Indian and one Englishman.

It is this specificity which gives *A Passage to India* its greatness. Readers looking for *The* Passage to India will be frustrated at the narrative tone of equivocality and non-involvement, and by the lack of significance in the juxtaposition of the stories of Mrs Moore, Adela, Fielding and Aziz. One may make much of the bee and Mrs Moore and Godbole, but in itself it counts for little until put up against the incident in 'Temple' when Ralph and Fielding are stung by a swarm of bees and the 'symbolic' moment is merged into part of the central ongoing narrative. The recurrences between being and nothingness, the stylistic affirmations and withdrawals, are in themselves dry, academic exercises until they are linked to the developing relationship of Aziz and Fielding, the delicate minuet of advance and withdrawal, closeness and alienation. For all his teasing attempts, Forster has no intention to 'bathe it all in a spiritual light', as Virginia Woolf wished.

While Woolf too reached a similar stage of scepticism about the efficacy of large statements near the end of her fictional career, she never abandoned the form of art to the extent that Forster did. Fielding may err like Forster's earlier heroes in overvaluing the form of Italian art, but in his earlier novels set in Europe Forster felt compelled to think of answers and to invent ideal heroes. In the muddled setting of India he felt liberated to offer no hero in Aziz, but to concentrate instead on the subtle pressures which are inevitably exerted on friendship, from without and from within. Forster wrote his novel in the spirit he recorded in 1921 in India – 'It doesn't do to think. To follow the promptings of the eye and the imagination is quite complicated enough' – and his imaginative grasp of the phenomenon of friendship itself helped create his greatest novel. But does the novel expand at the end, or

leave us hearing great chords behind? I think not. The politic:
and metaphysical possibilities of the novel have finally been abar.
doned in favour of the individual human being, with whor
Forster's sympathies finally lie. The structure of the novel doe
not reverberate except as the memory of a series of conflict
between perspectives. The last section in particular seems to bea
little relation to the point which Aziz and Fielding have reached i:
their friendship. Neither man seems to relate to the festival at al.
The festival seems to signify a common, minimal humanity whic!
friendship tries to rise above, and if the mystery of such friendshi;
cannot be achieved then at least the two men can attain the clea
sense of community which the Moslem or English society offers
The equality of Fielding's wife is not a psychological affront t•
Aziz (as Ursula is to Crich in *Women in Love*) but a social one. Th•
barriers to their friendship are not so grandly spiritual as ii
Lawrence – they are simply a matter of 'not then, not there' – bu
are perhaps more absolute because of that.

The greatest rhythm in the novel is not that created by the pat
terns of motifs or locations (Duncan Grant uses the 'rhythm of th•
line' to create a sensuous structure in his oriental sketch [Plat•
11]), but the rhythm of time. The central friendship is at th•
mercy of changing circumstances and, in the last section, the ga|
of two years seals its fate. Forster said in 1959, 'Proust has showr
me a little what it is to be both delicate and deep as a novelist.'[37]
In *A Passage to India* he has shown those qualities by letting the
passage of time finally pull Fielding and Aziz, and the pattern o!
the novel, asunder. But he has also learnt from Proust what |
discussed in chapter 1 as a way of shaping the reading time, too.
Here, as in no other Forster novel, the texture of the prose is
porous, constantly dissolving large statements into mockery and
silence. Even the possible friendship of narrator and reader is left
to wither and die. Thus the texture of Forster's last work of art is
at one with his subject, at last, although that subject is the impossibility of communication. The work itself is one vast
psychological volume, but like the Marabar Caves it unnerves
and challenges us by speaking only 'Boom'.

5   Forster and Woolf

Well, Morgan admires. This is a weight off my mind.
                                                    – Woolf, 1925[1]

Please tell me the names of the best novels.
                                                    – Forster, 1926[2]

One may as well begin with the personal relationship between
Forster and Woolf, since it underscored both the kinships and
antagonisms which they felt towards each other as artists and
literary theorists. According to Forster's biographer, after his
favourable review of *The Voyage Out* in 1915 she 'became very
dependent on his opinion'.[3] Certainly her relationship with him
was more 'professional' than with the other male members of the
inner circle of Bloomsbury. Forster was always on the fringe of
that circle, even though Woolf was able to number him among
'the enormous crowd of cultivated ones' at a party at Fitzroy
Square in 1911.[4] There was also the distance of literary achievement: although only three years older than Woolf, Forster at that
time (with *Howards End* recently published) was at the height of
his powers and fame, while Woolf was only struggling with drafts
of her first novel. In her essay 'Mr Bennett and Mrs Brown',
Woolf was to rank Forster among the Georgians, along with
Joyce, Eliot and Lawrence; yet, as Quentin Bell suggests, 'In a
sense he belonged to an older generation.'[5]

   In his personal behaviour Forster clearly intrigued as well as
disturbed Woolf. She noted chiefly his mercurial quality, likening
him at various times to a mouse and a butterfly. 'He is fantastic
and very sensitive,' she wrote in 1919, 'an attractive character to
me.'[6] His whimsicality reminded her of her own 'clumsiness and
definiteness', and like the general post-Cambridge Bloomsbury
milieu it probably had a beneficial effect in freeing up her own
considerable whimsicality. She recognised in Forster one of those
few blessed souls who, in her husband's terms, had the capacity of

'silliness'. But it was that same 'silliness' which made Woolf comment with scarcely concealed disapproval, 'Morgan goes to India, and I think for ever. He will become a mystic, sit by the roadside, and forget Europe, which I think he half despises. . . . He has no roots here.'[7] In 1926, perhaps responding to a new post-war, post-India mood in Forster, but perhaps also exercising her newfound confidence after the publication of four novels, Woolf described him as 'limp and damp and milder than the breath of a cow'.[8]

The crucial element in their relationship was sexuality. Woolf was familiar with the homosexual temperament, and found it far more congenial to her own highstrung, self-conscious sexuality than that of a heterosexual man. This perhaps explains the judgement of Forster's biographer that 'she liked him a good deal – rather more than, in his heart, he liked her'.[9] This is confirmed by Woolf's biographer:

> They were a little afraid of each other. Morgan Forster was, I think, happier with his own sex. He found Virginia's feminism disturbing and felt that there was something a little too sharp, a little too critical, about her. 'I don't think', he said, 'that she cared for most people. She was always very sweet to me, but I don't think she was particularly fond of me, if that is the word.'[10]

Certainly Woolf regarded Forster's homosexuality with frank concern and sympathy, as is shown in her comment about him of 1922: 'The middle age of buggers is not to be contemplated without horror.'[11] She united with Forster in writing a letter to the *Nation and Athenaeum* protesting the suppression of Radclyffe Hall's lesbian novel *The Well of Loneliness*. But another reason for Woolf's lack of 'fondness' for Forster is supplied by Leonard Woolf, recounting an incident near the end of her life:

> Morgan Forster asked her whether he might propose her for the London Library Committee. But years ago Morgan himself in the London Libary itself, meeting Virginia and talking about its organisation or administration, had 'sniffed about women on the Committee'. Virginia at the time made no comment, but she said to herself: 'One of these days I shall refuse.' So now on Thursday, 7 November 1940, she had some quiet satisfaction in saying No.[12]

Just as Woolf's ideas about sexuality had matured over the years, so had her views about fiction. In both cases Forster was a prime casualty in the battle. Unconsciously, perhaps, Woolf used sexual terms when she looked back on the parallel literary careers of herself and Forster in 1930 and proclaimed, 'E. M. Forster, the novelist, whose books once influenced mine, and are very good, I think, though impeded, shrivelled and immature.'[13] The damnation which follows the faint praise suggests a creative mind limited in sexual maturity. Considering Woolf's intimate knowledge of Forster's homosexuality, it seems unlikely that she was referring to the suppressed or unexpressed homosexual component in Forster novels. Even the publication of *Maurice* would not, as Forster thought, have affected her appraisal of his achievement; for Woolf disagreed with Forster on larger and more fundamental issues.

The critical argument between Woolf and Forster begins with his review of *The Voyage Out* in 1915. It reaches the intensity of a fully pitched battle in the years 1925–7, and Forster has the last word in his memorial lecture of 1941. By following this debate, we can see exposed the critical axioms sacred to each writer. We can also see that it was through this same process of debate with another writer who was a friend and lived in the same society, that both Woolf and Forster were able to clarify those axioms in their own minds.

In 1915 Forster praised *The Voyage Out* for its concentration on man alone: 'It is for a voyage into solitude that man was created.'[14] By 1925 and his essay on 'The Early Novels of Virginia Woolf', Forster's admiration for Rachel Vinrace's pilgrimage had not diminished, but he modified his praise of the novel with a rather ominous challenge to Woolf's subsequent fiction:

It is a noble book, so noble that a word of warning must be added: like all Virginia Woolf's work, it is not romantic, not mystic, not explanatory of the universe. By using a wrong tone of voice – over-stressing 'South America' for instance – the critic might easily make it appear to be all these things, and perhaps waft it towards popular success! His honesty must equal the writer's; he is offered no ultimate good, but 'life; London; this moment in June'; and it is his job to find out what the promise entails.[15]

What sounds like a challenge to the reader of the novel intrinsically turns out to be a challenge to Woolf to make clear just what
this 'life' holds that is worth reading about, since Forster continues, 'Will *Night and Day* help him?' That novel he dismisses for
its archaic classicism, and he moves quickly on via *The Mark on the
Wall* to praise *Jacob's Room*. While conveying his dissatisfaction
with Woolf's developing style of 'inspired breathlessness' in a
stream which seems to be going nowhere, Forster also praises the
character of Jacob for (to use his own later terminology) its
roundedness. This 'solid figure . . . monument . . . colonnade' is
miraculously raised from the ashes of the novel's style.

Forster is attracted to *Mrs Dalloway* because of 'the outline of
this exquisite and superbly constructed book', but he recognises
that he must not rend the 'shimmering fabric' with such crude
equations concerning 'mysticism, unity beneath multiplicity,
twin souls'. His growing dislike of this surface of life without
rounded characters is made explicit in his conclusion, in which he
condemns Woolf for not creating characters 'with Victorian
thoroughness' to live as whole human beings. (The phrase
'human beings as a whole and as wholes' is a deliberate imitation
of the language of G. E. Moore.) Forster clearly has more concern
for whole characters than whole works of art, yet he ends his
article with an ingenious conceit when he describes English fiction
as a picture gallery with windows, where one can see alternately a
still life, a portrait, or a view of Persia out the window. While the
concept of the novel as a framed work of art is of little importance
to Forster here, another painterly quality is, that of perspective or
point of view. He is concerned that the reader of a Woolf novel
has no longer a sense of proportion, of those pictures foregrounded upon the walls of the gallery, and those views out the
window. 'She wants to destroy the gallery' and fuse the fore and
backgrounds, replacing the shaping element of perspective by
'something more rhythmical. *Jacob's Room* suggests a spiral whirl-
ing down to point, *Mrs Dalloway* a cathedral.'

In this essay, Forster can be seen in the process of fashioning
new critical tools to deal with Woolf's new fiction. Yet, even as he
hesitatingly tries out the concepts of 'rhythm' and shape, he remains loyal in the body of the essay to the traditional concept of
rounded character. He remains true to human beings, whether
they be in the novel or sitting reading it.

In the spring of 1927 Forster delivered the lectures which

became *Aspects of the Novel*. There, with the same evidence of Woolf's genius before him (except for the recent publication of *To the Lighthouse*, which he does include), Forster equates Woolf with Sterne, labels them 'fantasists', and satirises their 'rather deliberate bewilderment':

> the mark on the wall turns out to be a snail, life is such a muddle, oh dear, the will is so weak, the sensations fidgety ... philosophy ... God ... oh dear, look at the mark ... listen to the door – existence ... is really too ... what were we saying?[16]

Understandably concerned to defend herself, Woolf responded in November of that year with a review of Forster's book in which she castigates him for his vagueness:

> If we cannot pin Mr Forster to a creed we can commit him to a point of view. There is something – we hesitate to be more precise – which he calls 'life'. It is the humane as opposed to the esthetic view of fiction. It maintains that the novel is 'sogged with humanity'; that 'human beings have their great chance in the novel'; a triumph won at the expense of life is in fact a defeat.'[17]

Because Forster cannot define what he means by 'life', we are, says Woolf dryly, 'back in the old bog'. She drives home her attack by observing that Forster says almost nothing about words or the medium of the literary artist, and that 'Beauty occurs but she is suspect'. She ends with both a condemnation and a challenge: 'There is not a critic alive now who will say that a novel is a work of art and that as such he will judge it.'

Forster replied to Woolf in a letter in the following way:

> Your article inspires me to the happiest repartee. This vague truth about life. Exactly. But what of the talk about art? Each section leads to an exquisitely fashioned casket of which the key has unfortunately been mislaid and until you can find your bunch I shall cease to hunt very anxiously for my own.[18]

Although Woolf was concerned that her friend should take her criticism so hard, she did defend herself in her reply by arguing, validly, that it was Forster, not Woolf, who was presuming to write a book about fiction. The onus was on him to find more precise critical tools. Woolf found Forster's habitual uncertainty (and, by the evidence of his request to her of the previous year, which is the second epigraph for this chapter, his sheer ignorance) less endearing when it came to public pronouncements on the novel.

Only a month after this Woolf followed up her review with a long article entitled 'The Novels of E. M. Forster', which she carefully prefaced with comments about the dangers of writing about one's contemporaries: 'we are at best only building up a theory which may be knocked down in a year or two by Mr Forster himself'.[19] From his first novel Woolf recognises that Forster 'is also the most persistent devotee of the soul', although she is more impressed by the Austen- and Peacock-like touches of comedy in *Where Angels Fear to Tread*. *The Longest Journey* reveals the novelist's conflict of interests: 'satire and sympathy; fantasy and fact; poetry and a prim moral sense'. The beauty which Forster sees is in the world and not in the work of art, and his novels construct the 'cage' of everyday life 'whence he must extricate her'. The difficulty becomes one of perspective, and here Woolf turns Forster's image of the picture gallery upon himself. Forster attempts to see the portrait and the still life irradiated and made 'luminously transparent' by the universe seen behind through the window. Unlike Ibsen, says Woolf, Forster fails to fuse the two perspectives, the real and the symbolical.

This failure extends to *Howards End:* 'Elaboration, skill, wisdom, penetration, beauty – they are all there, but they lack fusion; they lack cohesion; the book as a whole lacks force.' Again, Woolf uses Forster's word 'whole' deliberately applying it not to character but to the novel as a work of art. *Howards End* fails to be a 'masterpiece' because its creator cannot maintain a consistent perspective. *A Passage to India* presents again a 'model' of English society, but here 'set against a bigger and more sinister background'. The double vision has almost become single; 'Mr Forster has almost achieved the great feat of animating this dense, compact body of observation with a spiritual light', but again it fails.

Woolf's article, then, while it hoped vainly for future fulfilment from Forster, was uncompromising in its judgement. Whatever steps Forster took to suggest a unifying structure for his novels by way of sections or parabolic completion, Woolf's response was chiefly to the sensibility of the author, which she found wanting in consistency or encompassing vision. It was a more elegant, but no less explicit, version of her statement three years later that she found his novels 'impeded, shrivelled and immature'.

After an interval of thirteen years E. M. Forster delivered a memorial lecture on Woolf in 1941. It begins, if one has followed their relationship through as I have, with a note of implicit contrition. 'She liked writing', says Forster, as if to answer Woolf's charge that he said nothing about words. Her creations were 'analogous to a sensation', he continues, as if to answer the charge that he cannot consider the novel as a work of art. To be sure, he proceeds to warn his audience about the 'Palace of Art' which may trap the unwary aesthete, but only to exonerate Woolf. What saves her (and here again he seems to be answering her own praise for his wit and satire) is her appetite for 'writing for fun'.[20]

Forster's remarks on *To the Lighthouse* also show that he has taken up Woolf's challenge and become a critic who can judge a novel as a work of art. It gives 'the pleasure only art can give' of inhabiting a real world and a world where there is pattern, simultaneously. *The Waves*, too, is praised as an 'extraordinary achievement' of patterning which avoids 'arty-ness'. While he does little to recognise a pattern in the 'poetic vagueness' of *Between the Acts*, he stresses it again in Woolf's biography of *Roger Fry*. But then Forster, unrepentant after all, returns to state what he conceives to be Woolf's 'problem: can she create character?' The answer is that, while she is a poet and can catch the moment, she is not a novelist who can catch a character.

Forster then considers *her* character, emphasising repeatedly her detachment from life. She might have Rhoda imagine 'the square upon the oblong' but never would she completely realise abstractions and consider them as political realities worth fighting for. She might be a caring feminist but there was 'an admirable hardness' and lack of sympathy. This second half of the essay is a natural corollary of the first, in which Forster finally admitted Woolf's artistry. For Forster, to be an artist necessarily meant detachment from society, from life. Although he tries hard not to judge this attitude, again using Woolf's aesthetic terminology to protest that he is no painter who can yet see a pattern in Woolf's achievement, he ends his essay with a memorable image: 'And sometimes it is as a row of little silver cups that I see her work gleaming. "These trophies", the inscription runs, "were won by the mind from matter, its enemy and its friend." ' An apparently gracious salute, this image can be interpreted (and has been by feminist critics) as a deliberate diminution of Woolf's achievement. The notion of a battle between mind and matter is one which Woolf used in her criticisms of Forster's novels; there the problem was indeed one of conflicting allegiances in the creative artist's vision. But Forster's image suggests that Woolf's novels are nothing more artistic in themselves than mass-produced 'little' cups, and that they are mere markers for a personal struggle which the artist waged (this personal aspect is dealt with at length when Forster focuses on Woolf's insanity). It is to see Woolf's works as the carpet concealing the figure of Woolf herself. Looking at her novels for human beings, and finding none, Forster fills them with the nearest human being at hand, Woolf herself.

One wonders what Woolf would have thought of this final summation, and how she might have responded. Her reaction would surely have been other than that of 1925 when, on the evidence of Forster's comments on her work up to *Mrs Dalloway*, she confessed, 'I always feel that nobody, except perhaps Morgan Forster, lays hold of the thing I have done.'[21] Even in *Mrs Dalloway* what attracted Forster was not so much 'the framework of a summer's day' as the two fates of Mrs Dalloway and Septimus Smith which 'go spiralling' down within it.[22] The promising formal imagery gives way in Forster's essay to an admiration for the treatment of that highly human disease of madness.

The distinctions between the aesthetic ideas of Forster and Woolf will be more apparent by the end of this volume, but they may here be neatly symbolised by comparing, finally, essays by both of them on the same painterly rather than literary subject: the works of Sargent.

In 1919 Woolf wrote an essay about the Royal Academy, describing her reactions to an exhibition:

> It is indeed a very powerful atmosphere; so charged with manliness and womanliness, pathos and purity, sunsets and Union Jacks, that the shabbiest and most suburban catch a reflection of the rosy glow. 'This is England! these are the English!' one might exclaim . . . .[23]

Woolf's outrage at the implicit assumption in these paintings about the value – or rather lack of value – of ordinary, daily life culminates in her viewing of Sargent's *Gassed* [Plate 12], which 'at last pricked some nerve of protest, or perhaps of humanity. . . . Mr Sargent was the last straw.' Woolf flees the exhibition with its gaudy and brainless birds', and ends the essay, 'No doubt the reaction was excessive; and I must leave it to Mr Roger Fry to decide whether the emotions here recorded are the proper result of one thousand six hundred and seventy-four works of art.' The satirical point is obvious: none of these paintings revealed a true vision of life, not even *Gassed*, which struck Woolf as the most obscene because it pretended to be the most realistic. But her outrage was more that these paintings were concerned totally with content, in whatever unexamined way, rather than with form.

It happened that Forster in 1925 went to see a Sargent exhibition, and his essay recounting his reactions, entitled 'Me, Them, and You', demonstrates his distance from Woolf's position. Both writers heartily condemned the Royal Academy style of painting, but both singled out *Gassed* for special comment. Forster writes,

> You had been plentiful enough in the snow outside (your proper place), but I had not expected to find You here in the place of honour, too. Yours was by far the largest picture in the show. . . . You were of godlike beauty – for the upper classes only allow the lower classes to appear in art on condition that they wash themselves and have classical features. . . . Many ladies and gentlemen fear that Romance is passing out of war with the sabres and the chargers. Sargent's masterpiece reassures them. He shows that it is possible to suffer with a quiet grace . . . .[24]

Like Woolf, Forster finds in *Gassed* a reference to the common man; like her, he protests at his adulteration and sanitisation. But the terms of the protest are quite different. Woolf quits the gallery in disgust and laments the total lack of aesthetic sense, but Forster takes the opportunity to venerate 'You' and assert that among the common people occurs the life that matters: 'and far away, in some other category, far away from the snobbery and glitter in which our souls and bodies have been entangled, is forged the instrument of the new dawn'. That 'life' which Woolf found so

unsatisfactorily located in *Aspects of the Novel* is here the life of the
man in the street or in the trenches. For Forster the obscenity of
Gassed is that it arouses sentiment rather than anger: for Woolf it
obscenity is its assumption that out of such stuff art can be made
at all. Here the two writers take their stands. For Forster life consists of people and the larger universe, and he thinks so little of the
picture gallery that he can use that very image to refer to that
'real', common life which is the stuff of fiction. For Woolf the stuff
of fiction may be Mrs Brown, but the end of fiction is the work of
art: neither Jacob nor the view from the room, but the room itself.

6 Woolf and Painting

Not a single educated man's daughter . . . is thought capable of teaching the literature of her own language at either university. Nor is her opinion worth asking . . . when it comes to buying a picture for the National Gallery. [1]

A glance at Woolf's essays, letters or diary should be enough to convince one of the importance of painting in her life. far more than music, it offers the most common analogy for her career and aspirations as a writer. Also her closest friends were painters and critics: Vanessa Bell, Fry and Clive Bell. This chapter will establish this intimate connection and also suggest some of the ways in which Woolf found the enterprise and product of painters a useful sounding-board for the development of her own ideas about the novel.

In 1901 painting ranked a dismal third in the young Virginia Woolf's hierarchy of the Muses: 'The only thing in this world is music – music and books and one or two pictures.' [2] Three years later, she made the comparison between literature and painting which was to endure throughout her life in one form or another. She envied the lifestyle of the painter whose 'work is done in the open . . . whereas a poor wretch of an author keeps all his thoughts in a dark attic in his own brain, and when they come out in print they look so shivering and naked'. But she treasured the complexity of literature in contrast to the simple products of painting: 'Pictures are easier to understand than subtle literature, so I think I shall become an artist to the public, and keep my writing to myself.' [3]

Although Woolf was involved in the Post-Impressionist exhibitions of 1911–12, her gallery-visiting then and in subsequent years was not a matter of pure aesthetic enjoyment. Typically in 1912, she responded to the artists rather than to their amazing, controversial art: 'The Grafton, thank God, is over; artists are an abominable race.' [4] After a visit to the National Gallery in 1918

even her developing sense of fine-art aesthetics did not prevent
her from desiring to convert the pictorial into the literary:

> I see why I like pictures; it's as things that stir me to describe
> them. . . . I insist (for the sake of my aesthetic soul) that I
> don't want to read stories or emotions or anything of the kind
> into them; only pictures that appeal to my plastic sense of
> words make me want to have them for still life in my novel.[5]

A year later she commented on the visit to the Royal Academy
which resulted in her comments about Sargent's *Gassed*, calling it
'a very amusing and spirited place. I get an immense deal of
pleasure from working out the pictures.'[6] While Fry might
applaud Woolf's attempt here to take pictures seriously, there is
still something slightly scornful and reductive in her tone, as if
paintings can only be pretty puzzles over which to while away an
idle afternoon. There is no mention here of the 'aesthetic ecstasy'.
Indeed, around that time Woolf made her opinion clear in a flip-
pant but basically serious letter: 'Literature is the only spiritual
and humane career. Even painting tends to dumbness, and music
turns people erotic, whereas the more you write the nicer you
become.'[7] Woolf always had the feeling that the difficulties of
literature made a writer, if not nicer then at least more
thoughtful, sophisticated and tentative than a painter. But,
precisely because of this, she also retained a lingering jealousy for
the freer, more confident life of the painter: 'Why are writers so
much less well equipped for life than painters? . . . Instead of
controlling life . . . we writers merely contemplate it.'[8]

At times Woolf felt dismayed at the divorce between the two
arts. In 1922 she wrote to Jacques Raverat, 'We are so lonely and
separated in our adventures as writers and painters.'[9] But two important biographical accidents helped to bridge this gulf in
Woolf's career: her close friendship and subsequent aesthetic
education with Roger Fry, and her affection and sympathy for the
work of her sister Vanessa.

The extent of Woolf's admiration for Roger Fry is symbolised
in her biography of him, a labour of love indeed. 'I'm so in love
with him,' she wrote, 'and see dimly such a masterpiece that can't
be painted, that on I go.'[10] Forster reviewed the book in this way:
'Mrs Woolf preaches best when she does not preach, and her

accurate account of her friend's life, her careful analysis of his opinions, have as their overtone a noble and convincing defence of civilisation.'[11] Certainly Fry civilised Woolf in her attitudes to painting. she called his *Cézanne* a 'miracle' and judged him 'the only great critic that ever lived'. But Woolf meant 'literary critic' as well, for it was largely through discussion with him about concepts of art, and through his appreciation of her successive books, that Woolf found the impetus and direction for her artistic development. She wanted to dedicate *To the Lighthouse* to him, and in a letter replying to his response to that novel she affirmed, 'You have kept me on the right path, so far as writing goes, more than anyone.'[12]

Woolf was exposed to Fry's views in three ways. First there were the trips to the Continent, where Fry explained and brought to life the art treasures of museums and archaeological sites. During a trip with him to Greece in 1932, Woolf called Fry 'the best admirer of life and art I've ever travelled with'.[13] (A dim taste of what Woolf was responding to is left to us in Fry's *Sampler of Castile*.) The second way was through the theoretical publications of Fry and Bell. Woolf was well informed on the aesthetic debate of the War years. In 1914 she read Bell's *Art* and wrote to him, 'I liked the chapters of theory more than the historical chapters. . . . There are a great many things I don't agree with, where I understand. But it's great fun.'[14] When she came to research the Fry biography, Woolf concluded that 'Clive did pilfer a good deal without acknowledgement from Roger.'[15]

But most impressive to Woolf were Fry's lively discussions about art and literature, particularly during those years 1916–20 which encouraged Woolf to take a new direction in her fiction, towards *Jacob's Room* and beyond. Woolf described with exhilaration Fry's performance when he analysed Maynard Keynes's Cézanne, *Pommes:*

What can 6 apples not be? . . . There's their relationship to each other, and their colour, and their solidity. To Roger and Nessa, moreover, it was a far more intricate question than this. It was a question of pure paint or mixed; if pure which colour; emerald or veridian; and then the laying on of the paint; and the time he'd spent; and how he'd altered it, and why, and when he painted it – We carried it into the next room and

> Lord! how it showed up the pictures there, as if you put a real
> stone among sham ones. . . . The apples positively got redder
> and rounder and greener.[16]

In a letter describing the same incident, Woolf said, 'The artists
amused me very much. . . . I've never seen such a sight of intox-
ication. Roger was like a bee on a sunflower.'[17]

More exciting even than this were the times when Fry and
Woolf discussed literature. In 1916 Woolf reported with glee that
she could perceive a convert in the war between painters and
writers: 'I predict the complete rout of post impressionism, chiefly
because Roger, who has been staying with us, is now turning to
literature, and says pictures only do "to look at about 4 times".
He has lent us two of his works.'[18] At this stage, it is interesting to
note, Woolf was not contemplating that literature might in fact
follow the Post-Impressionists to create an analogous form. Such
an idea must have had its seeds in the kinds of discussion which
Woolf describes lovingly in her diary:

> We discussed literature and aesthetics. . . . I said one could,
> and certainly did, write with phrases, not only words; but that
> didn't help things on much. Roger asked me if I founded my
> writing upon texture or upon structure; I connected structure
> with plot, and therefore said 'texture'. Then we discussed the
> meaning of structure and texture in painting and writing. Then
> we discussed Shakespeare, and Roger said Giotto excited him
> just as much . . . .[19]

> We discuss prose; and as usual some book is had out, and I
> have to read a passage over his shoulder. Theories are
> fabricated. Pictures stood on chairs.[20]

How one wishes there had been a tape recorder present at such
occasions. Nevertheless, the close link between Woolf's theorising
about fiction and her developing understanding of painting is here
undeniable. Her major fiction owes a huge debt to Roger Fry,
'not only the most charming but also the most spiritually gifted of
mankind. . . . O if we could all be like Roger!'[21]

Although she occasionally commented on Fry's own paintings,
Woolf was far more absorbed in the work of her sister Vanessa,
who in turn, through her close personal as well as pedagogical

elationship, was heavily influenced by Fry. [Plate 13] The two
tephen sisters decided at an early age that they would each make
. profession of their chosen art. At first Woolf simultaneously
nvied and dismissed Vanessa as she did all painters, because she
ad an easier time of it: 'As a painter I believe you are much less
onscious of the drone of daily life than I am, as a writer. You are
. painter. I think a good deal about you, for purposes of my own,
nd this seems to me clear. This explains your simplicity.'[22] By
917 Woolf's interest in her sister's successes was also tinged with
personal jealousy, as she wittily revealed in a letter to her sister
recording a conversation between herself, Fry and Bell:

> *R.:* Vanessa really gets more and more amazing – I mean her
> character.
> *Clive:* Yes. She's quite sublime.
> *V.W.:* Her natural piety has greatly increased.
> *R.:* And then her painting. Sickert says he'd rather have her
> picture of apples than a Chardin. She's gone miles ahead of
> anyone. . . .
> *V.W.:* We've talked enough about Nessa – [23]

But at the same time, 1918, Woolf revealed an incident to her
sister which has an important bearing on her development as a
stylist. She sent Vanessa *Kew Gardens*, hoping that she would
design a cover for it (Roger Fry eventually did this). The story
itself marks a breakthrough in method for Woolf and it was,
obviously, intimately bound up with her relationship to Vanessa
and her paintings. Woolf says in her letter,

> Tell me what you think of the story. I'm going to write an
> account of my emotions towards one of your pictures, which
> gives me infinite pleasure, and has changed my views upon
> aesthetics. . . . Its a question of half-developed aesthetic emo-
> tions, constantly checked by others of a literary nature – in fact
> it's all very interesting and intense.[24]

In a subsequent letter Woolf related how a painting by Vanessa of
a vase and long flower made Woolf 'conceive the room as a whole,
in relation to your picture'[25]; and as a result she tried to find the
right fabric to recover a yellow checked chair which clashed with
the painting in the room. Woolf asked tentatively if this sensitivity

to colour might betoken the awakening of an aesthetic sense in her. Woolf's uncertainty is quite astonishing, but this incident and the success of *Kew Gardens* confirmed her in her movement, fostered by Fry, towards combining the arts of painting and literature. Her real fondness for the artistic instinct had always been there, as is shown by her readiness to listen to Fry on literature; or, as she wrote to Vanessa, the fact that she 'accepts your or Duncan's view of writing absolutely seriously'.

Woolf's confidence in her abilities as an art critic quickly grew; it was the English language which let her down. In 1920 she wrote to Vanessa of a new picture: 'I think it one of your finest – such a solid, entirely impersonal, and – I see my command over artistic language is still too poor to let me launch out. What I mean is "starry"; do you understand?' [26] In 1926 she described a painting at Charleston in similar terms as 'one of flashing brilliance, of sunlight crystallised, of diamond durability'. [27] But at the same time she was dissatisfied with the sterility of the larger design, arguing that her sister 'faltered' or 'flattened' when she reduced tone and colour to bare bones. A comment of the following year suggests that Woolf sensed something central missing in Vanessa's work, since she then asserted in apparent contradiction:

> All your pictures are built up of flying phrases. . . . Your problem will now be to buttress up this lyricism with solidity. We are both mistresses of our medium as never before: both therefore confronted with entirely new problems of structure. . . . I should like you to paint a large, large picture; where everything would be brought perfectly firmly together, yet all half flying off the canvas in rapture. [28]

Confirmation of this creeping dissatisfaction, a sense of the soul missing between the lyricism and the design, came in Woolf's 1930 review of her sister's exhibition. It is a brave, sincere piece, revealing as much about the writer as about the subject. It is cast in the form of a quest, a personal history recounting Woolf's attempt to find a verbal meaning in Vanessa's 'uncompromising art'. [29] There are no clues about the subjects of the paintings or about their creator, so that her art, considered as a puzzle, cannot be 'solved'. But this is because solutions are verbal, linear: 'Her vision excites a strong emotion and yet when we have dramatised it or poetised it or translated it into all the blues and greens, and fines and exquisites and subtles of our vocabulary, the picture itself escapes. It goes on saying something of its own.' Woolf admits, in effect, that Vanessa's paintings have a significant form, leaving us with an original, satisfying emotion which must be (though she does not label it) aesthetic ecstasy. The honesty of the review comes at the end, when Woolf frankly admits that for her, this perfection is *not* enough. She ends with the question, 'Is morality to be found there?' The formulation is crude, exhausted almost, but the conclusion is firm: art without life is not as exciting as art with life.

It is to Woolf's credit that she was able to distinguish her own desires from her sister's complete fulfilment of her intention. In 1938 she wrote to her, 'How I wish I were a painter!' after complimenting Vanessa on a new canvas which was 'firm as marble and ravishing as a rainbow'.[30] The image echoes Woolf's image of the ideal fiction, 'granite and rainbow', but there is in literature an extra possible dimension which makes the verbal achievement of this ideal a far more difficult task than it is on canvas.

The importance which Woolf placed on the element of human drama or familiarity with the natural world in painting can be seen by a short glance at her other artistic preferences. Of her immediate circle, the order of preference after a visit to the Omega workshops indicates this clearly: 'I was chiefly impressed by the Gertlers; Vanessa, too, very good: Duncan, I thought, a little pretty.'[31] She thought Sickert was the 'greatest English painter living',[32] making it clear in an essay that it was not as (what Fry would call) an illustrator that she prized him, but for a more abstract sense of the human predicament: 'That great stretch of silent territory. . . . We could not express in words the effect of those combinations of line and colour.'[33] Of the other painters admired one might list Tintoretto, Poussin, the English landscape-painters, Cézanne, Matisse and John. But a most illuminating example of Woolf's aesthetics comes from her reaction to sculpture. In 1918 she viewed some Rodins at the Victoria and Albert Museum and reported, 'I didn't think at all highly of them, except from the literary point of view, and even so they're not as good as Epstein's.'[34] Two years later she wrote to Vanessa about some Negro carvings:

dismal and impressive, but Heaven knows what real feeling I
have about anything after hearing Roger discourse. I dimly see
that something in their style might be written, and also that if I
had one on the mantelpiece I should be a different sort of
character – less adorable, as far as I can make out, but
somebody you wouldn't forget in a hurry.[35]

Here we see that, under Fry's tutelage, Woolf's aesthetic sense is
able to encompass the rugged sculptures of Epstein, but she
retains enough of the human (or, to refer to her essay on Vanessa,
'moral') sense to reject African primitivism, a style Fry was
championing in England. Between her rejection of the highly
literary Rodin and the 'pre-literate' Africans lies the realm of
experience which Woolf wanted to explore in her fiction.

There are two general ways in which Woolf's involvement with
painting was applicable to her theory and practice of fiction. They
are fused in her own best fiction, but it is as well to tease them
artifically apart here, because it will help to isolate that second
feature which only the greatest paintings have but which fiction
can achieve so much better, in her view.

There is first the immediate sense of aesthetic ecstasy, the sheer
beauty of colour, shape and tone. Writing to her sister in 1938
Woolf complained, 'One should be a painter. As a writer, I feel
the beauty, which is almost entirely colour, very subtle, very
changeable, running over my pen, as if you poured a large jug of
champagne over a hairpin.'[36] This vivid image stresses the
difference between a spatial and a temporal medium, a difference
Woolf attempted in her early work to overcome by the sheer
brilliance and insistence of her prose. Even in such an early work
as *The Mark on the Wall*, Woolf welcomed graphic illustrations to
aid her in her effort to create a speaking picture. She was very
disappointed when Pelican rejected Dora Carrington's woodcuts
for the volume – 'They added greatly to the charm of the work
which will look very blank without them.'[37] All the dustjackets of
Woolf's novels, however, were designed by Vanessa Bell or Fry,
as a vestigial reminder of this first, immediate affinity between
Woolf's fiction and painting.

The immediate perception of a painting is analogous to Woolf's
idea of life as a series of vivid moments, that 'semi-luminous halo'
or 'transparent envelope' which is our consciousness in each
successive moment. To render this on paper was one, immediate

way of capturing 'life'. The pictorial rendition of life is apparent on almost every page of Woolf's novels, but its naturalness in her own consciousness is nowhere better illustrated than in the autobiographical pieces in *Moments of Being*.

It is not simply a question of setting the scene for us, the readers, as when she described the St Ives Regatta as a French picture.[38] It is rather the Proustian necessity in Woolf, as in most of us, to recollect the past by means of scene-making: 'Scene making is my natural way of marking the past. Always a scene has arranged itself; representative; enduring. . . . In all the writing I have done, I have almost always had to make a scene.'[39] And so in *Moments of Being* Woolf recalls her own Proustian moment in the flower garden of Talland House, when everything was 'whole'.[40] Woolf recognises that it is the physical environment, the 'round apples red, lemoncoloured leaves seen just as vividly',[41] which gives a vivid sense to each passing moment. But she also recognises that a series of these moments will not convey to us a sense of her life, because the past is transformed in its present recollection. 'If I were a painter,' she says in a sentence clearly echoing her famous definition of life, 'I should make a picture that was globular; semi-transparent . . . curved shapes, showing the light through, but not giving a clear outline.'[42]

Woolf confesses to us that it is when the present slides over the depths of the past that she feels most fully alive,[43] but in this aptly titled 'Sketch of the Past' she cannot compose the fragments of her memory into a verbal equivalent for that sensation. A pictorial equivalent might be something like Monet's series of waterlilies, the depths constantly threatening the serene lilies with the motions of time. But here Woolf has not the time or the energy 'to spend upon the horrid labour that it needs to make an orderly and expressed work of art; where one thing follows another and all are swept into a whole'.[44]

If she will not compose herself for us, neither is Woolf able to compose the members of her family. As before, her protestations about the difficulty of the task vividly point to the terms in which she saw her own fictive task. Her sister Stella is 'more beautiful than pictures' with the 'ripple of sweetness and laughter over a shape, dimly discernible, as of statuesque marble'.[45] Her mother presents an even more complicated problem than this familiar granite and rainbow division of essence and life, because she manifested herself differently for each observer:

What figure or variety of figures will do justice to the shapes which since then she has taken in countless lives?

If one could give a sense of my mother's personality one would have to be an artist. It would be as difficult to do that, as it should be done, as to paint a Cézanne. [46]

In this recollection Woolf does not paint a Cézanne, but perhaps in *To the Lighthouse* she does.

This difference in the portrayal of character between frozen portrait or caricature and living, evanescent presence is really a distinction between space and time. This same dichotomy informs the second general area of application of painting to Woolf's novels. From the outset, Woolf saw the novel as a construction with a distinct form. In 1908 she wrote to Clive Bell, 'I shall reform the novel and capture multitudes of things at present fugitive, enclose the whole, and shape infinite strange things.' [47] Painting, especially as seen by Fry as a matter of significant form, had much to say about the shaping of strange things. As Woolf observed, 'Painting and writing have much to tell each other: they have much in common. The novelist after all wants to make us see.' [48] We have seen that before the 1920s Woolf felt that the painter was engaged essentially in a different task from the novelist, however. The drama of light and shade was not the same thing as the drama between men and women. The form of line and curve was not the same as the development of plot. But it seems that, independent of Fry and Mauron, Woolf was working towards a bridging-concept very similar to the 'psychological volume' as early as 1924. In that year she wrote to Jacques Raverat, 'I rather think you've broached some of the problems of the writer's too, who are trying to catch and consolidate and consummate (whatever the word is for making literature) those splashes of yours.' [49] Concerning Fry's ideas in *The Artist and Psychoanalysis*, and those of Percy Lubbock in *The Craft of Fiction*, Woolf wrote to Fry in September of that year, 'It is emotion put into the right relations; and has nothing to do with form as used of painting. But this you must tidy up for me when we meet.' [50] All this was clarified in her review of Lubbock:

When we speak of form we mean that certain emotions have been placed in the right relations to each other; then that the novelist is able to dispose these emotions and make them tell by methods which he inherits, bends to his purpose, models anew, or even invents for himself. Further, that the reader can detect these devices, and by so doing will deepen his understanding of the book. [51]

In her own criticism, Woolf rarely contented herself with pointing out the 'devices' in the way that Fry would point to a slide with his cane. Instead, she would move the opposite way, as it were, elucidating the vision by painting a picture rather than elucidating the design by writing an essay or talking. This may seem like an avoidance of the temporal question of what happens as one reads a novel, the reaction of one emotion upon the previous, the rhythm of the prose or the plot, and so on. But Woolf was acutely aware of what I elsewhere term 'the reading-process'. In an essay entitled 'How Should One Read a Book?' Woolf stresses the difficulty of judging and comparing. 'The thirty-two chapters of a novel', she says, 'are an attempt to make something as formed and controlled as a building; but words are more impalpable than bricks; reading is a longer and more complicated process than seeing.' [52] What we must do after reading a novel is to wait for the dust to settle, and than perhaps 'we see the shape from start to finish.' Finally 'there they hang in the mind, the shapes of the books we have read' [53] and the characters we have learnt about become familiar people 'sharply outlined in morning light'. [54] It is a rare moment this, when a book 'swims up complete in the mind' like a 'bare body against the sky'; [55] it is the moment when design is transformed into vision.

Woolf's literary criticism, then, is a sophisticated attempt to preserve the meaning of the temporal experience of reading the novel in a spatial metaphor. We find an obvious example of it when she speaks of the sense of the countryside in Brontë and Hardy: 'Through the half-shut eyes with which we visualise books as a whole, we can see great tracts of Wessex and of the Yorkshire Moors . . . the element we mean is rubbed deep into the texture and moulds every part.' [56] In *Robinson Crusoe* Defoe 'has roped the whole universe into harmony' [57] by focusing, as in a still life, on a mundane object like an earthenware pot, set against the background of the stars. In De Quincey's 'most curious re-arrangement of the landscape nothing must come too close'. [58] Of Conrad she writes, 'Picture after picture he painted thus upon the dark background.' [59]

Her critique of Lawrence is particularly complicated. She feels he gives us a 'coloured and stereoscopic representation of life', arranging his scene like a painter for the right contrasts and highlighted details. But Lawrence 'lacks the final power which makes things entire in themselves';[60] his vision is not inherent in his design, but overlaid. Woolf's sense of the writer's relationship to his work was acute, and is again based on the painterly analogy. The writer must be clear enough of his work to arrange it so that its juxtapositions and balances convey his 'meaning': 'There is a station, somewhere in mid-air, whence Smith and Liverpool can be seen to the best advantage; the great artist is the man who knows where to place himself above the shifting scenery.'[61] This sounds like the problem of the artist choosing a window in James's house of fiction, but Woolf would never be satisfied with the solution of, say, placing the centre of consciousness in the mind of one particular character. The question of the artist's perspective was almost a metaphysical one, and Woolf described the new novel in just these terms: 'The new novel will stand back from life. . . . Instead of enumerating details [the novelist] will mould blocks'.[62] Admittedly this is a late essay, but it shows the direction of Woolf's thought, and her consistent emphasis on control of form.

There are several undefined, crucial terms in Woolf's important enunciation of her literary aesthetics, in particular the idea of 'right relations' for the placing of emotions. In what sense 'right'? In the world of fiction, I think what Woolf was groping towards was an idea analogous to the idea of aesthetic rightness or beauty in painting. If the spatial, sensual criteria could no longer apply, perhaps a sense of 'truth' or rightness could. Woolf praised Ibsen for illuminating his subject – 'The thing we are looking at is lit up, and its depths revealed. It has not ceased to be itself by becoming something else.'[63] It is this sense of illumination that Woolf uses constantly in her creative and critical writing. It is an image which has its origins in the visual, but has an almost religious overtone of 'meaning' to it as well, and it was just this extra 'moral' dimension which Woolf felt literature could impart to life, and which only the rare painting could. To achieve that sense of illumination, of a flower, a moment in a character's life or of Julia Stephen, required the ability to paint a likeness but also to place or set that likeness in a framework of intelligible meaning. That is how the sense of form operates for Woolf in fiction, and it

is a sense which can be grasped only when the temporal experience of reading is finished and all the disparate elements come
together for a moment, to be held by the lucky reader likc a
Cézanne which he has recreated for himself.

Patricia Stubbs, a feminist critic, has argued that Woolf's
aesthetic theories 'actually devitalised her fictional world'.[64] The
selective evidence assembled here suggests that, on the contrary,
Woolf's aesthetics were both the inspiration and goal of her successive canvases. But to talk any further in the abstract of significant form, unity, wholeness, psychological volumes and the
reading-process would be unproductive. The test in the next
chapter (as in chapter 4) will be whether an approach to the novels
within the framework suggested here and in my first two chapters,
can illuminate them in ways not yet suggested by the more traditional psychological and biographical criticism of Woolf.

7 Woolf's Novels

THE VOYAGE OUT (1915)

> *Virginia's view of the world is perfectly artistic, but isn't there some danger that she may forget that an artist, like God, should create without coming to conclusions?*[1]

The tortuous evolution of Woolf's first novel, from 1907 to 1914, is told in detail in De Salvo's *Virginia Woolf's First Voyage*. What emerges is an unsatisfactory record of an emotional journey of emancipation, a 'curious amalgam of two stages of the novel's earlier phases . . . feverishly but imperfectly fused'.[2] Looking back in 1920, Woolf admitted as much: 'Such a harlequinade as it is – such an assortment of patches – here simple and severe – here frivolous and shallow – here like God's Truth – here strong and free-flowing as I could wish. What to make of it, Heaven knows.'[3] Woolf's use of the word 'harlequinade' is instructive, suggesting as it does both the fantastical nature of the boat journey to South America, and the 'particoloured' effect of the style of writing, changeable in the way she describes. The question of form became uppermost in her own mind, and it is interesting to see how a mind reared on nineteenth-century notions of form struggled to adapt itself to the Bloomsbury world of Post-Impressionist exhibitions and quite a new conception of form in art.

The art critics were closely involved with the evolution of the novel. In 1910 the first Post-Impressionist exhibition opened, and in 1911 Woolf travelled to Turkey with Fry and Bell. Fry at this time was talking with Woolf about the demands of 'authenticity' in literature and the avoidance of simile, but more important was Woolf's relationship with Bell. Their correspondence concerning *The Voyage Out* is documented in an appendix to Bell's biography, and, though caution should be exercised in using comments which were made about earlier drafts of the novel, one can see in Bell's comments of 1908 a focus on the central problem of the artist's relationship to her material: 'To give a sense of matter need one make so much use of words like "solid" and "block" – they become irritating: imaginations too, must they glimmer and shimmer always or be quite so often "shadowy"?'[4]

Replying to this, Woolf describes writing the 'bald' novel in a dreamlike state, then going over it to 'deepen the atmosphere – Giving the feel of running water, & not much else'.[5] Further on in the letter she describes her intention in the early part 'to bring out a stir of live men & women, against a background'. One can see here Woolf's concern for point of view – how to incorporate the central experience of her heroine Rachel, and how to get her and the setting into perspective. The Ambroses, Dalloways, all the shipboard guests, and the residents of Santa Marina, are themselves a background against a tropical background for the story of Rachel, whose emotional development provides the atmosphere, the 'running water'. The relationship of the subjective consciousness to external reality, which is Rachel's great problem in the novel, is also Woolf's great problem as an artist. How was she to portray both the 'solid' setting and the 'shadowy' imaginations of her characters?

On the most general level, Woolf would move her heroine deeper and deeper, geographically, into the fantastical world of Harlequin. From the opening journey down the Thames, we move as in Conrad's *Heart of Darkness* into ever-increasing unfamiliarity of sight, sound and weather. The unusual setting of the Atlantic with its storms and loneliness prepares us for Dalloway's sudden embrace, just as the jungles of the South American interior prepare us for Rachel's spiritual pilgrimage. As Beverly Ann Schlack has shown in her analysis of Woolf's literary allusions, she also colours the very text of the novel by hedging it about with references to the symbolic spiritual journeys of Dante's Virgil, Shelley's Adonais and above all Milton's lady in *Comus*.

It is true that this inward journey which dominates the second half of the book is layered uneasily atop an initially realistic theme of a girl's struggle for social and even political independence, symbolised by the references to the *Antigone*. Here, in the relationship of Dalloway and Rachel, Woolf played out her own rebellion against her father. This social revolution turns into an existential quest – the world of Jane Austen is forced to marry the world of Emily Brontë – but, whatever the resulting harlequinade of style, the two themes together provide what unity there is in the novel. The 'running water' takes Rachel from innocence to experience to death. It must have been that central drive which Forster responded to when he reviewed *The Voyage Out* and praised its form: 'Here at last is a book which attains unity as surely as *Wuthering Heights,* though by a different path.'[6]

Forster's modification of this view in his 1925 essay 'The Early Novels of Virginia Woolf' is a perceptive indication of why Rachel's spiritual odysseys, whatever form they take, fail in the last analysis to provide a significant form for the novel. There he praises the novel's ending and calls it noble:

> It is not romantic, not mystic, not explanatory of the universe. By using a wrong tone of voice – over-stressing 'South America' for instance – the critic might easily make it appear to be all these things, and perhaps waft it towards popular success! His honesty must equal the writer's; he is offered no ultimate good, but 'life; London; this moment in June'; and it is his job to find out what the promise entails.[7]

One might speculate on what appealed to Forster in this novel, given that it did not have the rhythm and the sense of opening out of his favourite books of prophecy. Probably he responded to the Austenian portrayal of English society with all its foibles, to the devoted portrayal of one young, questioning life, and to the (unconscious) anti-art stance of the book itself. However, Forster does not go on in his essay to 'find out what the promise entails', because there seems to be no significance beyond this to Rachel's abhorrence of love and eventual death.

Here Woolf does not use any of the methods she later perfected for imposing significance through form on a novel. There is no central image like the lighthouse or the waves; there is no structural shape in the meandering plot or the twenty-seven chapters; there is not even the dancelike progression of lovers that she was to use in the next novel (cf. Grant's aquatic voyagers in Plate 14). Nothing is juxtaposed in the plot save the vague memory of Dalloway's kiss during her courting with Terence, and nothing is juxtaposed in the sense of an illuminating dramatic confrontation. Even Terence and Rachel, together, seem tongue-tied and seen from a great and foggy distance. They keep repeating each other's words as if in a dream, and looking outwards to other, disparate members of the English party – to Mrs Flushing, St John Hirst, Helen Ambrose – rather than directly at each other to clarify their state of mind. The spare dramatic style which Woolf uses to document interaction is not buttressed either by a running motif (like the pageant in *Between the Acts*) or by a sustained and illuminating voyage into a character's consciousness, as in *Mrs Dalloway*. The typical ending to such a confrontation – here the two lovers at the crisis of the courtship – is a vague general gesture from the godlike narrator: 'The darkness poured down profusely, and left them with scarcely any feeling of life, except that they were standing there together in the darkness' (p. 294).

The soul and the physical world remain vastly divided and ignorant of each other. While this, it may be argued, is the very theme of the novel, it is as if the narrative persona is also bewildered by it all. We never linger long enough to get to know either dimension (even Rachel's own mind – in her illness, for example, we do not spend much time inside her head), but are – to use Woolf's phrase about Forster – twitched away to another scene or another perspective. It is little wonder that Clive Bell felt that the finished novel had not resolved his early criticisms about the division between solid reality and shadowy spirit, either in theme or in technique; he found 'grave faults' in it.[8] Woolf herself sensed the want of pattern when she wrote to Strachey in 1916, 'The whole was to have a sort of pattern, and be somehow controlled. The difficulty was to keep any sort of coherence . . . (is this possible in a novel?) Is the result bound to be too scattered to be intelligible?'[9] The colours remain scattered, and Harlequin's garb lies in a heap.

Nevertheless, we find *in* this first novel many references to painting and music; these will become the staple of Woolf's later fiction and here are pointers towards her later technique. To take music first: Rachel plays Bach fugues very well, feeling 'an invisible line seemed to string the notes together, from which rose a shape, a building' (p. 54). Later, when she plays to the guests,

As they sat and listened, their nerves were quieted; the heat and soreness of their lips, the result of incessant talking and laughing, was smoothed away. They sat very still as if they saw a building with spaces and columns succeeding each other rising in the empty space. They began to see themselves and their lives, and the whole of human life advancing very nobly under the direction of the music. They felt themselves ennobled, and

when Rachel stopped playing they desired nothing but
sleep. (p. 165)

This remarkable passage seems to support Rachel's opting for
music because it offers an ordered reality. She feels secure and
happy with 'the spirit of Beethoven Op. 112' (p. 33).

Terence and Rachel defend their respective Muses vocifer-
ously. 'Music goes straight for things', Rachel protests. 'It says
all there is to say at once. With writing it seems to me there's so
much . . . scratching on the match-box' (p. 210). Later, when
they are reading the letters of congratulation, Terence calls
Rachel's playing 'like an unfortunate old dog going round on its
hind legs in the rain!' and she protests, 'Think of words compared
with sounds!' (p. 297). Shortly afterwards, Rachel shifts the
analogy to painting, asking Terence if he thinks 'the world is composed entirely of vast blocks of matter, and that we're nothing but
patches of light' (pp. 297–8). This is an advance on Clive Bell's
stylistic criticisms, but hardly subtle. Still, it does suggest the deep
mistrust of her own craft which afflicted Woolf as she wrote. Her
words seemed like patches of light, like harlequins, compared
with the solid building of a Bach fugue. Terence is a would-be
artist who believes in the order to be revealed by art (here painting): 'He sketched for her portraits which fascinated her of what
other men and women might be supposed to be thinking and feeling. . . . According to him, too, there was an order, a pattern
which made life reasonable'(p. 304). However, he speaks for
Woolf when he expresses the limitations of literature and the difficulties of writing. He complains about the ignorance of women
in literature – 'It's the man's view that's represented, you see'
(p. 215) – and says that his own novel will be about silence, 'the
things people don't say. But the difficulty is immense' (p. 218).
He goes on to voice Woolf's artistic credo:

> As for the novel itself, the whole conception, the way one's seen
> the thing, felt about it, made it stand in relation to other things,
> not one in a million cares for that. And yet I sometimes wonder
> whether there's anything else in the whole world worth
> doing. . . . One doesn't want to be things; one wants merely to
> be allowed to see them. (p. 218)

It is appropriate in this novel that Woolf's spokesman should echo
the Conradian 'make them see', but the curious thing is that *The*

Voyage Out is hardly the kind of book Terence would like, except in so far as it gives the woman's view. Rachel muses on this conversation, considering the position of women and seeing it in visual terms, as if her aunts create 'a sort of beauty' by toiling away in submission and 'building up a solid mass, a background' (p. 216). Here the link is made between music and painting, with women creating the ordered framework within which men can shine. But it is painting above all the other arts which dominates in the novel as a storehouse of imagery. Even if the novel as a whole pays little attention to Bloomsbury aesthetics, Woolf was beginning to weave these concerns into her fiction on the conscious, discursive level.

Even literature is seen as one of the plastic arts. Rachel at the beginning is described as reading books, 'handling words as though they were made of wood, separately of great importance, and possessed of shapes'(p. 122), and near the end Terence reads Milton aloud, 'because he said the words of Milton had substance and shape, so that it was not necessary to understand what he was saying' (p. 331). But the painterly vision is ubiquitous in the novel. Woolf herself often steps back to paint a setting for the reader before entering again into the drawing-room or bedroom. A good example is after the peeking-scene at the hotel, when Woolf fills in the six hours of night by describing not only Santa Marina but also the 'Red and yellow omnibuses' (p. 109) in Piccadilly. And, on the first page, Helen Ambrose's blurred, tear-filled eyes can still comprehend the 'skeleton' of the true London beneath the beauty that clothes things (p. 7).

The Dalloways each expound their way of looking at things to Rachel. Mr Dalloway explains, 'Conceive the world as a whole . . . conceive the state as a complicated machine; we citizens are part of that machine' (p. 63). The subtlety of his vision is underlined later when he explains to Mrs Ambrose that his undergraduate years of philosophising were the greatest of his life (p. 71), and that philosophy is the centre of civilisation. But his application of Moorean principles to politics works only within preconceived bounds, which exclude the idea of the flux of time. Rachel, however, failing to perceive this, attempts to view the whole of history and not just the red portions of the globe in Dalloway's holistic fashion – 'the mammoths who pastured in the fields of Richmond High Street had turned into paving stones and boxes full of ribbon, and her aunts' (p. 64). Although expressed comically, this historical sense of unity, the effort to see time as well as space in some significant shape, is a recurring motif in the substance of Woolf's later novels, which all have characters thinking of a prehistoric England.

Mrs Dalloway's attitude to the arts is equally puzzling to Rachel, for she sees a 'perpetual conflict' between the arts and the sordid reality. It is an eminently reasonable view and fits in perfectly with her husband's leaving the real world to be ordered by politics and the world of the imagination to be separately ordered by art.

What precipitates the crisis between Terence and Rachel, and her subsequent willed death, is not a debate about the place of art in their lives at all but an ill-defined repulsion for physicality itself. But it is described most vividly in visual terms.

At an early stage, Terence considers marriage and imagines a series of paintings of the future (p. 244). This is an elementary use of the painting motif, but, soon after, he and Rachel enter a kind of hall of mirrors where their perspectives on themselves and each other constantly shift as they approach and recoil from physical contact with each other. As they talk the mist seems to lift from the world, which 'once more arranged itself beneath her gaze very vividly and in its true proportions' (p. 286). But the subsequent action is the beginning of this amazing process:

> She glanced curiously at Terence from time to time, observing his grey coat and his purple tie; observing the man with whom she was to spend the rest of her life.
>
> After one of these glances she murmured, 'Yes, I'm in love. There's no doubt; I'm in love with you.'
>
> Nevertheless, they remained uncomfortably apart; drawn so close together, as she spoke, that there seemed no division between them, and the next moment separate and far away again. Feeling this painfully, she exclaimed, 'It will be a fight.'

So it goes on, through the nightmare vision in the grass of Terence and Helen leaning above Rachel kissing, and her picture of a boat upturned in an English river which she keeps at bay by fixing her eyes on the figures of the party in the trees (p. 290). The effect of this experience in the innermost depths of the American jungle is to disorient Rachel completely. She struggles to get the sky horizontal again, but when she does her society appears as 'a little row of human figures standing patiently in the distance' (p. 288).

Later, on their way back downstream on the steamer, Terence and Rachel wonder if they are real at all, and look up at the stars:

> The little points of frosty light infinitely far away drew their eyes and held them fixed, so that it seemed as if they stayed a long time and fell a great distance when once more they realized their hands grasping the rail and their separate bodies standing side by side. (p. 293)

For Rachel the constricting demands of the physical soon become overpowering:

> She wanted many more things than the love of one human being – the sea, the sky. She turned again and looked at the distant blue, which was so smooth and serene where the sky met the sea; she could not possibly want only one human being. (p. 307)

The 'hopelessness' of the physical 'barrier' compels her to suggest they break off their engagement, and then

> The words did more to unite them than any amount of argument. As if they stood on the edge of a precipice they clung together. They knew that they could not separate; painful and terrible it might be, but they were joined for ever. They lapsed into silence, and after a time crept together in silence. Merely to be so close soothed them, and sitting side by side the divisions disappeared, and it seemed as if the world were once more solid and entire, and as if, in some strange way, they had grown larger and stronger.
>
> It was long before they moved, and when they moved it was with great reluctance. They stood together in front of the looking-glass, and with a brush tried to make themselves look as if they had been feeling nothing all the morning, neither pain nor happiness. But it chilled them to see themselves in the glass, for instead of being vast and indivisible they were really very small and separate, the size of the glass leaving a large space for the reflection of other things. (pp. 307–8)

The first thing to observe about this remarkable sequence is the unsureness of Woolf's omniscient style, vaguely embracing both characters and resorting to the habitual 'so that it seemed' to introduce an over-explicit simile of the author's. Secondly, the whole crucial sequence is accomplished virtually in silence, with the emphasis on how they see each other, the world, and how the world sees them. Even the word 'brush' (like the word 'stroke' in *To the Lighthouse*) has the double sense of a clothes brush and a painter's brush working on a portrait of the couple within the frame of the mirror. They struggle to place themselves in relation to each other and the universe: separate, joined, together, indivisible, separate, larger, small.

The passage virtually dramatises the Sartrean theory of the *for-itself* and *for-others*. In Sartre's analysis of love, the self enters into a conspiracy with the beloved that each will see the other not as an object (solid, physical) but as a subject, a *for-itself*. The most fatal destroyer of this mutual lie is the looking glass, which reduces each subject to an object (which is why Sartre's Hell in *Huis Clos* has no mirrors – the reliance for identity on others who are not trusted lovers is agony). Here the portrait which Rachel and Terence attempt to paint in the glass, while avoiding the issue of their frustrating separateness of souls, only underlines their physicality, which is the other great hindrance (especially for Rachel) to their 'union'. The mirror is the reverse of Alice's looking glass: the couple had created a fairytale world where they were huge and the world tiny, but the mirror restores the repulsive world of reality to their stricken gazes.

It is ironic that in a novel which fails as an art object, the terminology of painting and perspective should be so crucial to the explication of the central relationship. In her first novel Woolf remains distinctly present as an Austenian narrator, dictating our responses and labelling what is 'solid' reality and what is inner 'shadow'. She capitalises on that tension in describing the dilemma of her heroine and her love affair which is precisely a matter of trying to reconcile the romantic spirit with the lustful flesh. But she fails to organise her material according to an aesthetic shape which would give a meaning and beauty to the whole. Instead, caught up in her material she rushes the story on into the extended climax of Rachel's fever and death, which resolves – in a way – the dilemma of the novel, but which at the same time destroys any aesthetic significance.

1   *Screen* (1913) by Vanessa Bell

2   *Screen* (1912) by Duncan Grant

4 *Charles Mauron* (1931) by Roger Fry

3 *Roger Fry Lecturing* (*c.* 1911) by Walter Sickert

6 *E. M. Forster* (1911) by Roger Fry

5 *G. L. Dickinson* (1925) by Roger Fry

7 *St Gregory Announces the Death of Santa Fina* (1475) by Ghirlandaio

8 *The Ascension of St John the Evangelist* (*c.* 1311–14) by Giotto

9　*The Barn* (*c*. 1916) by Roger Fry

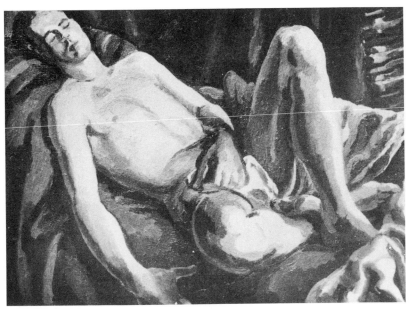

10　*Nude* (1923) by Duncan Grant

11   *The Hookah Smoker* (*c*. 1924) by Duncan Grant

12   *Gassed* (1918) by John Singer Sargent

13   *Virginia Woolf* (*c*. 1912) by Vanessa Bell

14   *Bathing* (1911) by Duncan Grant

16 *Figure in a Glass Case* (1938) by Duncan Grant

15 *The Studio Door, Charleston* by Vanessa Bell

18 *The Countess* (1912) by Duncan Grant

17 *46 Gordon Square* (*c.* 1908) by Vanessa
Bell

19   *Studland Bay* (1911) by Roger Fry

20   *Studland Beach* (1911) by Vanessa Bell

21 *Abstract Kinetic Collage: Painting with Sound,* detail (1914) by Duncan Grant

22 The dust-jacket for *The Years* (1937) designed by Vanessa Bell

24 The dust-jacket for *A Writer's Diary* (1953) designed by Vanessa Bell

23 *Ennui* (*c.* 1917) by Walter Sickert

NIGHT AND DAY (1919)

> *We had thought that this world was vanished for ever, that it was impossible to find on the great ocean of literature a ship that was unaware of what has been happening. Yet here is* Night and Day *fresh, new, and exquisite, a novel in the tradition of the English novel. In the midst of our admiration it makes us feel old and chill: we had never thought to look upon its like again!*[10]

Katherine Mansfield's review of Woolf's second novel drew the just analogy with Jane Austen, but protested that even within these terms Woolf's characters lacked life or conviction. Woolf said herself that she enjoyed writing the novel, that it was 'much more mature and finished and satisfactory' than *The Voyage Out*, and that she had indeed faced the new spirit, being as original and sincere as most modern writers.[11] Her sense of the modern vision, however, seems from her diary to have been confined to what her husband called the 'melancholy philosophy' of the novel, rather than to considerations of form or the techniques of portraying character.

E. M. Forster agreed with Mansfield's charge that Woolf shines her light at her characters deliberately, rather than through them (an image prophetic of Woolf's own definition of life as 'a luminous halo') when he wrote that *Night and Day* was 'a deliberate exercise in classicism'.[12] He felt she was using Austenian tools alien to her nature, and was relieved that she did not do so again. He was more polite to her in person, as Woolf anxiously records his reaction in her diary. There, though he complained that 'none of the characters is lovable', he 'admired practically everything' else.[13] And Woolf was warmed by Clive Bell's praise – 'a work of the highest genius'.[14]

After the exhaustions of *The Voyage Out*, Woolf consciously approached the novel as what Quentin Bell calls 'a recuperative work'. But it was more than an easy imitation of a Jane Austen love minuet; it was the beginning of her exploration of the novelist's craft as a visual composition, in two senses.

There is first of all the scaffolding of the novel, marked by the progression of the plot and by an analogous conversion of that temporal principle into the spatial principle of the arrangement of chapters. The novel has thirty-four chapters, and the plot falls into four phases, like a minuet indeed, with its four principal dancers, Ralph, Katherine, Cassandra and William. In chapter 11, at the end of the first third, which has the characters meeting each other in different combinations, the marriage of Katherine and William is announced. In chapter 18, the centre of the novel, Ralph and Katherine meet by chance in Lincoln, each character with a partner they like but do not love. Nevertheless the marriage is reaffirmed. In chapter 24, two-thirds of the way through, William and Cassandra are paired off, opening the way for the rightful pairing of Katherine and Ralph to close the dance.

More important than this spatial form, however (a form which in its classical purity no doubt pleased Clive Bell), is Woolf's experiment with technique. In a letter to Lytton Strachey she said, 'Dialogue was what I was after in this book' – amplifying her ideas later, 'the things one doesn't say . . . how far do our feelings take their colour from the dive underground? I mean, what is the reality of any feeling?'[15] The two problems are inseparable, of course – Woolf went on to puzzle over the question of 'form, which must sit tight (too tight in *Night and Day*, too loose in *The Voyage Out*)'. But, within the classical lines she had invented for herself in this novel (perhaps as a concession to her fragile mental state), Woolf explored the relationship between dialogue and the 'stream of consciousness', and the ways a writer could relate the two.

Because Woolf stands at a Victorian distance from her characters, she cannot dive into their consciousnesses and paint impressionistically, colouring the world as each character sees it. Nevertheless, she is acutely conscious of the 'colour' from underground which modifies and complicates the things her people say to each other in the novel. The result is not a concentration on *oratio obliqua*, but a high degree of stating a character's painterly vision of how things stand. It is like a frozen moment of the stream of consciousness, that medley of musical rhythm and fine art, without the music.

The dedication of the novel to her sister Vanessa should point us to the painterly preoccupations of *Night and Day*. The dedication reads, 'But, looking for a phrase, I found none to stand beside your name', suggesting the opposition between words and the physical world (or painting), which is not excluded from the novel itself. In the very first chapter, Katherine introduces her grandfather to her future lover:

Denham found himself looked down upon by the eyes of the great poet, Richard Alardyce, and suffered a little shock which would have led him, had he been wearing a hat, to remove it. The eyes looked at him out of the mellow pinks and yellows of the paint with divine friendliness, which embraced him, and passed on to contemplate the entire world. The paint had so faded that very little but the beautiful large eyes were left, dark in the surrounding dimness.   (p. 8)

The image of the Victorian paterfamilias still dominating his children with his own vision must have been close to Woolf's own experience. Certainly the whole Hilbery mansion is devoted more to the art of poetry – the pen, the desk – than to painting; the portraits are there only to remind one of the eyes of the past. It was against that same literary past that Vanessa had to struggle to free herself for her vocation and her technique. As for Katherine, 'she had no aptitude for literature. She did not like phrases' (p. 38). She regards poetry as indicative of an introspection and self-expression from which she shrinks. Even William Rodney, although he delivers a speech on metaphor, cannot express himself in words, but 'there had emerged some passion of feeling which, as he spoke, formed in the majority of the audience a little picture or an idea' (p. 49).

But, being non-verbal, Katherine, much later in the novel, finds in the same portrait of her grandfather a moving kinship:

The sensual lips were slightly parted, and gave the face an expression of beholding something lovely or miraculous vanishing or just rising upon the rim of the distance. The expression repeated itself curiously upon Katherine's face as she gazed up into his. They were the same age, or very nearly so . . . for the first time she realized him for herself, and not from her mother's memory. He might have been her brother, she thought.   (pp. 337–8)

Katherine, for much of the novel, relates not to people but to mind-paintings. She goes to the British Museum, 'and she con- jured up a scene of herself on a camel's back, in the desert, while Ralph commanded a whole tribe of natives' (p. 80). In William's room, 'Suddenly a picture presented itself before her, without any effort on her part as pictures will, of herself in these very

rooms. . . . It was a picture plucked from her life two or three
years hence' (p. 141) Her most elaborate painting, fairly throbbing with significant form, is a group portrait of Mary, Ralph,
William and Cassandra:

> Her mind . . . seemed to be tracing out the lines of some sym-
> metrical pattern, some arrangement of life, which invested, if
> not herself, at least the others, not only with interest, but with a
> kind of tragic beauty. . . . They were the lantern-bearers,
> whose lights, scattered among the crowd, wove a pattern,
> dissolving, joining, meeting again in combination.   (p. 332)

This last sentence could stand as a perfect description of the form
of *Night and Day*.

Ralph, too, thinks in images. After his first meeting with
Katherine he goes away deciding that she 'will do' as a model for
his life study. He 'required this vision of her for a particular purpose. He increased her height, he darkened her hair' (p. 17).
When he learns of Katherine's engagement, he loses the ability to
create a form significant to himself: 'The world had him at its
mercy. He made no pattern out of the sights he saw' (p. 161).
Later still, alone in his room, he takes his 'relics' – a photograph
of a Greek statue, a note, a flower – 'and set himself to visualize
her so clearly that no deception or delusion was possible' (p. 408).
The result of this arcane rite is that Ralph is able to summon
Katherine forth and commune with her, so he thinks. Most
importantly, the exercise propels him to declare out loud in words
for the first time, 'But I'm in love with you.' Here the dive
underground is initiated by a conscious visualisation exercise.
The crucial words are reached through a picture. The final pages
of the novel describing the real union of the two lovers are a
panoply of visual invention. First Ralph actually draws for
Katherine a 'little dot with the flames round it' (p. 522), crudely
symbolising the 'luminous halo' which Woolf was later to say is
the real quality of lived life. This is then, in a remarkable passage,
transformed by Woolf the narrator into a vision containing the
two lovers:

> Quietly and steadily there rose up behind the whole aspect of
> life that soft edge of fire which gave its red tint to the
> atmosphere and crowded the scene with shadows so deep and

dark that one could fancy pushing farther into their density and still farther, exploring indefinitely. Whether there was any cor-respondence between the two prospects now opening before them they shared the same sense of the impending future, vast, mysterious, infinitely stored with undeveloped shapes which each would unwrap for the other to behold . . . . (pp. 522–3)

Later still, Ralph appears to Katherine as 'a fire burning through its smoke, a source of life' (p. 533). He feels 'he had stepped over the threshold into the faintly lit vastness of another mind, stirring with shapes, so large, so dim, unveiling themselves only in flashes, and moving away again into the darkness' (pp. 534–5) until finally all is resolved. Ralph tries to verbalise his vision of all the other characters but cannot; nevertheless, 'They appeared to him to be more than individuals; to be made up of many different things in cohesion; he had a vision of an orderly world' (p. 536). We have worked through, then, from the fiery, abstract colours of twin visions of the lovers to a vision with significant form. It is a remarkable passage in which Woolf encompasses the powerful, even threatening passion of young love, and the more reflective sense of new clarity. And it is all done in visual terms, the characters themselves viewing life as an abstract, Expressionist painting. Whether it is the narrator viewing her characters, a character viewing himself, or his beloved, or the future, the imagery is consistently pictorial, and the epiphanic moment described as one in which the subject composes itself into a whole with significant form.

Other characters in the novel also 'view life' at crucial moments. Cassandra, spiritually as well as aesthetically unedu-cated, looks in the mirror at Katherine as she dresses:

and as she enveloped herself in the blue dress which filled almost the whole of the long looking-glass with blue light and made it the frame of a picture, holding not only the slightly moving effigy of the beautiful woman, but shapes and colours of objects reflected from the background, Cassandra thought that no sight had ever been quite so romantic. (p. 365)

Here Katherine composes herself as a framed portrait in the pre-sent moment. But her mother recalling her past sees time, too, spatially: 'Mrs Hilbery, her eyes growing blank, peered down the

enormously long corridor of days at the far end of which the little
figures of herself and her husband appeared fantastically attired,
clasping hands upon a moonlit beach, with roses swinging in the
dusk' (p. 511). And Mary Datchet, helping her rival Katherine
search for Ralph, looks into the future with a painter's sense of
the vanishing-point of perspective: 'She imagined a point distant
as a low star upon the horizon of the dark. There for her too, for
them both, was the goal for which they were striving' (p. 478).

For much of the novel, then, it seems as if, in order to illustrate
her concern with the relationship of feelings towards others to the
deeper flux of personal existence 'underground', Woolf paints
one picture as narrator and then sets up another one 'inside' a
character's imagination. This is Woolf's general way of exhibiting
what Katherine perceives is 'this astonishing precipice on one side
of which the soul was active and in broad daylight, on the other
side of which it was contemplative and dark as night' (p. 358).
The visual imagery is striking, but it prevents Woolf from exploring the supple interplay of the two forces in time. Later she would
evolve her characteristic 'stream of consciousness' style so that the
reader might go with the consciousness as it dives and surfaces
constantly. The free indirect speech between the dialogue would
become less discursive and less 'disciplined', and often the pictorial imagery would give way to freer association or to imagery in
fantastical narrative.

But there are moments even here when Woolf is able to explore
the unpredictable nature of human consciousness. When
Katherine, for example, is setting off to find her lover Ralph, she
gets sidetracked by the bustle and beauty of the London streets
around her:

> the changing tumult had the inexpressible fascination of varied
> life pouring ceaselessly with a purpose which, as she looked,
> seemed to her, somehow, the normal purpose for which life was
> framed. . . . The blend of daylight and of lamplight made her
> an invisible spectator, just as it gave the people who passed her
> a semi-transparent quality, and left the faces pale ivory ovals in
> which the eyes alone were dark.   (p. 466)

Faced with this canvas, she is seized with exhilaration and must
call herself back to the worrying task at hand. Or Ralph, almost
proposing to Mary:

He had been building one of those piles of thought, as ramshackle and fantastic as a Chinese pagoda, half from words let fall by gentlemen in gaiters, half from the litter in his own mind, about duck shooting and legal history, about the Roman occupation of Lincoln and the relations of country gentlemen with their wives, when, from all this disconnected rambling, there suddenly formed itself in his mind the idea that he would ask Mary to marry him. The idea was so spontaneous that it seemed to shape itself of its own accord before his eyes. (p. 239)

This image from the underground replaces the conscious sculpture of the moment, and Ralph almost ruins the novel. It is only his habit of distinguishing small and big talk which saves him.

The fact that Ralph's idea 'shapes itself' indicates the general valuation of the spoken word and the pictorial image in this novel. Katherine's great-grandfather may have been a poet, but she is no wordsmith, and her escape from the well-read Rodney is fortunate. Truths occur to characters only when they are visualised, not verbalised. Even Mary, the most sensible and 'prosaic' of the foursome, experiences her illumination of Ralph's love for Katherine in the form of a well-lit canvas: 'the light of truth, she seemed to frame the words as she rose to go, shines on a world not to be shaken by our personal calamities' (p. 243). That sentence suggests the morality Woolf has built into this experiment in style. To see the world steadily and whole means just that – to *see* it, as a painting (as in Vanessa Bell's tranquilly illuminated interiors [Plate 15]). Mansfield, looking for technical innovation, missed the fact that in *Night and Day* the innovation is still at a theoretical level; language is criticised, but only conceptually. However, the novel's bias, both in form and in content, in favour of the visual arts must have been what pleased Clive Bell and to a lesser extent Forster.

Of course, the visual arts can mislead the heart. Most of the complication and tension in the novel is built on this fact. The seductive chiaroscuro effects of all those wintry evenings and shadowy meetings transform but often falsify the realities of daylight. The novel works towards a new synthesis of the two elements of the novel's title. True love is when the world is illuminated not by the fluctuating light of nature, which the

Impressionists exposed and captured so masterfully, but by a steady artificial light. And it is a landscape, not a page of words, which is to be illuminated:

> Books were to be written, and since books must be written in rooms, and rooms must have hangings, and outside the windows there must be land, and an horizon to that land, and trees perhaps, and a hill, they sketched a habitation for themselves upon the outline of great offices in the Strand and continued to make an account of the future upon the omnibus which took them towards Chelsea; and still, for both of them, it swam miraculously in the golden light of a large steady lamp. (p. 537)

JACOB'S ROOM (1922)

> *The blobs of colour continue to drift past; but in their midst, interrupting their course like a closely sealed jar, rises the solid figure of a young man. In what sense Jacob is alive . . . we have yet to determine. But that he exists, that he stands as does a monument, is certain . . . .* [16]

In 1923 Virginia Woolf recorded in her diary that her close friend Roger Fry was impressed by her new novel *Jacob's Room*; 'only he wishes that a bronze body might somehow solidify beneath the gleams and lights – with which I agree'.[17] More recent critics have generally agreed that the novel, while an interesting sourcebook for Woolf's developing theories and motifs of fiction, fails in its depiction of the central character to give the wished-for 'bronze body'. Allen McLaurin emphasises the opposition between the sculptured solidity of Jacob's room and the evanescence of his character, 'all movement like a flickering light'.[18] Alice van Buren Kelly seeks to retain Jacob at the centre of the picture, if only as a 'visionary presence', with the other characters 'flickering across the surface' of his life.[19] Hermione Lee, whose analysis of the novel comes closest to the interpretation I am about to offer, must also find a real Jacob at the centre – this time a Wordsworthian hero, whose efforts to sustain an imaginative life give significance to the 'room of the universe' and even to the book itself.[20] The three-dimensional analogy of a sculpted, 'round' character has proven as stubborn a concept to shift as its actual Greek model, even in the recent study by Ralph Freedman, which begins promisingly with a discussion of the philosophical realism of the Cambridge philosopher dear to Bloomsbury, G. E. Moore. Unfortunately, questions of objective reality and subjective consciousness are finally eschewed for a traditional literary interpretation of the novel as a mixture of epic and social comedy. Jacob, failing as a hero, remains only an 'aesthetic surface' of 'interpersonal relations'.[21]

The use of spatial dimensions of surface and depth, flatness and roundness, can lead to confusion in the consideration of any novel and above all this one, Woolf's first experiment in form. The initial mistake is to assume that here we have a conventional dichotomy between a narrated story and a 'real' character, with the story as a surface revealing Jacob's 'depths'. It would be better to abandon such preconceptions when approaching *Jacob's Room*. Certainly Woolf herself felt she was attempting something new, 'one thing opening out of another' in order to 'get closer and yet keep form and speed, and enclose everything, everything'.[22] All Woolf's comments are to do with form, and if an analogy from another art form must be used as an aid to explication, it should be drawn not from sculpture but from painting. David Daiches was close to the truth about *Jacob's Room*, although he meant the comment derogatorily, when he said, 'The book was written for the sake of the impressions, of the fluid rendering of experience – one might say, for the sake of style.'[23] S. P. Rosenbaum, in an excellent background article, was clearly aware of the truth when he called it 'an anti-novel'.[24]

Jacob's Room is an amazing departure from the conventionality of *The Voyage Out* and *Night and Day*, in both form and subject. In both these novels, love is the explicit means to true vision. In *Jacob's Room* Woolf explores a single character who steadfastly avoids the conventional romance. In contrast to the central figures of the previous novels, Jacob does not reach out to others for new perspectives on himself and the world. Consequently his vision of the world is never challenged and quickened into clarity by emotional conflict with another person.

Structurally, too, Woolf has abandoned the scaffolding of a narrative drive towards thwarted or fulfilled love. Instead of having the characters reveal themselves in conscious painterly devices, Woolf herself draws on the techniques of painting to convey her vision. One important such technique is chiaroscuro. In an essay on Sarah Bernhardt Woolf wrote, 'Are we not each in truth the centre of innumerable rays which so strike upon one figure only, and is it not our business to flash them straight and completely back again, and never suffer a single shaft to blunt itself on the far side of us?'[25] Woolf's characters in the earlier novels illuminate each other, metaphorically, by being vividly *there* to the life around them. Ralph appeals to Kathrine when he draws himself as a flame with a halo around it, and this image becomes central to Woolf's theory of fiction when she speaks of life as a 'luminous halo'. Jacob is a new kind of protagonist in that he does not reflect the light but remains a dark silhouette on the brightest summer day. For an artist he is therefore a difficult figure to paint, just as for a woman or a man he is a difficult figure to love. While in the earlier novels the characters function as amateur painters, Jacob is the subject of a painter, and the play of light and dark over him reveals his character figuratively.

Woolf provided a kind of acrostic clue to the nature of *Jacob's Room* when she wrote in her diary that it would be as if three of her stories, *Kew Gardens*, *The Mark on the Wall* and 'An Unwritten Novel', were to 'take hands and dance in unity'.[26] What would such a combination be like? There would be an equal emphasis on the objective world – the people in Kew Gardens, Minnie Marsh – and on the subjectivity of the narrator. There would be a balance between the feeling of triumphant exhilaration at the end of *Kew Gardens* and the self-conscious defeat of the other two stories. Above all there would be what the three stories lack (*Kew Gardens* could go on for ever; the other stories finish circumstantially): unity. 'What the unity shall be', wrote Woolf in that same diary entry, 'I have yet to discover.' The answer is provided in a note at the beginning of the manuscript: 'Yet what about Form? Let us suppose that the Room will hold it together.'[27] As I suggested at the outset, we can take the 'room' to mean several different things, and it is worth exploring each of them.

If we take the 'room' as meaning the inside of Jacob's head with its mental furniture, then we do not get very far and are liable to end up feeling as disgruntled as many of the critics. The parameters of Jacob's mental existence are pretty well defined in the opening scenes: the entwined lovers and the sheep's skull, sex and death. In his short life Jacob will find only one other dimension to his being, the intellect. But both sex and intellect seem to stir him weakly and fitfully: as a child he was interested in collecting insects, an occupation suggesting (especially when one remembers the fate of the collector of rocks in Woolf's story 'Solid Objects') an automatic, unreflective mind; and, while Cambridge seems to excite him a little, his intellectual discussions have the same precocious emptiness of those in the final section of Joyce's *Portrait of the Artist*. His resistance to such appealing sexual mates as Clara Durrant or Bonamy suggest that his sexual appetite is just as meagre. Perhaps his emotional life is stunted by the traumatic experience of being jilted by Florinda, for it is a moment when we see deepest into Jacob's heart: 'It was as if a stone were ground to dust; as if white sparks flew from a livid whetstone, which was his spine; as if the switchback railway, having swooped to the depths, fell, fell, fell. This was in his face' (p. 89). Even though he is a young man, this experience inures Jacob to further adventures such as the one with Sandra Wentworth Williams, and he assumes the pose of old age with his pipe and newspapers, his quotations from Marlowe and his Home Rule for Ireland. Our final clue to the crampedness of Jacob's 'personal space' is his lack of an aesthetic sense: in his reaction to Cruttendon's canvas – 'A pretty solid piece of work. . . . But what I wish you'd explain ... ' (p. 120) – one can almost feel Woolf's despair.

If we consider the room as Jacob's surroundings, the people and places which make up the England for which he died, we meet a similarly alarming coldness and disconnectedness. The vistas of Cornwall, the Scilly Isles, Cambridge, London and Greece are fascinating enough, but they seem like a slideshow, unrelated to the people who inhabit them. Those people are either pathetic in their fate – Mrs Flanders in her loneliness, Clara's spinsterhood, Florinda pregnant and desperate, Timmy at work in his Ministry office, the artist Jinny gone mad and Cruttendon painting his orchards 'savagely, in solitude' (p. 124) – or horrific in their predatoriness – the man-eating Sandra, the worshipping Fanny, the sinister heads of state with their skulls 'bald, red-veined, hollow-looking' (p. 164).

The third view of the room is to consider it as Woolf's painting of the world. 'Nobody sees anyone as he is . . . they see a whole – they see all sorts of things – they see themselves' (p. 28), writes Woolf. In *Jacob's Room* she has not attempted to see Jacob as he is and failed; she has attempted to see him as a whole, in his context as well as in the context of her own work of art. The novel begins with an account of painting, as Charles Steele tries to include a moving Mrs Flanders as 'a hasty violet-black dab' in his landscape. If this is a cautionary parable about the attempt to see the world aesthetically, there is an even more cautionary incident in the opening lines, when Mrs Flanders, writing her letter, looks up with tears in her eyes and sees a blurred landscape; what is more, her falling tears blur her page. The original last line of the novel, 'The room waved behind her tears',[28] suggests that Woolf intended to emphasise the problem of an involved yet true vision. In Moorean terms, subjective consciousness gives a 'diaphanous' or translucent quality to what we assume to be reality. As a painter, Woolf has set herself the task of being objective about Jacob: but how to give us more than a 'hasty violet-black dab' in her effort to capture Jacob's elusive reality?

As Jacob declines into respectability, he is seen reading 'these pinkish and greenish newspapers . . . thin sheets of gelatine pressed nightly over the brain and heart of the world. . . . How miserable it is that the *Globe* newspaper offers nothing better to Jacob Flanders!' (p. 93). The newspapers do not record the translucent quality of subjective experience, but merely make mechanical copies of fact, those 'features of our landscape' (p. 92), as Woolf puts it. Newspapers may be contrasted with letters, those 'stays and props' of our subjective life which, inefficient as they may be, sometimes succeed in registering and conveying the subjective flux: 'If bound together by notes and telephones we went in company, perhaps – who knows? – we might talk by the way' (p. 88).

Woolf's assessment of the medium of print may be translated into the medium of paint, as Woolf herself suggests. The public facts in the morning papers are like a bad landscape painting, recording but not illuminating. *Jacob's Room* has its share of lifeless landscapes, too. With a similar intent, but more strikingly, Woolf fills the novel with still lifes. Jacob's room is the most memorable of these: 'Listless is the air in an empty room, just swelling the curtain; the flowers in the jar shift. One fibre in the wicker chair creaks, though no one sits there' (p. 36). Jacob himself registers the scene like an amateur still-life painter during dinner with the Durrants: 'Opposite him were hazy, semi-transparent shapes of yellow and blue. Behind them, again, was the grey-green garden, and among the pear shaped leaves of the escallonia fishing-boats seemed caught and suspended' (p. 54). Here, as if a camera were recording the aura of an angel, Jacob's passionless gaze registers the crucial 'semi-transparent' quality of the human beings opposite him simply as an annoyingly unfocused 'dab'. When Woolf is being the painter, she admits perplexity when faced with human forms: 'What was shaped by the arms and bodies moving in the twilight room?' (p. 41) Later, indeed, she resigns her brush to the reader when (reminding us of the affinities between literature and painting by her pun on the word 'sketch') she invites us to 'fill in the sketch as you like' (p. 91).

Although *Jacob's Room* is a remarkably static book, Woolf does succeed in animating her larger Room. Roger Fry's description of Cézanne's still lifes as 'dramas deprived of all dramatic incident'[29] could well apply to Woolf's technique of word painting. The space around Jacob seems filled with objects and particularly with people; one critic has counted over 160 characters in the novel.[30] Faces, 'far back, round, pale, smooth, bearded, some with billycock hats on' (p. 70) appear in Rembrantesque profusion, and the play of light on faces and bodies is as remarkable as in that painter's portraits. The light on Jacob's face and figure is specially highlighted, so that we can understand both Fanny and Florinda seeing him as statuesque (Fanny indeed visits the British Museum to ogle the Ulysses and dream of Jacob).

But Woolf does not succeed simply in bringing to life the canvas around Jacob; she also conveys 'some emotion of actual life', the characteristic Woolfian notion that physicality and surfaces are not simply 'shallow' but morally degraded. Filled with sexual desire, Jacob 'observed Florinda. In her face there seemed to him something horribly brainless – as she sat staring' (p. 76). Florinda's own attachment reaches no deeper than the play of expression on Jacob's face – 'I don't like you when you look like that.' Laurette's Madame, too, 'had about her that leer, that lewdness, that quake of the surface (visible in the eyes chiefly) which threatens to spill the whole bag of ordure' (p. 99). Such strong language alerts us to the importance of Woolf's belief in the danger of trusting in human appearances. The dichotomy between surface and depth is extended in the novel along the lines of the dichotomy which can be found throughout Woolf's creative and critical writing: between the shawl and the skull, the granite and the rainbow. So Woolf paints the tombs of St Paul's, but values above them 'the leathern curtain of the heart' opening wide (p. 62); the great dome of the British Museum is not so important as the lives of the cleaners and janitors (p. 103). The idea is epitomised in the paper flowers which open on touching water: 'Real flowers can never be dispensed with. If they could, human life would be a different affair altogether' (p. 79).

If we place Jacob and the way he sees his room, then, within the larger frame of Woolf's Room of the world, we find a conflict of styles. At the centre, though hardly foregrounded, is an indistinct dark dab, a person who does not reflect rays, 'flashing them straight and completely back again' like normal objects. Around him are the objects which he notices (including people): shapes with surface only, over which the light plays in pretty but meaningless patterns. Finally there is the larger world of life, which does have beauty and a deeper meaning, a meaning inaccessible to Jacob or to many in his world (Grant's *Figure in a Glass Case* seems to me a perfect visual metaphor for the novel [Plate 16]).

In her appreciation of the paintings of her sister, Vanessa Bell, Virginia Woolf wrote about her effort to achieve the pure, Fryean aesthetic emotion; to see 'the picture, serene and sunny, and very still'. But she ended her essay bravely and unequivocally:

> Perhaps by degrees – who knows? – one would become an inmate of this strange painter's world, in which mortality does not enter, and psychology is held at bay, and there are no words. But is morality to be found there? That was the very question I was asking myself as I came in.

Jacob's Room is not 'just a pretty picture' but a work with a profound moral. That moral is conveyed partly in the figurative aspects which I have been isolating, but more importantly in the elements which are peculiar to the novel form. Like the Greek statues which are never finished at the back (p. 141), Woolf's novel gives us not only the present inhabitants of England but through the medium of words leaps back into the past to suggest the ancient heritage which began before the primeval swamps. From the Cook's Tour of Scarborough (pp. 15–16) to the anthropological vista of London, from the tour of Cambridge to the history of Athens, Woolf capitalises on the ability of her medium to range about in past time as well as to present the vivid present. At one point she even takes us into her confidence to tell us of 'a lonely hill-top where no one ever comes' (p. 128) which she longs for at this very moment. Just as she emphasises her own contingency in space and time, Woolf emphasises the historical accidence of Jacob's room. It is a technique learned from Sterne, and one which she uses to assert the same moral values. Uncle Toby survived his war, but, just as the moment when he received his wound at Namur has become an eternal present for him round which everything else revolves, so the moment of Jacob's death in the trenches is the real historical moment around which the whole novel revolves. Woolf stresses this by introducing early on and at many successive points the sound of the gunfire in the night. Unlike Chekhov's breaking string, this repeated sound has the remorseless inevitability of history, reminding us of the privileged historical perspective from which both Woolf and her readers are viewing Jacob's life. 'The flight of time which hurries us so tragically along' (p. 145) constantly limits the apparent potentiality of young Jacob, as unknowing and unseeing he descends into the maelstrom of the Great War. As if to hammer home her meaning to the point of torture, Woolf calls Jacob 'Flanders' and reminds us halfway through the book that 'now Jimmy feeds crows in Flanders' (p. 91).

The novel, then, is far more a lament for a generation of Englishmen than it is for Woolf's brother Thoby Stephen, who died in 1905. But, like Mansfield's *Prelude*, Woolf's protest is deliberately and beautifully oblique, and being couched in aesthetic terms it also offers a solution.

The novel rises to two climaxes, both equally important in the way they clarify the implicit moral statement of the stylistic treatment of the Room so far. In the first, Woolf asks 'How far was Jacob Flanders at the age of twenty-six a stupid fellow?' (p. 146). 'So we are driven back to see what the other side means – the men in clubs and Cabinets – when they say that character drawing is a frivolous fireside art, a matter of pins and needles, exquisite outlines enclosing vacancy, flourishes, and mere scrawls' (p. 147). Here Woolf forestalls conventional criticism of her own novel by asking us whether we think her drawing of Jacob is a mere scrawl or something more intelligible. While we debate the answer, she gives us the alternative view of life offered by these men of state: a bland account of modern warfare, the hideous destruction of tin soldiers on land and sea – 'one or two pieces still agitate up and down like fragments of broken matchstick' (p. 148). Is it better, Woolf asks, instead of struggling to see into the heart of things and people by means of painterly technique, to draw back and observe life through field glasses? The equation made is obvious. To disbelieve in the existence of subjectivity, of the 'semi-transparent envelope' surrounding each individual, is to open the way to fatal abstraction. The 'men in clubs and Cabinets' are men like Richard Dalloway, with whom Woolf had had this debate in her earlier novel *The Voyage Out*, in the person of Rachel Vinrace. 'Conceive the world as a whole', Dalloway insists (p. 63); but Rachel cannot 'combine the image of a lean black widow, gazing out of her window, and longing for someone to talk to, with the image of a vast machine'.

Neither can Woolf reject Jacob in his room. Her affirmative answer to this horrific climax comes a few pages on when Jacob himself asks, 'What for?' In answer Woolf moves from the abstractions of philosophy to the specific realities of daily life: 'In Surbiton the skeleton is wrapped in flesh' (p. 154). Her comment is not satirical but in dead earnest, as the following description of daybreak over London makes clear. 'The Bank of England emerges; and the Monument with its bristling head of golden hair . . . sunlight strikes in upon shaving-glasses.' Finally everything is revealed in a common blaze of glory:

> The bright, inquisitive, armoured, resplendent, summer's day, which has long since vanquished chaos; which has dried the melancholy medieval mists; drained the swamp and stood glass and stone upon it; and equipped our brains and bodies with such an armoury of weapons that merely to see the flash and thrust of limbs engaged in the conduct of daily life is better than the old pageant of armies drawn out in battle array upon the plain. (p. 155)

The passage is reminiscent of a passage by Sterne which Woolf singled out for praise in her introduction to *A Sentimental Journey*, describing the streets of Paris:

> all the world in yellow, blue, and green, running at the ring of pleasure. The old with broken lances, and in helmets which had lost their vizards, the young in armour bright which shone like gold, beplumed with each gay feather of the east,

all – all – tilting at it like fascinated knights in tournaments of yore for fame and love.

The stirring martial imagery of the passages makes it plain that the authors regard the daily battles and triumphs as being far more glorious and exhilarating than the more lethal substitutions of the 'red, fat' men in government. Certainly, after this climax there is little left for the novel to do but document the feelings of bewildered loss among Jacob's friends. Standing out from this coda is the passage describing the heads of state with their 'bald, red-veined, hollow-looking heads' (p. 164) who presume to control the course of events. Nowhere in Woolf's fiction is her allegiance to the common life against the machinations of state more violently stated.

It is understandable that Woolf should have felt during the composition of *Jacob's Room* that her book was 'an eyesore',[31] because the canvas was incomplete. Here at the end of the novel, however, she draws her threads together, completes her pattern, and hangs her canvas on the wall. She wanted, she said, 'to provide a wall for the book from oneself'[32] without becoming restrictive as an authorial presence in the manner, say, of James Joyce, whose world she described elsewhere as a 'bright yet narrow room'. Her authorial comments throughout the book should not be seen as intrusions, since they are part of the very texture and technique of painting, just as the two climaxes I have described are not argued by her but juxtaposed so that the viewer can draw the conclusion. Neither does the book break into two halves, a book about Jacob and a book about Woolf's views on the Great War. Rather, I think, Woolf is suggesting a psychological, almost an aesthetic, explanation for why so many like Jacob went willingly to Flanders. Jacob's own world is a world without interiority, without relationship with people or things. It is a still life of stilled life, like the landscape provided by the newspapers he so avidly digests. From a youthful world vibrating with life – the moment on the boat travelling to the Scilly Isles, perhaps his first moments of love for Florinda – Jacob has descended willingly into the world of the politicians, a world of abstractions and death. When Mrs Flanders asks what to do with his shoes, Woolf is reminding us that Jacob was there, when he was alive, only in the minimal sense of occupying his clothes. Certainly the friends who

grieve for him are grieving not so much for the loss of a loved one
as for the sudden realisation of the fragility of their attachment,
the emptiness of the object of their feelings.

Jacob, then, emerges as a pre-war type. There is much in him
of the Cambridge Apostles, whom Woolf was able to observe
through her Bloomsbury friends – at least those Apostles who
failed to claim the Moorean salvation of friendship and aesthetics.
As Woolf described them in her biography of Roger Fry,

> There is no evidence . . . that the young men who read so
> many books and discussed so many problems ever looked at
> pictures or debated the theory of aesthetics . . . .
> Perhaps, then, when Mr Benson talks of the pallor of the
> Apostles, he hints at something eyeless, abstract and austere in
> their doctrines.

Jacob's vision of life remains at the level of his undergraduate
essay 'Does History Consist of the Biographies of Great Men?'
He continues to believe so, and dies a pawn of that kind of
history.

But we have not yet come to the 'moral' which I suggested is
contained in the form of the novel – that element which Woolf felt
so keenly was absent from her sister's pictures. The moral lies in
Woolf's wishing to 'provide a wall' at all for Jacob. For all Jacob's
obtuseness and inhumanity, he was alive and did possess the
value and fascination of any human being in Woolf's eyes. 'There
remains over something', Woolf admits, 'which can never be conveyed to a second person save by Jacob himself' (p. 69). Jacob
never conveyed this, and 'Yet', she goes on, 'over him we hang
vibrating.' Roger Fry uses the word 'vibrating' ubiquitously in
his art criticism, as in this description of Cézanne: 'The perpetual
slight movements of the surface, the vibrating intensity and shimmer of the colour . . . gives to this austere design the thrill of
life.'[33] Again, this description could be applied to *Jacob's Room*. It
is the painter who gives to the still life or to Jacob the quality of
vibrating life through her technique. While her subject in this
novel is singularly unrewarding from this point of view, Woolf's
constant effort to divine and capture the living in the scene is in
itself an example of the effort required in us as we live our daily
lives. In a much-quoted passage from the novel Woolf says,

Why are we yet surprised in the window corner by a sudden vision that the young man in the chair is of all things the world the most real, the most solid, the best known to us – why indeed? For the moment after we know nothing about him.

   Such is the manner of our seeing. Such the conditions of our love.   (p. 68)

Critics have commonly taken this passage as Woolf's rueful recognition of the vagaries of human attention and the impossibility of writing her novel. I see it instead as a realistic affirmation of the potentialities in human consciousness for both aesthetic apprehension and real fellowship. The difficulty and riskiness of human attachments are no reasons for opting out of them, as Jacob seems to do. Likewise, the difficulty and riskiness of achieving the artistic vision are no reasons for abandoning the artistic enterprise, for out of those very difficulties a work of art may be constructed. The real centre of *Jacob's Room* is the artist, whose documented efforts and occasional successes (like the passage describing dawn over London) provide a positive counterpoint to the implicit moral criticism of Jacob and his world.

   In 1926 Roger Fry wrote in *Transformations*,

Even in the novel, which as a rule has pretensions to being a work of art, the structure may be so loose, the esthetic effects may be produced by so vast an accumulation of items that the temptation for the artist to turn aside from his purpose and interpolate criticisms of life, of manners or morals, is very strong. Comparatively few novelists have ever conceived of the novel as a single perfectly organic esthetic whole. [34]

Virginia Woolf was one of those novelists, and with *Jacob's Room* she managed to create a whole from an uncompromising subject and a form which seems constantly on the verge of self-destruction. She achieved unity by incorporating her own vision as part of the design, balancing Jacob's room with her own Room and the failure of one generation with the success of another. Certainly, while it contains many landscapes and still lifes, *Jacob's Room* has not the significant form of lines and spaces which Fry was looking for. Its form arises from this balance of psychological volumes: Jacob's detachment, Woolf's engagement; Jacob's lethargy, Woolf's energy; Jacob's ignorance, Woolf's wisdom; finally, Jacob's death and the living achievement of *Jacob's Room*.

In her later novels, Woolf was able to attribute the task of seeing things whole to one of her characters (Mrs Dalloway, Lily Briscoe) or to signpost the whole by means of a clear structure (*The Waves*). What is remarkable about *Jacob's Room* is that she was able to combine her aesthetic concerns with a critique of the Great War without stepping outside of her canvas; she still manages to show when the impulse to tell must have been very great. Having rejected the old stable ego of character, she refuses to capitulate to the Laurentian 'unseizable forces' of the politicians or, analogously, of the stream-of-consciousness novelists. While Jacob is a failure and almost sabotages his own novel, Jacob's potential and the eventual triumph of form in the novel offer a third way through the manner of our seeing. Faced with Jacob's empty shoes, we should not wish for a bronze body with which to fill them; instead, we should gaze steadily at the emptiness and wonder at the waste.

MRS DALLOWAY (1925)

> *And Hutton (a very bad poet) always felt that Mrs Dalloway was far the best of the great ladies who took an interest in art.*   (p. 195)

In June 1925 Woolf recorded in her diary the reactions of her friends to *Mrs Dalloway*. While Clive Bell and others thought it 'a masterpiece', Lytton Strachey felt that although it was 'a whole' there was 'some discrepancy in Clarissa herself'.[35] Strachey felt that Mrs Dalloway was an unworthy centre for such a novel, and Woolf admitted that she did feel some 'distaste' for her.

It is understandable that the author of *Eminent Victorians* should find this novel disagreeable in subject matter, and equally understandable that Forster should admire it – this, records Woolf, was 'a weight off her mind'.[36] For Mrs Dalloway belongs to that silent rank of English matrons so deeply appreciated by Forster and forming, in the characters of Mrs Herriton, Mrs Failing, Mrs Wilcox and Mrs Moore and so on, a major theme

and focus in his novels. 'It is a civilised book', Forster said in his
memorial lecture, and perhaps his understanding of that key
Bloomsbury word 'civilisation' was different from Strachey's. For
Forster saw in the English society around him civilisation, while
for Strachey it was an ideal rarely approximated in England, and
certainly not achieved since 1914. Strachey did however recognise
that the novel was a whole, and it was this formal achievement,
rather than any praise for an attitude taken towards Mrs
Dalloway, that must have pleased Woolf. Her business was to
select, arrange and present the London she experiencd in the
1920s. Civilised or not, there it must be.

In 1922 Woolf recorded, '*Mrs Dalloway* has branched into a
book; and I adumbrate here a study of insanity and suicide; the
world seen by the sane and the insane side by side.'[37] The evolution of the subject from one woman who goes insane to two
characters whose stories are virtually disconnected, has been well
documented. What impresses me from the diary is the insistence
on structure:

> I want to think out *Mrs Dalloway*. I want to foresee this
> book better than the others. . . .

> The design is so queer and so masterful. I'm always hav-
> ing to wrench my substance to fit it.

> . . . *The Hours* and my discovery: how I dig out beautiful
> caves behind my characters: I think that gives exactly
> what I want; humanity, humour, depth. The idea is that
> the caves shall connect and each comes to daylight at the
> present moment.

> I think the design is more remarkable than in any of my
> books.

> Suppose one can keep the quality of a sketch in the fin-
> ished and composed work?[38]

The last quotation, from 1924, indicates Woolf's confidence in
her design. She now wants to regain the feeling of spontaneity
within each section and in the movement from one section to
another. She described the revisions in a painterly way, 'as thus

one works with a wet brush over the whole, and joins parts separately composed and gone dry'.[39]

The joining-up of the various 'caves' in *Mrs Dalloway* is achieved in various ways. There is first of all the first appearance of the characteristic Woolfian style, described by Seymour Chatman in his analysis of the first sentence of the novel as 'the communal or sympathetic mode . . . indirect free statements which are indifferently attributable to either narrator or character'.[40] All the characters, because of such a style and the frequent use of such generalised pronouns as 'one', seem equally accessible to the narrator. From the sheer evenness of texture of the prose, a sense of community is evoked.

There are secondly the often noted geographical and temporal links. Avrom Fleishman has plotted the novel minutely in both time and space, according to the frequent clues dotted through the novel.[41] The bells, the sign-writing plane, the car, the woman singing: all these devices link the gallery of characters who are all living during this one June day in London. Thirdly there are the dramatic links, when characters either meet, pass, notice, hear about each other, or have mutual acquaintances. Sir William Bradshaw is the mutual acquaintance who finally brings the story of Septimus to Clarissa's attention, but before the party it is Peter during his wanderings in Regent's Park who provides the main link between the two stories. And here Woolf is able to establish both an accidental connection and a far more alarming (and significant for the themes of the novel) mutual ignorance between the players. Peter wakes up from his dream, for example, to notice a little girl running off and crashing into 'a lady's legs. Peter Walsh laughed out' (p. 73). The lady is Rezia, and, as she watches in turn 'the kind-looking man' showing the girl his watch, she is sunk in her own predicament. Perhaps the most remarkable example of this deliberate conjunction of disjunctions comes when Septimus kills himself, and Rezia lying in shock sees the dark, malignant body of Dr Holmes stooping over her: 'One of the triumphs of civilization, Peter Walsh thought. It is one of the triumphs of civilization, as the light high bell of the ambulance sounded' (p. 167). The 'wet brush', then, does not always smooth the transitions from one scene or point of view to another, but stresses either the communal or the separate, alternately.

The effect of these links, or rather of the many heterogeneous points of view, is to provide what Fleishman calls 'carefully constructed perspectival situations'.[42] There are representatives from almost every class in London, from Lady Bruton to the old hag by the Underground. Peter provides the personal link between Clarissa and the Smiths; Dr Bradshaw provides the professional connection. To balance the upper-class perspective of Clarissa's own world, especially the party scene, we have the opening scene where the mysterious car mingles with the populace, and later on Miss Kilman is introduced to give, again, the 'Leonard Bast' element.

Of course Clarissa is the centre and often the focus for these perspectives, but before considering her I should like to point out one major artistic device by which Woolf links the classes and perspectives, and establishes a major theme. The sun as a leit-motif has been well explored, but more remarkable is the pervading imagery of the pastoral, chiefly in trees and flowers. Although the novel is set firmly in the heart of London, it seems from the outset a book filled with plants. 'June had drawn out every leaf on the trees' (p. 9), and Clarissa feels that she will survive death, 'she being part, she was positive, of the trees at home' (p. 11). She felt 'laid out like a mist between the people she knew best, who lifted her on their branches as she had seen the trees lift the mist' (p. 12). A quarter of the way through the book comes the first climax, the reunion of Peter and Clarissa, and she sees Peter's love Daisy as 'a lovely tree in the brisk sea-salted air of their intimacy' (p. 51). At the centre of the novel we focus on Septimus and his appointment. We are told that Septimus had 'flowered' into manhood before going to France. Three-quarters of the way through, Septimus and Rezia have their moment of communion before Dr Holmes barges in, and Septimus feels her mind, 'like a bird, falling from branch to branch, and always alighting, quite rightly; he could follow her mind' (p. 162). Because images of trees and flowers occur with such regularity through the novel, I have selected these ones in order to illustrate at the same time the larger structure of the book. The communion of Peter and Clarissa parallels that of Septimus and Rezia, and each is associated with trees. Trees suggest pastoral tranquillity and the interconnectedness of branches, or human minds.

At this point a distinction must be made between trees and flowers. Flowers are more ordered than trees, more beautiful but more fragile. Clarissa opens the novel buying flowers, but it is while she is in the flower shop, surrounded by Miss Pym's cultivated beauty, that she hears the 'pistol shot' of the car backfiring outside. Later Richard brings her cut roses, which she treasures far above his 'Armenians' (p. 133). The women characters are defined by their attitudes towards flowers: Clarissa loves them but can only bear to see roses cut; Sally Seton gaily cuts off the heads and floats them in a bowl for an immediate, transient beauty (p. 38); Rezia buys some dying roses from a poor man in the street (p. 116); and Lady Bruton poses with Hugh's red carnations, 'holding them rather stiffly with much the same attitude with which the General held the scroll in the picture behind her' (p. 116). In this last example the analogy is clarified: flowers, the staple material for still life, are beautiful but destined soon to fade. For Lady Bruton, the momentary posture is all; for Rezia, human beings come first. Clarissa's attitude lies somewhere between the two.

At this point reference must be made to Shakespeare's *Cymbeline*, the play from which Woolf takes the verbal leitmotif of the novel, 'Fear no more the heat of the sun'. The quotation, familiar to both Clarissa and Septimus, is a beautiful lament over the (imagined) dead body of Fidele (Imogen). Arviragus, one of the mourners, strews the stage with flowers: 'With fairest flowers/ Whilst summer lasts, and I live here, Fidele, / I'll sweeten thy sad grave' (IV. ii. 218–19). Immediately after the song the 'imagined' body of Posthumus (really Cloten) is brought in, and when Imogen revives she weeps over the beloved. Later, the real Posthumus wakes in prison and reads Jupiter's prophecy: 'when from a stately cedar shall be lopp'd branches, which, being dead many years, shall after revive, be jointed to the old stock, and freshly grow, then shall Posthumus end his miseries, Britain be fortunate, and flourish in peace and plenty' (V. iv. 140–5). While Woolf's novel cannot be paired off against Shakespeare's play, we have here a cluster of images and ideas which, as the leitmotif suggests, inform Woolf's novel and direct us to the heart of her purpose.

The scene of the beautiful lament is, of course, the forested hinterland of Roman Britain, and the play itself is a highly patriotic pastoral comedy. The name of Septimus at once suggests a parallel with Posthumus, and his Italian wife Rezia echoes the Italian connections of Posthumus. Like Posthumus, Septimus is a noble and slighted warrior. He is also an avid Shakespearean scholar: 'He went to France to save an England which consisted almost entirely of Shakespeare's plays and Miss Isabel Pole in a green dress walking in a square' (p. 95). The dress which Clarissa chooses to wear at her party is green, too, though it loses its colour in the sun (p. 42). This image connects Clarissa to Septimus within the novel (we first meet Clarissa walking through London in the greenness of June). But the extrinsic connection, via Shakespeare, is to Cymbeline that 'stately cedar', and all that is best in England.

The pervasive imagery of trees in this scene of 'life; London; this moment of June' suggests that England be seen as a flourishing tree. Clarissa herself stands erect, 'stiffens' as the car goes by with its pattern of trees on its pulled blinds. But Septimus represents those 'hearts of oak', the menfolk of England, who as branches have been lopped off in the holocaust of the Great War. In the flower imagery, Septimus is like the cut-flower arrangements of Sally Seton, looking glorious in uniform (like the young boys who, horrifyingly, are even now parading the streets of London – pp. 57–8) but soon to wither and die. When he flings himself downwards on the railing, he is felled like the branch of a tree. Clarissa has had her own experience of such a death, when her sister Sylvia (ironically named for a wood) was 'killed by a falling tree (all Justin Parry's fault – all his carelessness) before your very eyes' (p. 87). It was this episode, Peter remembers, which compelled Clarissa to adopt an atheistic stance, 'doing good for the sake of goodness'.

Clarissa's reaction to her sister's death is an exact preparation for her reaction to the news of the death of Septimus which, again, is the result of the carelessness of the ruling classes. She feels 'somehow very much like him – the young man who had killed himself. She felt glad that he had done it; thrown it away while they went on living' (p. 206). The American edition makes her reaction more explicit, with the addition of the lines 'He made her feel the beauty, made her feel the fun.' Septimus's death confirms Clarissa's belief in the importance of doing good for the sake of goodness, and of standing firm like a tree for the sake of England. The flowers which she bought for the party in the first line of the novel may die, but she herself, in the last line of the novel, is there, tall and stiff like a noble tree. Septimus, among his messages to the world, warned against chopping down the trees, but Clarissa accepts the necessity of pruning perhaps. The tree of England is the healthier for the loss of the branches, not in the callous sense of a ruthless destruction of all new growth, but in the increased awareness of the *value* of new growth, and its fragility. Septimus, after all, had 'flowered' like a budding branch, and the flower may fall the more easily.

Mindful of the centrality of these ideas when she wrote the introduction to the Modern Library edition of *Mrs Dalloway* in 1928, Woolf described books as 'the flowers of fruit stuck here and there on a tree which has its roots deep down in the earth of our earliest life'. The sentence has extraordinarily rich repercussions in considering the novel's themes or aesthetic design. All the main characters in *Mrs Dalloway* are afflicted with love, usually a hopeless or unfulfilled love, and their plight is summed up in the meaningless lyric of the old hag by the Underground:

like a wind-beaten tree for ever barren of leaves which lets the wind run up and down its branches singing

ee um fah um so
foo swee too eem oo

and rocks and creaks and moans in the eternal breeze.   (p. 90)

Septimus's love for Evans, Miss Kilman's for Elizabeth, Hugh's for his wife, Mrs Bradshaw's for her husband, Rezia's for Septimus, Clarissa's and Peter's for each other, Clarissa's for Sally: all of these relationships have been frustrated and cause pain in the pursuance or the memory. In a similar way, Posthumus's passion for Imogen is the very cause of his undoing. This basic, romantic passion is seen by Woolf as a timeless, inexpressible yearning and tragedy. The passage about the old woman is a remarkably poetic, imagistic rendering of this truth, with its vision of prehistoric London stretching back even beyond the Roman Britain of Cymbeline, to the wild wilderness where Imogen's lament is sung. For the old woman death is seen as a release from love's torments, just as Septimus chooses it to escape from his dashed love for Evans.

Of course one must be careful to define what one means by love. In all these cases it is the personal, perhaps physical passion, but Clarissa herself distinguishes it from the love she feels for her husband. 'Love destroyed too', she observes, thinking of Peter's affairs (p. 140), and then of Miss Kilman. In this meditation central to the novel, Clarissa goes on to consider the old lady in the house opposite: 'here was one room; there another. Did religion solve that, or love?' (p. 141). Clarissa, by rejecting Peter and taking Richard, has rejected sexual love as a way of crossing the barrier between the rooms and chosen rather a reasonable friendship. She sleeps in a separate room, but Richard travels across London to be with her at lunch.

Before rejecting Clarissa's version of love, one must consider those alternative methods of relating to the people around one which others from her class practise. The extreme example is Bradshaw, with his policy of 'proportion', which, as Woolf makes perfectly clear in an intrusive diatribe on the subject, is in fact a doctrine of 'conversion'.[43] His relationship with his wife is reduced to a photograph (not even a portrait) of her in evening dress, above the mantelpiece in his rooms. He has lost all sense of personal contact and relates only to an abstract vision of the community as England or empire (hence the force of Woolf's observations about the principle of conversion operating in India and Africa). The female counterpart of Sir William, closer to Clarissa, is Lady Bruton. She entertains menfolk at lunch and poses for them, but she is seen as engulfing everything she touches:

> whatever it be, this object round which the essence of her soul is daily secreted becomes inevitably prismatic, lustrous, half looking-glass, half precious stone; now carefully hidden in case people should sneer at it; now proudly displayed. Emigration had become, in short, largely Lady Bruton.   (p. 121)

Likewise she swamps the menfolk, even Richard Dalloway. She 'has the papers' ready for him when he loses his parliamentary seat – presumably some colonial post which she has in mind for him so that he may, like her ancestors whose portraits Richard admires, do his duty. Lady Bruton is surrounded by portraits of her family, men of action, 'who had done their duty' (p. 123). Lady Bruton is the living principle of duty, or conversion of one's desires and loves to one single love – for England. Certainly there is a complete absence of a sexual ambience at her lunches; Clarissa need have no fear.

Bradshaw and Lady Bruton, then, would summon the lady from her window next door and demand proof of her service to the Empire. Clarissa is content to let her be, marvelling at her separateness rather than swamping her. But Clarissa is not wholly for the individual either. Her sense of love concerns the society around her, considered not as individuals nor as England but as a 'party' of people. When she stiffens at the sight of the Prime Minister's car, it is because she is reminded not of the flag but of her impending party which he will attend. When she hears the bells, she is reminded not of the glories of England but of the passing of a common time which unites her with all the people of London 'this day in June'. When she hears of Septimus's suicide, she is reminded of the wrongness of both the other ways – of personal passion and of patriotism – and the incident reconfirms her middle way.

Septimus, then, functions not in some general way as a symbol of 'insanity' (whatever that may mean) but as the symbol of two ways of bridging the gap between one room and another: personal love, and conversion to the mass cause. By recounting his experience of the war as a matter not of tactics, bombardments, trenches and the rest of it, but of a simple love for one other man, Woolf sets the one principle against the other other and finds them both wanting. The impossibility of their mutual survival – Septimus's love for Rezia or Evans and his love for his country – drives him down on the railings. Just as Shakespeare's *Cymbeline* exposes the dangers of passionate love (misapprehension, jealousy) and patriotism (bloody battle), so Woolf's novel exposes the inadequacies of personal love or the religion of jingoism as answers to her Clarissa's question – 'here was one room; there another'.

Clarissa's answer, from the first line of the novel, is a party, a community affair which nevertheless encourages individuality, with the right kind of hostess. Clarissa's party, handled as only she can handle it, allows the individuals attending to air their distinctive views (and we get them in the novel). It is the counterpart to the early scenes in the streets of London, particularly the event of the sign-writing aeroplane, when all over London people interpret the common perception in different ways: the sign in the sky both unites the people and distinguishes them.

But that cryptic sign, and the old woman's song, have another significance as signs in the texture of the novel as a work of art: they are indecipherable. They are the linguistic equivalent of the raw stuff of experience, the daily 'life' with which all the human beings in London have to deal. They, like the life of London, represent an epistemological challenge to the onlookers: how are hey to interpret it all? This brings me back to the phrases Woolf used in her introduction, about the novel being the flower on a ree, because this novel is a flower in the sense of a working answer to the basic problems posed at the outset. *Mrs Dalloway* noves from consciousness to consciousness, asserting at the same ime the spatial and temporal proximity of its actors, and the subective separation into different worlds. We start and end with Mrs Dalloway in particular only because she, in Woolf's view, has achieved a unified vision appropriate to her own station. In response to the disaster of the patriotic mass movement which resulted in the Great War, and in response to the failure of personal passion in Septimus, Peter, Miss Kilman and Sally, Clarissa gives her party. The party, like a flower, seems a beautiful and perhaps frivolous crown to it all; it comes like a flower, too, to crown the novel. Yet, in its limited way, it is recognised as a genuine and sophisticated response by Woolf. It succeeds because Clarissa is the perfect hostess. The novel that bears her name ends with her, but seen only from a distance by one of the guests: 'For there she was.' She provides a locus for so many people, neither swamping nor rejecting them (even Bradshaw). She has become what Peter predicted, 'the perfect hostess', or as she sees herself in the mirror:

> she alone knew how different, how incompatible and composed so for the world only into one centre, one diamond, one woman who sat in her drawing-room and made a meeting-point, a radiancy no doubt in some dull lives, a refuge for the lonely to come to, perhaps . . . . (p. 42)

But Clarissa is also aware in this passage of the other parts of herself, the sides she rarely shows. Walking down Bond Street 'she had the oddest sense of being herself invisible; unseen; unknown' (p. 13), a being divided between this secret inner freedom and the outward show for which she is not even Clarissa but Mrs Richard Dalloway. Some, of course, like Peter himself, would see this split existence as inauthentic; indeed, he had decided when Clarissa objected to Sally Seton's liberal ideas of sexual conduct that it was 'the death of the soul' (p. 66). But what redeems Clarissa and makes her, even in Peter's eyes, still the 'life and soul' of the party, is the knowingness with which she submerges her own character. The dress which she wears to the

party glows green only under artificial light; the party is not a true
pastoral scene, and Clarissa knows it. Nevertheless she looks forward to 'kindling, illuminating' that night, bringing warmth and
light to others and so to herself. She continues to have an inner
life – her complex response to Peter's visit proves that – but she is
also able, later on that day, to submerge personal attachments
and memories in the duties of being a party hostess. Her achievement is similar to that of the much-admired Lady Bexborough,
who held the telegram informing her of her son's death as she
opened the bazaar. Here, Clarissa holds the rekindled memory of
her youthful love as she stands at her husband's side in the service
of the larger community (it is significant that Lady
Bexborough is opening a *social* event).

Clarissa's achievement is not a tragedy but a triumph. Seen
spatially, there is a reciprocal movement of Clarissa's society
inward to her diamond-like, focusing point, and of Clarissa outward, permeating her society like a mist through a wood. It is a
reconciliation Clarissa has long since learnt, so that the novel as a
whole has no sense of urgency or increasing moral awareness.
Avrom Fleishman is correct in his summary of the novel until he
speaks of it as documenting 'the dawn' of some new achievement:
'It uses the conventions of the English social novel toward a
metaphysical aim – the dawn of an individual's conviction of her
own reality and the simultaneous evocation of that sense in the
reader.'[44] That evocation is due to the *form* of the novel, with
Clarissa framing it and forming the locus for the various sallies
into other consciousnesses. The exception, the story of the
Smiths, resonates in the manner of a subplot. Septimus's fight
with authority, his attempt to nourish personal attachment in the
mass patterns of public duty, reflects the cost of Clarissa's rejection, long since made, of Peter's individual demands. It is
Woolf's invention of Rezia which is the masterstroke in closing
the gap betwen the two plots, for she too embodies aspects of
Clarissa. In her desperate loneliness relieved only by the satisfac-
tions of a rudimentary yet social art form – her hatmak-
ing – Rezia suggests the kind of wife Clarissa might have become
had she sought constant access to Richard's mind, which, though
not insane, is as far from Clarissa's world in its preoccupations as
is Septimus's from his wife's. O. P. Sharma, in a feminist article
on the novel, perceives correctly that 'in Clarissa mingle the
manifold streams of consciousness in the novel'.[45] Septimus,

Peter and Sally represent the personal, emotional life which she has sacrificed; Richard, Hugh, the Bradshaws the extremes of the life for which she has opted. But Sharma is wrong to suggest that the novel is a feminist cry, with Rezia reminding us of the 'quiet pathos of Clarissa's cleavage from Richard' and the song of the old hag an affirmation of the female life force. These are aspects which Clarissa has consciously rejected, and there is no sense of tragic loss. On the contrary, the novel celebrates Clarissa's triumph. That triumph is reinforced by the odiousness of another female character, Miss Kilman (with her ominous feminist sur-name), who in attempting to convert Elizabeth almost crushes that love of life which animates her mother. Fortunately we see Elizabeth escaping her clutches and in her trip towards St Paul's repeating the spirit of Clarissa's earlier shopping-expedition, when she rejoiced not in classes or flags but in 'life; this moment in June'.

In this sense too *Mrs Dalloway* is a flower, the flower of Clarissa's life with all its perfume and charm. Even the return of Peter does not blight it. The form of the novel is appropriate because it takes one day in Clarissa's life, remaining embedded resolutely in the present. Even with the seductive invita-tions – first of Peter, then later, at the party, of Sally – to delve back into the past, Clarissa remains steadfastly illuminating the present moment. When Woolf talked in her diary of her new method of tunnelling behind each character, she did not specify the different kinds of tunnelling that go on in this and subsequent novels. For Peter it is a tunnelling into the narrow, dark labyrinth of the past; for Septimus a tunnelling into the nightmare chaos of the subconscious; but for Clarissa the tunnelling always stays somehow near the surface, engaged to what she is seeing or doing, or whom she is meeting or thinking about. For her, the tunnelling is what Woolf called the 'digging out of a beautiful cave'. In 1922 she asked 'whether the inside of the mind in both Mrs Dalloway and Septimus Smith can be made luminous – that is to say the stuff of the book – lights coming on it from external sources'.[46] The only lights playing on Septimus, those of Rezia, Bradshaw and the sign-writing plane, illuminate nothing because they can-not focus on anything. Clarissa's mind is made luminous, a semi-transparent envelope, because she is in harmony with her world. She does not puzzle over the meaning of life (the sign-writing plane) or the old human passions (the old hag's song). She focuses on London, the flower shop, the orderly progression of the bells, and the symbol of order and community (but for her, not nationalism), the Prime Minister's car. Her mind is best symbolised in the party, completely in harmony with Woolf's technique of writing about it: 'A general view of the world. The different groups: All sketched in.'[47] Alone of the partygoers, Clarissa moves to another room and takes in the lady opposite, as she takes in Septimus's death. The disparate classes and mental states are accepted by her and, like an artist, she sketches them into a larger fabric of 'life' this moment (cf. Vanessa Bell's interior/exterior at 46 Gordon Square [Plate 17]), which she can best nourish this moment and at this place in time – there, at the head of the stairs.

TO THE LIGHTHOUSE (1927)

> *We have, when reading it, the rare pleasure of inhabiting two worlds at once, a pleasure only art can give* . . . .[48]

Forster's admiration for *To the Lighthouse* was based not so much on the 'sonata form'[49] of its three sections as on the 'interest' of the chief characters. Certainly the novel began as a testimony to the (continuing) presence of Woolf's parents; this is apparent from the priorities in her diary:

> This is going to be fairly short: to have father's character done complete in it; & mother's; & St Ives; & childhood; & all the usual things I try to put in – life, death, etc. But the centre is father's character . . . .[50]

> Father's birthday . . . I used to think of him and mother daily; but writing the Lighthouse laid them in my mind.[51]

It is a short step from this to the interpretation of Lily as a dramatisation of Woolf herself:

> Lily is, surely, a surrogate for the author. . . . The author had to unite with words what Lily is represented as uniting on canvas. Lily needs both the colours and the cohesive form; her creator needed to present variegated impressions within a rigid

design. Moreover, Woolf had to express the multiform 'feminine' experience with words, those instruments of 'masculine' order. She represented with the tools of her father the vision of her mother.[52]

This is neatly put, but it would be truer to say that Woolf creates an aesthetic whole, and aesthetics were an idea which neither Mr nor Mrs Ramsay contemplated. Woolf's achievement is a third thing, and it is of a far more sophisticated dynamism than the canvas which Lily produces by the end of the novel. Lily, like the Ramsays, functions in no autobiographical way but as a psychological volume in the totality which is this novel.

Woolf's aesthetic aims, which overlaid and unsurped the psychological or nostalgic need in the writing, dominate her deliberations in the diary:

> The sea is to be heard all through it. I have an idea that I will invent a new name for my books to supplant 'novel'. A new —— by Virginia Woolf. But what? Elegy?[53]

> This theme may be sentimental. . . . I think, though, that when I begin it I shall enrich it in all sorts of ways; thicken it; give it branches & roots which I do not perceive now. It might contain all characters boiled down; and childhood; and then this impersonal thing, which I'm dared to do by my friends, the flight of time, and the consequent break of unity in my design. That passage (I conceive the book in 3 parts: 1. at the drawing-room window; 2. seven years passed; 3. the voyage) interests me very much.[54]

> I think I might do something in *To the Lighthouse* to split up emotions more completely. I think I'm working in that direction.[55]

> Since October 25th I have been revising and retyping (some parts 3 times over) . . . it is a hard muscular book.[56]

Coming at a time when Woolf was learning of Mauron's ideas about fiction aesthetics from Roger Fry, then, *To the Lighthouse* is not a family saga but an artistic attempt to mould psychological volumes into a satisfying whole – not simply by juxtaposition (she had done this in *Mrs Dalloway*) but by taking into account the reading-experience itself, and capitalising on the element which the reader shared with the world of the novel, and which is absent from a painting: Time.

The titles of the three sections reveal the central preoccupation of the novel with space and time: 'The Window', 'Time Passes', 'The Lighthouse'. Like *A Passage to India*, the novel comprises a triptych, and the central panel shares a concern with the bald realities of life which undercut the affirmations of the first section. Woolf's third panel, however, is (unlike Forster's) a true Hegelian synthesis of the previous elements. Unlike Forster's wise old woman who dies at sea in confusion, Mrs Ramsay's spirit moves the novel towards a satisfying, affirmative conclusion. The idea of progress, an onward drive towards the achievement of the last word, 'vision', is apparent in the title itself with its prepostion 'to', which carries none of the evasions and ironies of Forster's title.

Woolf avoids the charge of writing an 'art novel' by making her principal couple insensitive to aesthetics. Mrs Ramsay, during her walk into town with Tansley, is more interested in circuses than art galleries, and more excited by the view of the bay ('That was the view, she said, stopping, growing greyer eyed, that her husband loved' – p. 17) than by the efforts of the local painters intent on creating bad Monets: 'Since Mr Paunceforte had been there, three years before, all the pictures were like that she said, green and grey, with lemon-coloured sailing-boats, and pink women on the beach' (p. 17). To her credit, Lily Briscoe is not a follower of Paunceforte:

> The jacmanna was bright violet; the wall staring white. She would not have considered it honest to tamper with the bright violet and the staring white, since she saw them like that, fashionable though it was, since Mr Paunceforte's visit, to see everything pale, elegant, semi-transparent. Then beneath the colour there was the shape. She could see it all so clearly. . . .   (pp. 22–3)

The passage carries an implicit warning to those readers who would confuse Woolf's description of life – a semi-transparent halo – with the finished work of art, which should have a shape of steel. But, however noble her intentions, Lily's efforts are belittled by Mrs Ramsay, not from any aesthetic point of view but from the fact that Lily will not be a pawn in Mrs Ramsay's matchmaking plans:

> Lily's picture! Mrs Ramsay smiled. With her little Chinese eyes and her puckered-up face she would never marry; one could not take her painting very seriously; but she was an independent little creature, Mrs Ramsay liked her for it, and so remembering her promise, she bent her head.   (p. 21)

If Mrs Ramsay has little appreciation of aesthetic shape, her husband has even less about the shimmering surface of life. He reduces the vividness of lovely evenings to 'angular essences . . . this white deal four-legged table' (p. 26). Under that same pear tree which holds up, for Lily, this mathematical table, she experiences an epiphanic moment which predicts the larger movement of her mind throughout the novel. In comprehending William Bankes, she pours out 'the load of her accumulated impressions of him' (p. 27). Then, as another sensation, she feels that 'up rose in a fume the essence of his being'. Not only is this a fairly accurate description of the artistic process of Post-Impressionism, but Lily is able to extend this detached apprehension to include Bankes's opposite, Mr Ramsey. Finally, 'All of this danced up and down, like a company of gnats, each separate, but all marvellously controlled in an invisible elastic net' until the moment is lost in the report of Jasper's gun. It is a remarkable passage, moving as it does between Lily's comprehension of two psychological volumes and the awareness of the natural scene about her, her sense of human relationships finding clarification and solidity in a pictorial projection. By the end of the novel she will have learned how to contain Mr and Mrs Ramsay within a similar comprehension, and once again the 'net' or the suspended aesthetic whole will be subject to the destructive effects of each new passing moment.

For states of mind rather than states of art are what Woolf is pursuing here, and the great enemy of the comprehension of pattern is time. We move, for example, from Lily's vision outside the window to Mrs Ramsay inside, behind the window, coping with domesticity: sewing stockings, entertaining James, worrying about doors left open in the house, and the Swiss maid. In the midst of her revery she considers for a moment the phenomenon of entropy, which is a major motif in the novel, where things fall apart or, in Mrs Ramsay's words, 'spoil': 'What was the use of flinging a green Cashmere shawl over the edge of a picture frame? In two weeks it would be the colour of pea soup' (p. 30). That picture, we learn at the end of the section, is 'the authenticated masterpiece by Michael Angelo', but Mrs Ramsay prefers the still-life arrangement made up of objects used in living, like shawls. The colours of the reproduction presumably fade as well, but for her it is the fading shawl which reminds her forcibly of the corrosive effect of time on surroundings and on people.

Mrs Ramsay herself is that impossibility, a living work of art. William Bankes sees her as a clay Greek statue, 'straight-nosed', and refers to a trope of Renaissance painting when he imagines, 'The Graces assembling seemed to have joined hands in meadows of asphodel to compose that face' (p. 32). Bankes gets as close as anyone to defining her attraction. She has beauty, but, even as the workmen crawl over the hotel they are building within his sight, so she is not simply a well-built sculpture but a living thing, a 'quivering thing'. Woolf completes this extremely dense passage by summarising her point about the relationship between Mrs Ramsay and art:

> Knitting her reddish-brown hairy stocking, with her head outlined absurdly by the gilt frame . . . Mrs Ramsay smoothed out what had been harsh in her manner a moment before, raised his head, and kissed her little boy on the forehead. 'Let's find another picture to cut out,' she said.   (p. 32)

Art seems absurd in relation to her. Its only place is as something for James to practise on with his scissors.

From outside the window, again, Mr Ramsay observes his wife as if she were 'an illustration, a confirmation of something on the printed page' (p. 35). Later on, after picturing himself in a series of heroic Victorian poses – on mountain tops, across wild seas – he comes back to 'pay homage to the beauty of the world' (p. 38), but this is a long way from aesthetic appreciation. Ramsay sees her as an adjunct to himself, a complement in the real world. In comparison to this personal apprehension, we see Lily (and this is the last time we see her in action as painter in the section) achieving an aesthetic vision. Lily, looking at Mrs Ramsay, wonders if there is something additional to her 'perfect shape' (p. 49) – some 'inner, sacred inscription' (p. 50). While she recalls her love for Mrs Ramsay, she sees her as a dome shape, but shortly afterwards she explains to Bankes that in her painting the triangular shape is Mrs Ramsay reading to James. The change in abstract shape is important, because it signals Lily's transcendence of personal need and association to aesthetic appreciation – 'for the picture was not of them, she said' (p. 52). As she elucidates the principles of significant form to Bankes – 'it was a question, she remembered, of how to connect this mass on the right hand with that on the left' (p. 53) – she shares with him a moment of aesthetic contemplation unlike the earlier epiphany, which relied on personalities. This moment is not shattered by the sound of a gun, but quietly confirmed, 'surrounded in a circle' (p. 53), by the snick of her paint box closing.

It is part of Woolf's homage to her sister's abstract art that Lily's image of Mrs Ramsay as a triangle is close to the truth. Mrs Ramsay feels her essential self to be 'a wedge-shaped core of darkness' (p. 60). Mrs Ramsay, indeed, is the closest person in the novel to Lily's painterly vision, although she would always rank painting as merely an aspect of the demanding business of living. When she and her husband go out to look at the evening view, he interprets, imposes human meaning and becomes maudlin (' "Poor little place", he murmured with a sigh' – p. 66), while she sees the lights of the town and harbour 'like a phantom net floating there' (p. 65). Nevertheless, the crucial difference in the preoccupations of Lily and Mrs Ramsay is evident in the alternating viewpoints of chapters 12 and 13, where Mrs Ramsay sees Lily and Bankes as a marriageable couple, while Lily sees the Ramsays as 'symbols of marriage' (p. 69). The one is utilitarian, matchmaking; the other sees pattern and form (compare Fry and Vanessa Bell on Studland Beach [Plates 19 and 20]).

Mrs Ramsay's triumph, of course, is the dinner party, when she is able to bring art and life so close together. When the dinner is framed by candlelight and focused on the fruit-bowl centrepiece, the group becomes 'composed'. Carmichael and Mrs Ramsay look at the bunch of grapes (like those 'on the shoulder of Bacchus (in some picture)' – p. 90) differently, but their shared focus unites even them. The composition is blessed by the entrance of Paul and Minta, and the dinner – already a ritual – becomes a prothalamion, a celebration of fertility and life. In such an atmosphere, Lily's aesthetics, although she began the dinner more content with herself than any of the others seemed, and although she has reached – theoretically – the solution to her painting-block, are gently mocked. Recoiling from the implicit comparison between her spinsterly self and the radiant Minta, Lily concentrates on the salt cellar and insists: 'For at any rate, she said to herself, catching sight of the salt cellar on the pattern, she need not marry, thank Heaven: she need not undergo that degradation. She was saved from that dilution. She would move the tree rather more to the middle' (p. 95). Lily goes on to grumble inwardly about the necessity of love and hate, of human relations at all, but she recalls exactly this incident in the third section as part of her drive towards the aesthetic vision. She has escaped the morass of personal desire, need for Mrs Ramsay, and from the feeling of inadequacy in her self-sufficiency. The triumph here in the first section, though, is Mrs Ramsay's, as she apprehends the group as illuminated trout, swimming in a pattern (p. 99) and in a medium almost tangible – the medium of outgoing human love. Like all epiphanies, this one is subject to time, and it is broken when the still life is broken (p. 100). As she leaves the room, the scene is already becoming the past.

The section ends with Mrs Ramsay bestowing her gift of making the real beautiful on each member of her family. She covers the skull with her shawl for the younger children, turning their thoughts from the entropic effects of time to the beauty of the present moment. Prue sees her at the top of the stairs and echoes Peter Walsh with 'That's my mother' (p. 107), and finally she goes in to her husband. She shares his version of completeness in the literary perfection of a sonnet, but it is only when she goes to the window and agrees that they will not be able to make their journey that the day is completed. The human world is perfectly balanced, just as Lily's painting is at the end of the third section: husband and wife answer the first lines of the novel, each in their own way, and each in their own way triumph.

In the third section Lily must compose the Ramsays as opposite principles – male/female, rational/emotional, present/past – into her canvas. She must, as detached observer, do through aesthetics what those two could do through love. Her painting must be inclusive, which is why much of the section is taken up with her coming to terms with Ramsay. At the outset words are recognised as being not inimical but in a sense an element in her painting. Lily 'could not contract her feelings, could only make a phrase resound' (p. 137), but she yearns for the cognitive precision of language – if only she could 'put together' words or ideas she would reach the truth. Her painting must include his 'Perished. Alone' and also the 'grey-green light on the wall opposite. The empty places' (p. 138), the colour reminding us of Paunceforte's landscapes. All life, then, must be encompassed in the work of art, even bad painting. And it is when Ramsay has his conversation with her about bootlaces, when she recognises him as a personality as eccentric and comprehensible as any other human being, that Lily makes the breakthrough. Mellowed by his wife's death into a more accessible humanity, Ramsay becomes comprehensible to Lily, who examines his face closely in preparation for the portrait. With the missing link now accessible, Lily can start on the artistic process of capturing that 'sense of relations' (p. 147) between elements in the design, past and present.

Lily's method of painting is a combination of Expressionism and Impressionism, because only in this way can she match Mrs Ramsay's combination of life and art or, to put it in other terms, only in this way can she comprehend the past (Lily's own emotions and memories) and the present at once. Faced with a very Vanessa Bell-like still life, the 'white lampshade looming on a wicker table' (p. 148), she paints by spurting her own memories and ideas over the canvas like a fountain, and at the same time 'she modelled it with greens and blues' (p. 149). The image is appropriately sexual, because the androgynous painter must partake of male and female. Even here the imagery is deliberately confused, since the 'spurting' image suggests male ejaculation, while it is in fact associated with Mrs Ramsay's fountain of spontaneous life. Just as Ramsay's beak or scimitar plunged into that fountain in the first section, so here Lily's brush controls and models the canvas.

When she was alive Mrs Ramsay 'resolved everything into simplicity' for Lily (p. 150). She was able to say 'Life stand still here' and make moments remain in people's memories – such as Lily's and Tansley's – as in 'a work of art' (p. 150). Lily is now trying to repeat that magical manoeuvre, making something equally permanent 'in another sphere' (p. 151), but in order to do it in art rather than in someone's mind she must transcend that element which things out there are most at the mercy of – time. This is why Mrs Ramsay must be there in Lily's canvas – 'It must have altered the design a good deal when she was sitting on the step with James. There must have been a shadow.' Lily seems to begin her 'white canvas' afresh, painting two pictures into one, the then and the now. The pattern of the past gives Lily the framework she needs:

> The whole mass of the picture was poised upon that weight. Beautiful and bright it should be on the surface, feathery and evanescent, one colour melting into another like the colours on a butterfly's wing: but beneath the fabric must be clamped together with bolts of iron. It was to be a thing you could ruffle with your breath, and a thing you could not dislodge with a team of horses. And she began to lay on a red, a grey, and she began to model her way into the hollow there. At the same time, she seemed to be sitting beside Mrs Ramsay on the beach.   (p. 159)

This description can be compared to Fry's description of Cézanne's *Card-Players:* 'The feeling of life is no less intense than that of eternal stillness and repose.'[57] The image of 'hollowing out' is one Woolf used in her diary to describe her own writing-technique, and here it seems to refer to the exploring of the present scene in terms of the past and all the associations which the painter brings to the familiar scene. But the framework of the past is not enough to complete Lily's painting – she must have the life of the present, which includes Ramsay.

For a time, as Lily comes to terms with the past, she considers the other personalities at the holiday house and objectifies them – 'So much depends, she thought, upon distance' (p. 177). But Mrs Ramsay is still too close to her, and Mr Ramsay too distant. Finally acknowledging that she must achieve a balance between 'Mr Ramsay and the picture, which was necessary' (p. 178), Lily realises his wife one more time, in relation to him, and with what would seem to Lily her faults exposed. She had, for instance, 'the faculty of obedience to perfection' (p. 185); what is more, if she *had* painted she would have produced those soft Pauncefortean landscapes of white flowered valleys. At that moment, as if stumbling on the key, Lily sees Mrs Ramsay on the step and rushes forward to see Mr Ramsay in the boat. Her final line is her recognition of the balance of past and present, male and female, and so on, which is essential to the encompassing aesthetic experience. Allen McLaurin argues that the line is Mrs Ramsay,[58] and other critics have identified it with the lighthouse; but such literal attributions, like the efforts to reconstruct Lily's actual painting, are futile and irrelevant.

So far I have followed Lily's progress and the development of her aesthetic. But if the novel were only this it would be a rather insufferable theoretical account of, perhaps, the writer's own pilgrimage. It is, of course, much more than this. It accomplishes in words, with a perfection and affirmation unmatched in any other Woolf novel, the same aesthetic achievement as Lily's painting – only the novel is there in front of us to appreciate.

I have not yet mentioned the central section, 'Time Passes', because it is irrelevant to Lily's story but essential to the reader's. One would like to think that it was Fry or Bell who encouraged Woolf to write such a difficult passage and to insert it so boldly into an apparently seamless narrative. It fulfils magnificently its two purposes, in space and time. Temporally it covers ten years in ten chapters, beginning with the family going to bed and ending with Lily waking up. For the reader, then, it is ten years with the effect of one night. It is told in elegant, dense prose, almost indigestible at times compared with the fluent clarity of the inner monologues in sections one and three, and it is told from the point of view of an omniscient narrator or a nameless Everyman on the beach. The impact of time is registered as a busy entropic force, since for all its vacancy the house seems to be a riot of activity. By chapter 3 goodness exits and wind and destruction take over. By chapter 6 all possibility of the pathetic harmony between Nature and man has been abandoned:

> That dream, then, of sharing, completing, finding in solitude on the beach an answer, was but a reflection in a mirror, and the mirror itself was but the surface glassiness which forms in quiescence when the nobler powers sleep beneath. Impatient, despairing yet loth to go (for beauty offers her lures, has her consolations), to pace the beach was impossible; contemplation was unendurable; the mirror was broken. (p. 125)

Nature is rife with an insensible fertility threatening to topple the house into chaos, until the primaeval beings of Mrs McNab and Mrs Bast drag it back into the present order, with young George an ironical Father Time with his scythe and all three as a parodic Creator – 'It was finished' (p. 131).

The human events in the Ramsay family are reduced to parentheses, and the reversal of point of view is apparently complete.

However, each human event is preceded by a sympathetic occurrence in the natural world: wind and destruction precede Mrs Ramsay's death; spring 'like a virgin fierce in her chastity' (p. 122) precedes Prues wedding; it 'takes upon itself the knowledge of the sorrows of mankind' (p. 123) before her death; measured blows shake the crockery before Andrew is blown up; Carmichael's poems follow the quotation above when the mirror is broken. These coincidences move us from 'Time Passes' as a temporal phenomenon to one much more concerned with space and the artistic concerns of the rest of the novel.

Of course, the reader experiences the whole central section as the passing of a generation of the Ramsay family. But the deliberate foregrounding of the non-human world alters the relation of elements within the novel. Instead of the stifling intimacy of Woolfian inner monologue, the reader experiences the Ramsay family from a great distance and is able to consider and place them. The technique is appropriate also to the metaphysical concerns of Ramsay and the aesthetic ones of Lily, because it makes the reader meditate upon the relationship of the human to the non-human. The passage is a poetic answer to the question 'What happens to the cow in the quad when I'm not there?' as well as a verbal equivalent of an Impressionist still life. The disparity between ourselves and the natural world around us is something to be born with stoical resignation by thinkers such as Tansley, Bankes and Carmichael, or to be dramatised into perpetual combat by Ramsay. But Woolf's answer is the magic of art. Just as Mrs Ramsay, where possible, flings a shawl over the skull, so Woolf here suggests that there is a relationship between the natural and human worlds *if* you want to see it that way. The contingency is important, because I do not think that she is putting forward here any version of pantheistic mysticism. No; she is simply suggesting a spatial juxtaposition possible to the artistic mind.

On a larger level, 'Time Passes' has spatial significance in that it at once divides and connects the other two sections of the novel, functioning like Lily's final stroke or like Lily herself, who stands on the cliff between the window and the lighthouse. Those other two titles are spatial locations, but 'Time Passes' is a teasing use of our hopeful cliché which spatialises what is beyond space. With reference to the final moments of the novel, the section is that bit

of art which extrinsically helps the reader to connect past and present, Mrs and Mr Ramsay, in an aesthetic way similar to that in
which Lily intrinsically achieves her vision in her head and on her
canvas. And it gives the secret of union in itself, because it conveys the two truths: Mr Ramsay's overwhelming sense of
aloneness with the sudden, senseless deaths of the parentheses;
and Mrs Ramsay's sense of the unity of the moment, in the
resonance between what goes on at the Ramsays' holiday home
and what affects their lives elsewhere.

The function of the lighthouse in the novel confirms Woolf's
success in translating the spatial concerns of painters into the temporal world of print. To identify any character with it is a
mistake, for it stands alone rather as a symbol of subjectivity,
objectivity and the possibility of illumination. In *Night and Day*,
Ralph was obsessed with the image of a bird flying into the glass
of a lighthouse; he felt himself to be both light – 'steadfast and
brilliant' – and bird – 'whirled senseless against the glass'
(p. 418). This image of the moth or bird round a flame was a persistent one in Woolf's imagination, and, though it does not occur
specifically in *To the Lighthouse*, the simple main story line, getting
to the lighthouse, seems in this context to be fraught with
analogous dangers. Ramsay, indeed, as a man of action struggling from 'P' to 'Q' and on to 'R', sees the completion of the
journey as everything. As he leaps onto the rocks at the end like a
young man he cries, as it were, 'There is no God' (p. 131).

In the first part of the novel, however, he is like a bird beyond
the glass of the other lighthouse which is Mrs Ramsay, radiating
her beauty behind the window. 'Steadfast and brilliant', she
responds to the rhythm of the lighthouse beam, 'the long steady
stroke, the last of the three, which was her stroke' (p. 61). The
flash is here a symbol of each moment passing by, like the ticking
of a clock, and Mrs Ramsay is as content with the passing of time
as she is with the limitations of space (she does not want to *go*
anywhere):

Often she found herself sitting and looking, sitting and looking,
with her work in her hands until she became the thing she
looked at – that light for example. And it would lift up on it
some little phrase or other which had been lying in her mind
like that – 'Children don't forget, children don't forget'

– which she would repeat and begin adding to it, It will end, It
will end, she said. It will come, it will come, when suddenly she
said, 'We are in the hands of the Lord.'   (p. 61)

Here Mrs Ramsay transcends her worries about children and the
passing of time with a rhythmical assertion of well-being.
Although she immediately ridicules it herself, it is this instinctive
rapport with life and light and time which gives Mrs Ramsay her
serenity and charisma.

I should like to think that Woolf was inspired in her choice of
central symbol not by the very distant lighthouse at St Ives but by
Forster's description of the lighthouse of Pharos in *Pharos and
Pharillon*, in 1923. That lighthouse, he says, had in its top a
'mysterious mirror' which suggests Mrs Ramsay, not as a source
of light but as a reflector of the light of lighthouses and people
about her.[59] Forster also says, 'It beaconed to the imagination,
not only to ships, and long after its light was extinguished
memories of it glowed in the minds of men.'[60] And in 'The
Lighthouse' Mrs Ramsay's memory certainly funtions like this,
her husband's voyage being a kind of pilgrimage of penance and
homage to the object which was the source of their last quarrel
and which also stood for his wife herself.

Both the lighthouse image and the central section suggest permanent monuments to the supremacy of art. But the greatest
strength of Woolf's novel lies in the way it retains that reflexive
suspicion of itself which was to become more and more pronounced in her later novels. Lily's canvas will probably be hidden
in an attic and would in fact do nothing for the sensibilities of even
a Roger Fry. Similarly her own vision will be a fleeting thing. The
reader's vision, then, coming at the same moment as Lily's, when
she utters that final word 'vision' and completes the design, will
not persist in time. On reflection the unity of the novel is an
artistic fabrication concealing the difficult marriage of an interfering old woman and irascible man, and the lonely lives of some of
their acquaintances. But, by acknowledging the fragility of her
construction, Woolf in fact strengthens it. The last section devotes
as much time to the group on the boat as it does to Lily on the
lawn. The reader is torn in two directions and must be, like Lily,
Hydra-headed. He must focus on the window and the memories
of Mrs Ramsay in her past and Lily's present; and he must travel
with Ramsay and his children out across the bay into the future.

Cam and James are characterised at some length, to show that the pattern of the Ramsays' marriage is actually repeating itself: James, for all his rebellion, is an adventurer, a 'doer'; Cam is acquiescent, ready like her mother with sympathy. Time continues to pass, then, and Lily must include that element in her vision. From her diary it appears that Lily's and our aesthetic moment was secondary to the completion of this temporal plot: 'The problem is how to bring Lily and Mr R. together and make a combination of interest at the end. . . . I had meant to end with R. climbing on to the rock. If so, what becomes of Lily and her picture?'[61] Woolf's solution preserves that happy balance, with Lily's excitement gently mocked by old Carmichael, who comes over to her 'like an old pagan God, shaggy, with weeds in his hair and the trident (it was only a French novel) in his hand' (p. 191) to bless the occasion. The final mood is one of lightheaded exultation, made the more profound yet transitory by the perfect balancing of time and space both within the novel and in the way the shape of the novel and the reader's experience come together in a unison of completion.

John Roberts captures the importance of the novel as work of art when he describes *To the Lighthouse* as

> structurally like a pool which narcissistically reflects its theme. . . . Here again, as in *Mrs Dalloway*, we have time and space creating the frame within which the 'psychological values' find their final relationship. . . . This unity is itself the novel's meaning: Mrs Ramsay, though dead, still lives, not in the beauty of her flesh, which, like all merely associative emotions, must – according to Fry – dissolve and fade, but as the means by which order is brought out of chaos as the uniquely aesthetic principle which brings to a complete relationship all the parts within the system.[62]

To the Lighthouse is Woolf's greatest achievement in the balancing of psychological volumes, because both Mr and Mrs Ramsay are fully realised in terms of space and time. Mrs Ramsay resonates through time, each moment in the novel recalled and repeated like the beats of a lighthouse; Mr Ramsay provides the moulding element in space. It is his presence which inspires Lily to make her painting not a portrait of Mrs Ramsay but a landscape, drawing her attention out across the water to encompass the whole,

and helping her to convert the lighthouse 'stroke' to the final com
pletion of her design with one 'stroke' of the brush. Woolf indeed
'laid' the ghosts of her parents, by laying them out in their
appropriate forms; but Cam and James will return from the
lighthouse, and the waves will continue to crash on the shore.

ORLANDO (1928)

> *To the unrivalled sympathy and imagination of Mr Roger Fry
> owe whatever understanding of the art of painting I may
> possess.* (p. 7)

In 1927 Woolf published an essay entitled 'The New Biography',
in which she introduced her distinction between the 'granite-like
solidity' of truth and the 'rainbow-like intangibility' of personality.[63] Like many of her Bloomsbury friends, she was very
interested in biography, and the challenge to the biographer of
welding these two aspects of his subject into a 'seamless whole' is
a problem within the work analogous to the extrinsic problem for
the novelist of balancing content and form. For the biographer,
the life provides the given frame, so that the aesthetic question
seems not to arise. But to capture within that frame the evanescent personality demanded an artistic skill as subtle as that which
attempted to marry the novel and significant form, and in the
hands of Woolf and her friends biography became indeed a work
of art. It is useful, then, to follow Woolf's theory and her practice
in her major 'biography' *Orlando*. We shall find that her solution
to the biographical problem involved using the insights of Charles
Mauron of a few years earlier concerning psychological volumes.
By spatialising personality within the frame of the work rather
than of the life, an aesthetically satisfying portrait might be
accomplished in prose.

But to return to that essay: Woolf argues that the biographer,
faced with the sheer historical problems of the impenetrability of
the human personality, must become an artist in order to
illuminate his subject: 'He chooses, he synthesises; in short, he
has ceased to be the chronicler; he has become an artist.'[64] Woolf
makes explicit reference to the novelist:

Truth of fact and truth of fiction are incompatible; yet he
[the biographer] is now more than ever urged to combine
them. For it would seem that the life which is increasingly
real to us is the fictitious life; it dwells in the personality
rather than in the act. . . . Thus the biographer's
imagination is always being stimulated to use the
novelist's art of arrangement, suggestion, dramatic effect
to expound the private life. [65]

The occasion of this essay was a review of Harold Nicolson's
Some People. That same year Woolf was contemplating a curious
biography as a tribute to her close friend and Harold's wife, Vita
Sackville-West. 'How I could revolutionise biography in a night',
she wrote to her. [66] The result was *Orlando*, described by Vita's
son Nigel as 'her most elaborate love-letter'; but it is also much
more than that. The idea of a fantastic biography featuring a
man – woman who lives for 400 years certainly appealed to Woolf
as a way of being able to write about her friends without incurring
their wrath – 'It might be a way of writing the memoirs of one's
own times during people's lifetimes', she mused in her diary. [67]
But it was already a way of bridging the gap between the granite
and rainbow, the personalities of her closest friends and their
meanings, or what they added up to. Her diary comments,
therefore, become more and more concerned with the style of the
book itself. 'Unity of tone very important,' she noted, [68] and,
looking back on the book: '*Orlando* taught me continuity and
narrative and how to keep the realities at bay. . . . I never got
down to my depths and made shapes square up, as I did in the
Lighthouse.' [69] I think that what Woolf means is that she did not
consider real characters in real dramatic conflict in *Orlando*. But
her novel is certainly not of the type of the entries beloved of her
father and original of Mr Ramsay, with the alphabetical 'P, Q,
R' order of the *Dictionary of National Biography*. *Orlando* is not a
work of art which resonates in depth with the patterns of human
inter-relationships (that was to come next in *The Waves*). But it
has an extended shape on the surface, stretching in space and
across time, which amounts finally to a portrait of its creator,
Woolf herself. Her friend Lytton Strachey, in his 1918 preface to
Eminent Victorians, argued that 'the art of biography' was for the

biographer 'to lay bare the facts of the case, as he understands them'. In *Orlando* we get Woolf's understanding of human nature and history in an elegant work of art.

As in *Jacob's Room*, which in comparison with *Orlando* is like an artist creating what she can purely out of the granite, Woolf lets the reader share her problems as a modern biographer. Most of these comments come appropriately in the last, Victorian section. Concerning time, Orlando's middle-aged reflection 'Nothing is any longer one thing' (p. 215) opens the way for Woolf's *ad patrem* conclusion: 'The true length of a person's life, whatever the *Dictionary of National Biography* may say, is always a matter of dispute. For it is a difficult business – this timekeeping; nothing more quickly disorders it than contact with any of the arts' (p. 216). This is because the arts consider the rainbow for their subject, and the rainbow of personality has been recognised in modern times to be split into the facets of the spectrum. The problem extends to perception of the outside world – 'Nothing could be seen whole or read from start to finish' (p. 217) – and to perception of self: 'For if there are (at a venture) seventy-six different times all ticking in the mind at once, how many different people are there not – Heaven help us – all having lodgement at one time or another in the human spirit?' (p. 217). This modern relativity and multiplicity of perceptions and selves engages the reader in a constant philosophical battle and at the same time establishes, implicitly, a reason for the fantastic psychological volume which is Woolf's Orlando, for she at least has two selves, and is outside the timekeeping of the *DNB*.

Woolf uses her medium to point up the absurdity of the mimetic mode in a long disjointed report of the reflections of Orlando's various selves. While the sequence ends with the ironic comment that the chaos is caused only because she is a woman, the real reason is given at the beginning, where Woolf mocks our belief that there is a true or 'Key' self within us:

> Orlando was certainly seeking this self, as the reader can judge from overhearing her talk as she drove (and if it is rambling talk . . . it is the reader's fault for listening to a lady talking to herself; we only copy her words as she spoke them, adding in brackets which self in our opinion is speaking, but in this we may well be wrong).   (p. 219)

This method of advancing the ideas of the novel (such as a plea for a more liberal attitude to life styles) through a running debate with the reader about novelistic style is masterfully handled by Woolf. At one stage in Orlando's Victorian career, Woolf gives us the months of the year and explains that Orlando is at present doing nothing, but that a biographer's task is apparently to document the granite, however colourless: 'Thought and life are as the poles asunder. Therefore – since sitting in a chair and thinking is precisely what Orlando is doing now – there is nothing for it but to recite the calendar, tell one's beads, blow one's nose, stir the fire, look out of the window, until she has done' (p. 189). Refus-- ing to follow Henry Fielding in his supremacy over time, Woolf here mockingly follows the Arnold Bennett (or a host of Victorian novelists) who refused to look inside Mrs Brown in the railway carriage – and we must endure the results.

The way literature can shape and limit our imaginations is personified in Nick Greene, once the energetic Elizabethan scribbler who dismissed his contemporaries Shakespeare and Jonson, and now the Great Victorian Critic, revering Shakespeare and cursing his own age. The overall impression which Orlando gets from his and the age's vision of literature is that 'one must never, never say what one thought' (p. 201). Here again the direct link is made between a stylistic choice and a way of life: plodding mimesis is matched by hypocrisy and dull respectability. But Woolf supplies her own answer stylishly in the following sequence, which describes in fantastical imagery what turns out to be the process of conception, labour and childbirth. 'Hail, happiness!' cries Woolf, 'whether it is what the male novelist says it is' (p. 208) or whether, she implies, it may be a loosening of the imagination and the irruption of totally new forms of fiction.

Woolf's stand as artist and as social critic is, as always, conservative. She wants to conserve the best in fiction and biography, as in English society. Orlando, her surrogate artist in the novel, finds her peace like Lily Briscoe, not like Miss La Trobe, by accepting her changing society as a background and doing her own imaginative work at her own pace:

The transaction between a writer and the spirit of the age is one of infinite delicacy, and upon a nice arrangement between the two the whole fortune of his works depends. Orlando had so ordered it that she was in an extremely happy position; she need neither fight her age nor submit to it; she was of it, yet remained herself. Now, therefore, she could write, and write she did.   (p. 188)

Orlando's poem, of course, is 'The Oak Tree', a poem with its roots firmly in the English countryside and which becomes associated with Orlando's home. As she goes out to bury her poem beneath the oak tree she is composed and sure, 'for she was now one and entire, and presented, it may be, a larger surface to the shock of time' (p. 226). There is a hint here, as in Woolf's last novel, of Forster's pastoralism, that security and wholeness might be found beyond the busy streets of London in the conjunction of a house and a tree – Howards End, or Vita's own Knole. But we must remember that 'The Oak Tree' may be no work of art. It has a personal significance and value, even if one does not go so far as Clifton Snider and argue that the tree has a Jungian meaning, 'symbolic of Orlando's psyche. As it grows, so does Orlando.'[70] Indeed, one suspects that Woolf would probably regard it as a very bad poem; she certainly does not reproduce it in *Orlando*. But it serves its personal purpose for Orlando, and as a symbol it has its place in Woolf's work of art.

Woolf's own answer to the question of how to give an artful shape to her work will not be found in the granite of biography or even the organic growth of an oak tree. She makes her struggle, as I have shown, part of the experience of the novel itself, but it is certainly not the case that this conflict between biographer and artist is one 'from which the artist always emerges victorious'. James Naremore goes on to argue that *Orlando* is like Woolf's other novels, where 'granite gives way almost entirely to rainbow';[71] but the remarkable granite of Orlando obtrudes obstinately. Indeed, to resolve the conflict in this way, says Woolf at the outset, would be to become a novelist, 'to smooth out the crumpled silk and all its implications' (p. 52). One remembers the Augustan tea party where a disgruntled Mr Pope says something and the whole gathering disbands. Unlike Pope, and unlike Forster, Woolf does not intrude in that way into *Orlando*, although her own feminist concern must have made the temptation great. Remembering Roger Fry's complaints about the novelist who is too easily tempted to interpolate his own opinions about life into his text, Woolf remains teasingly difficult to locate as a narrative presence. She leaves London society undescribed, because, as she claims, that would require a novelist:

At one and the same time, therefore, society is everything and society is nothing. Society is the most powerful concoction in the world and society has no existence whatsoever. Such monsters the poets and the novelists alone can deal with; with such something–nothings their works are stuffed out to prodigious size, and to them with the best will in the world we are content to leave it.   (p. 136)

It is interesting to note that in her remaining novels Woolf would indeed try to capture this elusive 'society'. But for the moment she will remain a biographer, the perfect hostess like Lady R, who for seventeen years said nothing memorable and all went well (p. 141).

But it is not quite that simple. As we have seen, Woolf does involve herself as author, putting her problems before the reader. But she does so not as one attempting to record the social history of Europe; rather, her musings are meant to reflect the kind of mind of her hero. By inventing such a fantastical subject, Woolf has freed herself from the biographical restraints of fact. This restraint, she explained in her essay 'The Art of Biography', limited Lytton Strachey when he tried to turn Elizabeth and Essex into a work of art.[72] That essay also gives several clues to her intention in *Orlando*. She praises the freedom given by 'the invented character' who allows the writer to create a world 'rarer, intenser, and more wholly of a piece'. At the same time, the modern biographer, knowing more about history and psychology, 'must be prepared to admit contradictory versions of the same face' to bring out 'a richer unity'.[73] The unity which she aimed at in *Orlando* was a vision of the androgynous mind, and both the granite and the rainbow, the fantastical life history and the fantastical, musing style, are meant to convey that same unity.

'Our simple duty', protests the narrator of *Orlando* in much the same way as the creator of *Eminent Victorians*, 'is to state facts as far as they are known, and so let the reader make of them what he may' (p. 46). But by inventing a character who lives through several ages with different social and sexual mores, and who changes sex at mid-point, Woolf has freed herself from biographical facts and invented a whole new set. It is at that elementary level that the artistry begins, so that she can stand back as hostess rather than as interpreter, arguing, 'For though these are not matters on which a biographer can profitably enlarge, it is plain enough to those who have done a reader's part in making up from bare hints dropped here and there the whole boundary and circumference of a living person' (p. 51). It is the reader, then, who will give a significant form to Woolf's work of art, which is to say, to Orlando him/herself, since, Woolf goes on, he is 'compounded of many humours'. This amalgamation of opposites by the reader not only brings him to appreciate the diversity of soul which can exist within one person, but the *act* itself is like those flexible, synthesising acts of mind of the androgynous vision.

Woolf supplies the reader with enough structural antithesis for the androgynous attitude to start working. The first ninety pages of the novel show us a male Orlando, over a 130 years or so, falling out of love with himself as a man, moving from a passionate affair with a Russian lady to disgust at the amorous advances of what proves to be the Archduke Harry in disguise. His sex-change ushered in by the masquelike procession of Our Ladies of Purity, Chastity and Modesty, begins the central section of the novel, fifty pages, when Orlando moves from being the dominating lover of a gypsy to the repressed woman in Pope's Augustan court. She returns to England, crying, 'Praise God that I'm a woman', at almost the exact centre of the book. This central section ends when Orlando, outraged at Pope's misogyny, dresses up as a man to explore London. The last section of the book shows Orlando coping with the male chauvinism of Victorian society and, with the help of the experience of childbirth, winning through to an acceptance of the biological demands of either sex and a liberated union with Shelmerdine. This section also covers about 130 years, so the novel as a whole is like a mirror separated by a central section of conversion and ambiguity. That ambiguity is nicely epitomised in the device of Archduke Harry, who was homosexually attracted to Orlando when he was a man, but whose disguise destroyed his chances and prompted Orlando's flight. Now a woman, Orlando finds him repulsive. This is just one of many plot devices whereby Woolf upsets the normal stereotyped behaviour between the sexes, suggesting that frank homosexual attraction (Platonic, as it were) might satisfy the androgynous urges of human beings more successfully than the socially ordained separation into either one sex or the other.

While Orlando undergoes a huge biological shift, the irony is that his personality remains constant throughout the novel. We

are aware of this partly because his vision is so closely allied to the
fluid, ever-varied reflections of the narrator. As Herbert Marder
says, 'Orlando's dramatic change of sex is only a single
manifestation, however, of a fact which had been established
much earlier. Orlando is androgynous from the beginning, as the
opening sentence of the book hints.'[74] In the middle of the novel
Woolf makes this point clear:

> it is clothes that wear us and not we them; we may make them
> take the mould of arm or breast, but they would mould our
> hearts, our brains, our tongues to their liking. So, having now
> worn skirts for a considerable time, a certain change was visible
> in Orlando, which is to be found if the reader will look at page
> 111, even in her face. If we compare the picture of Orlando as a
> man with that of Orlando as a woman we shall see that though
> both are undoubtedly one and the same person, there are cer-
> tain changes. . . . Had they both worn the same clothes, it is
> possible that their outlook might have been the
> same. (pp. 132–3)

The difference between the consistent style of the novel and the
violent breaking of the plot into two halves is a reflection of the
disparity between Orlando's consistently androgynous inner
spirit, and the perversions which society attempts to force on him
outwardly in social behaviour and dress. The granite of Orlando's
figure, like a sculpture, is crudely picked at by society's chisels,
while the beautiful rainbow of his soul remains constant (Duncan
Grant's *Countess* is similarly evanescent and solid [Plate 18]).

Near the end of *Orlando* Woolf describes the present age and
mentions 'the walls were bare so that new brilliantly coloured pictures of real things like streets, umbrellas, apples, were hung in
frames, or painted upon the wood' (p. 210). This reference to the
Bloomsbury artists and their interior decorating does not go by
uncommented on, for, while it suggests 'something definite and
distinct about the age', Orlando perceives 'a distraction, a
desperation'. Here, I think, Woolf is making a claim for her art
above that of her sister and colleagues. Painting can only depict
what is, like the photographs which Woolf included in the original
editions of *Orlando*. They cannot penetrate below the surface,
beneath the clothes; they can draw the human body either as one
sex or as another. Only the novelist can portray the androgynous

body or the androgynous mind in all its ambiguity and complexity, and still make of it 'a richer unity'. In his Hogarth essay, Charles Mauron described the psychological volume as a complex to be treated analogously to the painter's problems of space. It must not be too simple, but must reflect 'all the forms of our inner life. . . . It ought to admit of all spiritual possibilities.'[75] What started as a highly personal *jeu d'esprit* in *Orlando* became an extremely useful exercise for Woolf in portraying a psychological volume in fiction. By creating a fantastical subject she avoided the biographical problems of reconciling truth and personality, and by isolating Orlando (save for one or two friends) she avoided the novelist's problem of dramatising and encompassing the soul in society. But she did discover that a unity could be imposed on her material through her style rather than through the forcible connecting of personalities like Septimus and Mrs Dalloway, or the artificial links of the bells of London or the intrusion into the scene of an artist like Lily Briscoe to make the connections for her. The reader could be left to do much more of the work of unification, and the hesitations and authorial puzzles of *Jacob's Room* could be turned to much clearer account as the encompassing of deeper ambiguities and more contradictory complexities. By deliberately spreading *Orlando* thinly upon her canvas Woolf discovered that she could, through the interplay of granite and rainbow during the reading-process, suggest deeper truths than all those modern painters with their 'brilliantly coloured pictures'.

THE WAVES (1931)

> *Now and again their songs ran together in swift scales like the interlacings of a mountain stream whose waters, meeting, foam and then mix, and hasten quicker and quicker down the same channel, brushing the same broad leaves. But there is a rock; they sever.* (pp. 93–4)

Forster called *The Waves* Woolf's greatest book, and David Daiches called it 'at once the subtlest and the most rigid, the most eloquent and the least communicative, of Virginia Woolf's novels.'[76] It stands like an abstract sculpture among the more recognisable forms of her other novels, and, while with Forster we might acknowledge the daring, difficult achievement of its experimental form, we might also as readers confess with Daiches to puzzlement, bafflement or exhaustion. A look at the evolution of the novel will reveal that Woolf too was acutely conscious that this extreme departure from the novel form would create a unique reading-experience, and that readers would have to follow her in creating a new vocabulary to deal with the vision.

In 1927, listening (significantly) to the intricate marriage of expression and form in some late Beethoven, Woolf contemplated 'the play–poem idea: the idea of some continuous stream, not solely of human thought, but of the ship, the night etc'.[77] For the next few years Woolf saw this book as having an essentially domestic base, focusing on a couple, but also recording the activities of the moths about them, In 1929 she was musing, 'Islands of light – islands in the stream . . . life itself going on . . . two different currents – moths flying along, the flower upright in the centre; a perpetual crumbling and renewing of the plant.'[78]

It is tempting to see the moths of the early working-title as the six characters of *The Waves*, and the unifying entity – 'she' or perhaps the flower – as Percival. At any rate, there was always the worry of shape and how to get it. In the previous passage Woolf demanded a beginning, middle and climax, and earlier she determined, '*The Moths* will be very sharply cornered. I am not satisfied though with the frame.[79]

During the following two years her desire to get the stream itself, 'the moment whole' saturated with 'nonsense, fact, sordidity',[80] 'things oddly proportioned',[81] came to be shaped under the demand for 'design'.[82] The sea interludes are first mentioned in February 1930: 'The interludes are very difficult, yet I think essential; so as to bridge and also to give a background – the sea; insensitive nature – I don't know.'[83] Woolf's awareness of the reading-process can be seen in those two ideas of bridge and background, the former a term referring to the reading-time of the reader, the latter a spatial reference to the conceptual notion of the novel. The question 'how to comport it – press it into one' is soon answered by reference to the visual arts. 'The pressure of the form' becomes 'a mosaic',[84] and in a wonderful image Woolf asserts, 'I have got my statues against the sky.'[85]

The reference to the characters as statues is significant, especially when one finds Woolf's reaction to the *Times* review, praising her 'characters' when 'I meant to have none'.[86] But the word 'mosaic' is the perfect clue to the work, I think. It comprehends the individual speeches, unique and separate yet part of a larger whole. During revisions Woolf found the book 'resolving itself into a series of dramatic soliloquies. The thing is to keep them running homogeneously in and out, in the rhythm of the waves.'[87] 'Rhythm' was a word she used again when pondering the unity of the novel, referring once more to the reader's experience – she wished 'to make the blood run like a torrent from end to end'.[88] Clearly the unifying image is the waves themselves: they are there not only in the interludes, explicitly, but also implicitly in the rhythm of reading the rest of the novel. Her most explicit statement of this idea comes in 1931, when the final manuscript was ready, 'the thing stated':

> What interests me in the last stage was the freedom and boldness with which my imagination picked up, used and tossed aside all the images, symbols which I had prepared. I am sure that this is the right way of using them – not in set pieces, as I had tried at first, coherently, but simply as images, never making them work out; only suggest. Thus I hope to have kept the sound of the sea and the birds, dawn and garden subconsciously present, doing their work under ground.[89]

Having put such weight on the reading-experience itself, having guided the reader's reflections by manipulating the immediate responses to imagery, shape, point of view, Woolf feared that the novel might be, although 'compact', too heavy, 'inspissate'.[90] She waited more anxiously than ever for the reaction of her husband, the common reader, and was most relieved when he declared it (again choosing the painterly image carefully) a 'masterpiece'.

For *The Waves* is the most painterly of Woolf's fictions, drawing most obviously and daringly on the ideas of the Post-Impressionists and Roger Fry which had absorbed Woolf's interest for the past twenty years. The technique of her earlier novels may be remarkable in the history of the English novel, but for her it was a way of coming closer to quotidian reality. In *The Waves* she deliberately turns her back on that technique, adopting a prose style which is grammatically simple by contrast, but curiously arch and archaic in diction. 'We feel', says Daiches with some regret, 'that Virginia Woolf is deliberately depriving herself of the use of certain sensitive devices which her earlier work showed her using so effectively.'[91] It is part of a turning-away from subjective reality as something approachable and approximated through language, to an attempt to use form rather than material as a vehicle for her vision. Woolf herself was acutely aware of the parallels between this development and the painting-style of her Bloomsbury friends, when she wrote that she wanted it to be 'an abstract mystical eyeless book. And there may be affectation in being too mystical, too abstract; saying Nessa and Roger and Duncan and Ethel Sands admire that'.[92]

The most obvious formal feature of *The Waves* is the series of nine interludes in italics, which have a coherence to be expected when one learns that Woolf rewrote them all at once.[93] Reading them through all at once one appreciates the parallelism of form, in the openings for example: '*The sun had not yet risen*', '*The sun rose higher*', '*The sun rose*', '*The sun, risen . . .*', '*The sun had risen . . .*', and so on.

The interludes also use the same geography, although it is a curiously abstracted setting of sea, shore, garden and house. There are occasionally human figures, but the main population seems to be the birds and the unfortunate worms. What is most striking is Woolf's sustained attempt to mingle the qualities and activities of the elements: the waves (water), the sun (fire), the birds (air), the worms (earth). Each environmental detail is described, where possible, in images drawn from one of the other elements: for example, '*the sea blazed gold*', '*shallow pools of light*', '*waves breaking . . . like logs falling*', '*Tables and chairs rose to the surface as if they had been sunk under water*', '*all the blades of the grass were run together in one fluent green blaze. The trees' shadow was sunk to a dark pool at the root*', '*Darkness rolled its waves along grassy rides and over the wrinkled skin of the turf*'.

Along with this elemental landscape goes an elemental, brutish activity, centred on the birds pecking at the soft worms: '*Then one of them, beautifully darting, accurately alighting, spiked the soft, monstrous body of the defenceless worm, pecked again and yet again, and left it to fester*' (p. 63). This warlike imagery is made explicit in the analogy of the waves to turbaned warriors '*with poisoned assegais*' (p. 64) – an image which carries over into the following interlude, which begins by referring to the waves: '*their spray rose like the tossing of lances and assegais over the riders' heads*' (p. 92). The basic image in all of this is the blade cutting or the spear stabbing: the sunlight strikes, pierces and sharpens; it falls in wedge shapes upon the knife in the room; the corn is cut. Woolf gives us a material world where ignorant armies clash by night and day, the only movement being one of domination – either by a sudden thrust, or by the equally efficient smothering by clouds or darkness or flocks of birds. The final line – '*The waves broke on the shore*' – sums up this activity, being an image of ceaseless assault, a clarification or sharpening of the sea into the blade of the wave and its dissolution back into the general, elemental mass.

While the interludes trace the progression of one day from dawn until dark, there is not the same emphasis on the passage of time as there is, say, in the 'Time Passes' section of *To the Lighthouse*. One might sense, reading the novel now straight through rather than selectively, that each interlude sets the mood for the stage in the development of the six characters which follows. There is a general truth in this – the way youth is the morning, the time of greatest agitation in young adulthood filled with birds pecking at worms, middle age like the soft moth of afternoon, and so on. But more remarkable is the movement from an empty landscape to one densely populated, from matter to mind. This is accentuated by the fact that in the novel proper we get very little by way of scene-setting. But the emptiness of the interlude world is emphasised not only by the elemental concentration, but also by the way the human domain of the room is described.

To follow Woolf's descriptions of that room is like reading Roger Fry's descriptions of the still lifes of Cézanne:

> Each touch is laid with deliberate frankness, as a challenge to nature, as it were, and, from time to time, he confirms the conviction which he has won by a fierce accent, an almost brutal colour, which as often as not he will overlay later on, under stress of fresh discoveries and yet again reaffirm. These successive attacks on the final position leave their traces in the substance of the pigment, which becomes of an extreme richness and density. The paste under his hands grows to the quality of a sort of lacquer, saturated with colour and of an almost vitreous hardness.[94]

Compare, then, these successive descriptions:

The sun fell in sharp wedges inside the room. Whatever the light touched became dowered with a fanatical existence. (p. 94)

A deep varnish was laid like a lacquer over the fields. . . . The light which entered by flaps and breadths unequally had in it some brown tinge . . . . Here it browned a cabinet, there reddened a chair, here it made the window waver in the side of the green jar. (pp. 156–7)

The evening sun, whose heat had gone out of it and whose burning spot of intensity had been diffused, made chairs and tables mellower and inlaid them with lozenges of brown and yellow. Lined with shadows their weight seemed more ponderous, as if colour, tilted, had run to one side. Here lay a knife, fork and glass, but lengthened, swollen and made portentous. (p. 179)

The precise brush stroke was swollen and lop-sided; cupboards and chairs melted their brown masses into one huge obscurity. (p. 203)

Though the room is three-dimensional and changes in appearance as the day proceeds, we have the impression in each interlude of a flat canvas being painted through words to give a pattern of colour, volume and texture.

Or one might see the parallel with the still lifes of Vanessa Bell taking in the corners of rooms, or the sunlight across a floor. In February 1930, about the time when Woolf seized upon the idea of the interludes and was also composing the Hampton Court scene, she wrote that analysis of her sister's paintings which confesses to find them puzzling to one who 'knows nothing' of masses, relations and values. But 'there is emotion in that white urn', says Woolf; 'One feels that if a canvas of hers hung on the wall it would never lose its lustre. It would never mix itself up with the loquacities and trivialities of daily life.'

Like Vanessa's paintings, these interludes in *The Waves* refuse to get mixed up with the loquacities and trivialities which are documented in the lives of the six characters. They represent the elemental setting, constantly changing but only in terms of space and colour, against which human life plays itself out. They are the setting for the mosaic. But, more than that, they function in the reading-process as an elemental sea. The name 'interlude' is misleading since they begin and end the novel, and the speeches are actually set within them. The speeches are like waves rising out of this sea, and after riding on each one we sink back into the elemental progression, the cycle of the sun and moon, and (therefore) the cycle of the tides on the shore. The dawn, the flora and fauna of the garden, all the sensoria of the physical world, remain as ground (but underground) as we read, constantly qualifying what is thought, 'as doth eternity'.

In contrast to the earlier novels *Mrs Dalloway* and *To the Lighthouse*, *The Waves* is apparently full of speech. But the 'he saids' and 'she saids' of this novel are of a unique kind. While one speech may occasionally pick up from the image or idea of the previous one, the characters rarely actually speak to one another. What we have here is a version of the dramatic monologue as practised by T. S. Eliot in such poems as 'The Love Song of J. Alfred Prufrock'. Eliot, in fact, is the presiding genius of this novel, since so much of the imagery can be traced to his early poetry, and the character of Louis draws heavily on his biography (for Brisbane substitute St Louis). Just as Prufrock does not actually speak his speech out loud to anyone, even to himself, so Woolf's characters are expressing almost unconscious thoughts in a stylised way.

The degree and consistency of this stylisation, from character to character and from age to age, are also deliberate. A general impression is that the prose in *The Waves* is a curious combination of the simple and the mannered, with elementary vocabulary mingling with such words as 'immitigable' and Jinny's 'fulvous dress'. The syntax, similarly, moves between the simplicities of a Janet and John book to the tortured complex sentences of Bernard when he is theorising. By no leap of the imagination can one agree with Winifred Holtby that the prose has the supple rhythm of the sea:

> It has passed into time; it has passed into the swing and surge of Mrs Woolf's deliberate prose; it has passed into the hearts and minds of men and women, until the characters are tossed upon its restless waters, carried by the tide which is time to meet the final challenge of death. From cover to cover the novel is saturated in the sea. [95]

Indeed, in 1928 when she was contemplating the novel Woolf

noted that she had 'come to a crisis in the matter of style: it is now so fluent and fluid that it runs through the mind like water'.[96] In *The Waves* Woolf makes a determined effort to *avoid* fluidity, in favour of a jagged, rugged style more like a baroque ornament than the gushing romanticism promised by the interludes.

To consider the prose in this way, and taking into account also Woolf's claim that her personae were not to be 'characters', is to come at the novel in the appropriate way. The closest analogies are not with other novels but with morality plays or with psychomachia, where Man is represented in embodied facets within a formalised structue. A key element in that structure, as I have shown, is the way the human reflections are embedded like pieces of mosaic in the background of the sea, or matter. The pieces, nine in all, are also arranged in a pattern which one sees by standing back and appreciating the watershed gatherings: the farewell dinner for Percival, and the assembly at Hampton Court. These occupy the fourth and eighth sections. Since the ninth section, one fifth of the novel, is one long monologue by Bernard beginning, 'Now to sum up . . .', I think we can be justified in regarding the rest of the novel as an entity in itself. When we do this we discover the symmetry of the first dinner scene falling halfway through the novel, with Hampton Court at the 'end'. The first meeting represents the culmination of community, with the six personae arranged like rose petals around Percival. They are also about to enter the greater world after their educations, and the following four sections document their decline into middle age. This culminates in the gathering at Hampton Court, their last meeting, arranged almost as a penance by Bernard, who in his youth refused to go there with Percival. The ghost of Percival, long dead, hangs over them. They have made their own separate peaces with death, and have settled into the patterns of their lives.

To persist with the imagery of the sea, then, we can see in this structure the rise and fall of one great wave, or the incoming and outgoing of the tide. The tide is at the full during the farewell to Percival, and it recedes or the wave falls (falling being a constant image in the second half of the novel) afterwards.

This rise and fall, almost (as in Beckett's play 'Breath') like one intake and exhalation of breath, reminds us of the passing of time. If the interludes evoke a world of matter, the speeches show us beings acutely aware of time. 'This is here,' says Jinny, 'this is now. But soon we shall go' (p. 19). For all of the personae there is the problem of transience. Louis tries 'to fix the moment in one effort of supreme endeavour' (p. 32). Rhoda less excitedly considers 'this is here and now' (p. 55) as she shares the first moments of the summer holiday with all the human beings around her. Later she finds the present moment terrifying because she cannot see herself cohering in time as a personality: 'I do not know how to run minute to minute and hour to hour, solving them by some natural force until they make the whole and indivisible mass that you call life' (p. 111). At Hampton Court she is still wishing to 'escape from here and now' (p. 192), while Jinny voices the desire in another way with her paradoxical 'As if the miracle had happened and life were stayed here and now' (p. 193). Eternity or an hour, either way many of the personae wish to escape from the awful pressure of the passing moments. Even Neville whispers to his lover at the door, 'Let us abolish the ticking of time's clock with one blow. Come closer' (p. 155).

Bernard is a prose writer, unlike Louis the poet. He and Rhoda are, he thinks, 'authentics. . . . They toss their pictures once painted face downward on the field. On Louis's words the ice is packed thick' (p. 99). Bernard tells stories, describing (as Neville puts it) 'what we have all seen so that it becomes a sequence' (p. 31). He attempts to see patterns in time and so answer his question, 'What is this moment of time, this particular day in which I have found myself caught?' (pp. 96–7). His answer involves shared memories, which is why he turns from his engagement to the dinner with Percival, or from the birth of his son to arranging the dinner at Hampton Court. The personal, biological immortality he has found through the family in no way satisfies his spiritual longing to reconcile himself with the present moment.

For all this awareness of time, the novel is curiously out of time. Much of the speech is in the present tense and moves from image to image rather than telling a sequence of events. The constant 'saids' suggest a pattern already accomplished and laid down. Jinny predicts her future at school quite clearly (p. 19); Louis predicts Percival's death (p. 31); Neville at eighteen sees his future with alarming clarity: 'It would be better to breed horses and live in one of those red villas than to run in and out of the skulls of Sophocles and Euripides like a maggot, with a high-minded wife, one of those University women. That, however, will be my fate' (p. 50). Bernard quotes his own future biographer

(p. 65) with a little more awareness, but Louis seems to be predicting Virginia Woolf herself when he says early on, 'The time approaches when these soliloquies shall be shared' (p. 33). Yet, for all these presciences of the future, the novel is set (like so many of Woolf's) against a background of primordial swamps and violence. There are the stamping beasts in the desert, the stags clashing horns in the sexual dance, and Jinny's remarkable vision of London as 'sanded paths of victory driven through the jungle' (p. 166).

Against this panorama of time, Jinny is able to place herself purely as a sensual body. She had this ability at the first dinner, where on entering she 'seems to centre everything; round her tables, lines of doors, windows, ceilings, ray themselves, like rays round the star in the middle of a smashed window-pane' (p. 103). The imagery is spatial because Jinny exists primarily in space as a physical body. She is like Percival in that, Percival who is bored by Bernard's stories and provides an easy, accessible focus for the group because he is so totally *there*, in front of them.

For the thinkers a relationship with and within time is more difficult to achieve. Neville scorns prose or plot: 'It is not enough for them to wait for the thing to be said as if it were written; to see the sentence lay its dab of clay precisely on the right place, making character; to perceive, suddenly, some group in outline against the sky' (p. 169). He prefers to read a poem in his study, paring away to the essentials, bringing to the surface 'what he said and she said and make poetry' (p. 171). His tragedy is that this is not enough, and in the next paragraph he is waiting anxiously for a lover to come to his door.

Louis, for all his fastidious submersion of spiritual questioning to his business dealings, finds himself in old age rummaging in the attic of his mind, writing poetry and trying to make sense of the past. Just as Neville tried abortively to find a meaning with Jinny, Louis has spent time with Rhoda, to no avail: 'My destiny has been that I remember and must weave together, must plait into one cable the many threads, the thin, the thick, the broken, the enduring of our long history, of our tumultuous and varied day' (p. 173).

Susan has related to the people around her as a physical being, merging with her children and the daily round; for her there is no existential crisis, for 'I possess all I see' (p. 163). Bernard, similarly, wants a sense of community, but he is more acutely self-aware than Susan and must fight the battles which Louis only glimpses in solitude. Bernard always places himself in time as well as space. He realises that one's awareness of time is itself a transitory thing: 'And time lets fall its drop. The drop that has formed on the roof of the soul falls' (p. 157). Overlaying the habit of shaving comes the realisation that his youth has passed. Visiting Rome, city of the past, he sits on the ruins and waits like one of Forster's youthful heroes for an epiphany. He has one, albeit an anti-epiphany: 'But why impose my arbitrary design? Why stress this and shape that and twist up little figures like the toys men sell in trays in the street? Why select this, out of all that – one detail?' (p. 161). For once Bernard manages to drop out of time and pattern, and he gives his experience an image – the fin in the waste of waters. It is a desolate image, but one clear and unique in the ceaseless flux of the sea. Immediately he moves back into time, and Woolf describes it in two elaborate images drawn from literature and painting:

> Observe how dots and dashes are beginning, as I walk, to run themselves into continuous lines, how things are losing the bald, the separate indentity that they had as I walked up those steps. The great red pot is now a reddish streak in a wave of yellowish green.   (p. 161)

Bernard's life becomes, like a film, too fast for words to record.

Although the flux of time seems beyond the power of words' recall, words are the only way to vision for the thinking personae. Susan 'does not understand phrases' and does not need to. Neville insists, 'In a world which contains the present moment, why discriminate? Nothing should be named lest by so doing we change it' (p. 69). Yet he grows up lonely and unhappy, a student of literature who 'knew' when he was young that he would be 'a clinger to the outsides of words all my life' (p. 40).

Louis and Rhoda are more poetical and more at home with the insides of words. They have the only direct conversations in the novel, during each party (pp. 120, 194). But they use words not to link themselves to the community, rather to create an inner refuge – Louis in time (the beast stamping) and Rhoda in space (the far-off grove). Only Bernard seems to avoid 'the sharp tooth of egotism' by using his words to distance himself from himself and engage in life more subtly. During the party for Percival, for example, he is part of the group, but at the same time he is able to imagine India while the rest of them are focused on that one room and the circle of 'love and hate' which bind them together. While the others yearn for some absolute communion, abandoning 'I am this; I am that', Bernard is able to enjoy their company yet remain himself, and so later he is the one to organise the reunion, valuing the companionship of the group but still leading his own life with wife and family.

It is this flexibility which sets Bernard apart. The others have often extremely accurate insights into each other, but remain in general ignorance of themselves. Bernard is not only the butt of much of their criticism, but turns upon himself often as well, mocking his love of fine phrases, admitting, 'To be myself (I note) I need the illumination of other people's eyes, and therefore cannot be entirely sure what is my self' (p. 99). This Sartrean uncertainty about his own identity is what redeems Bernard and sets him apart. For him it is not a cause for anxiety or despair. He does not envy like the others Percival's integrity, which is based on a limited, physical, unthinking existence. He pleads permission to be rather than to act, to go down and explore his own psyche, to explore vertically as well as horizontally. Because of this, Bernard's images (like the fin) are often conscious, while the imagery associated with the other personae tends to persist from the initial statements when they are children.

Bernard is the most self-conscious of the six, not in his concentration upon his own navel but in his awareness of himself set in space and time. He is able to question without disintegrating:

> There is no stability in this world. Who is to say what meaning there is in anything? Who is to fortell the flight of a word? It is a balloon that sails over tree-tops. To speak of knowledge is futile. All is experiment and adventure. We are for ever mixing ourselves with unknown quantities. What is to come? I know not. But as I put down my glass I remember: I am engaged to be married. I am to dine with my friends tonight. I am Bernard, myself. (pp. 100–1)

While the other personae's speeches emanate from that blurred, subconscious area I tried to indicate by analogy with Prufrock's 'Let us go then', Bernard alone is fully self-conscious as he 'speaks'. His self-appraisal – 'a faithful, sardonic man, disillu-

sioned, but not embittered' (pp. 68–9) – is borne out by his
behaviour and that of his friends. He is able to feel and reason
and, as he observes, 'Very few of you who are now discussing me
have the double capacity to feel, to reason' (p. 65). Bernard's
winning combination of sensitivity and self-mockery qualify him
to deliver the final speech, but he also reveals in an important
scene another qualification. He has an ambiguous attitude
towards art itself.

After Percival's death, Bernard goes to the National Gallery
and Rhoda goes to a musical concert. Both characters are trying
to cope with grief, and, while all the characters could be grouped
in three pairs in a variety of permutations, one could make a
strong case for pairing Bernard and Rhoda as the two characters
most responsive to language and beauty. The two scenes
however, read like parodies of Forster's two essays 'On Not Looking at Pictures' and 'On Not Listening to Music'.   •

In the latter scene, Rhoda enters the concert hall sceptical of
the 'beetle-shaped men with their violins', but she finally achieves
an aesthetic apprehension of something more than goblins:

> what is the thing that lies beneath the semblance of the thing?
> . . . There is a square; there is an oblong. The players take the
> square and place it upon the oblong. They place it very
> accurately; they make a perfect dwelling-place. Very little is
> left outside. The structure is now visible; what is inchoate is
> here stated; we are not so various or so mean; we have made
> oblongs and stood them upon squares. This is our triumph
> this is our consolation.   (p. 139)

By contrast, Bernard goes to the paintings with their lines and colours, which, by their non-referentiality, allow space for him to
recall Percival and remembered sights. But he cries because 'they
cannot be imparted. Hence our loneliness; hence our desolation.'
Bernard seems to have reached the opposite extreme from Rhoda
The aesthetic emotion, being inhuman, has cast him back on the
human and reminded him of the irrelevance of art to human suf-
fering. Echoing Woolf's own envy of her sister, Bernard says,

> Painters live lives of methodical absorption, adding stroke to
> stroke. They are not like poets – scapegoats; they are not chain-
> ed to the rock. Hence the silence, hence the sublimity. Yet that

crimson must have burnt in Titian's gizzard. No doubt he rose
with the great arms holding the cornucopia, and fell, in that
descent. But the silence weighs on me – the perpetual solicitation of the eye.   (p. 134)

He complains that he cannot achieve the coherent aesthetic emotion, although 'arrows of sensation strike from my spine, but
without order'. Something deeper may be added to his understanding of life one day, but for the moment he is left with his
grief.

Was all that Bernard needed a Roger Fry at his elbow, or does
he stand for a more serious attack on the notion of aesthetic
pleasure? The answer will be found in Bernard's final speech,
which we must now discuss.

Bernard chats to us over a glass of wine during this third meal,
using the Jamesian image to place himself 'not from the roof, but
from the third-story window' (p. 207) observing the panorama of
life. His love of the everyday is balanced by the archetypal
memory of the gardeners and the lady writing, the life next door
or in the other room 'which is beyond and outside our own
predicament; to that which is symbolic, and thus perhaps permanent, if there is any permanence in our sleeping, eating,
breathing, so animal, so spiritual and tumultuous lives' (p. 213).

Bernard is clearly torn between the desire for pattern and the
desire for life. He buys a picture of Beethoven in a silver frame
only because he sees himself in the line of 'masters and adven-
turers'. The lives of his friends were certainly not an orderly symphony, and even his own sentences are but 'a string of six little
fish that let themselves be caught while a million others leap and
sizzle, making the cauldron bubble like boiling silver, and slip
through my fingers' (p. 220). To his wife at the window Bernard
says, 'Heaven be praised . . . we need not whip this prose into
poetry. The little language is enough' (p. 226). Just because of
Bernard's devotion to reality, the death of Percival shatters him.
The 'terrible pounce of memory' intrudes in the National
Gallery, and the meaningless of life leads him almost to despair:
'I to whom there is not beauty enough in moon or tree; to whom
the touch of one person with another is all, yet who cannot grasp
even that, who am so imperfect, so weak, so unspeakably lonely'
(p. 229).

The moment of reassembly at Hampton Court was the last

happiness in Bernard's life – 'we six, out of how many million millions, for one moment out of what measureless abundance of past time and time to come, burnt there trimphant. The moment was all; the moment was enough' (p. 239). That moment passed, and the cynical old man realises that 'the true order of things' when 'our life adjusts itself to the majestic march of day across the sky' is 'our perpetual illusion' (p. 233). Bernard heaves himself up from the table to go out and do battle with death, but he has no sense of self and no sense of art. 'I do not altogether know who I am – Jinny, Susan, Neville, Rhoda or Louis – or how to distinguish my life from theirs' (p. 237), he complains, and he has done with phrases: 'Life is not susceptible perhaps to the treatment we give it when we try to tell it' (p. 229).

It is a melancholy conclusion. Bernard's devotion to life has not sustained him, just as Rhoda's devotion to beauty cannot save her. Early on in the novel Rhoda, at the onset of menstruation, asked, 'To whom shall I give all that now flows through me, from my warm, my porous body? I will gather my flowers and present them – Oh! to whom?' (p. 48). After the concert she throws her violets into the waves as an offering to Percival (p. 141). Her gift of love, like Bernard's gift of words, avails nothing.

If the personae in *The Waves* end sadly, the novel does not. The last line, '*The waves broke on the shore*', makes a satisfying formal completion of a complex kind. To be symmetrical the novel should be seen without Bernard's long speech and without that last line. The opening line, 'The sun had not yet risen' would be balanced by 'Them, too, darkness covered' (p. 203), and Bernard would have the last observations about the difference between subjective and objective existence.

Why, then, do we have those last fifty pages? They are there to throw us back from art into life. Bernard actually addresses an acquaintance like the Ancient Mariner, actually pours out his life story. Woolf teases us with the question of how 'real' her novel is. Despite this disturbing intrusion of the real moment, we look forward to some triumphant summation from Bernard. Instead we get a weary repetition of what we already know, with the addition of such melancholy facts as the suicide of Rhoda. Even his rather worked-up exclamation at the end is undercut, not by the completion of the background pattern, but by the start of a new cycle, or the constant, indivisible flux itself.

The formal shape of the wave, then, has itself been shattered.

We are left with a mosaic of pieces which we had thought con-
stituted a whole but which remain six facets of life. Even the symmetry of the six is broken by taking one of the six, Bernard, out of
the pattern. He observes of his youth, 'You know that sudden
rush of wings, that exclamation, carol and confusion, the riot and
babble of voices; and all the drops are sparkling, trembling, as if
the garden were a splintered mosaic, vanishing, twinkling'
(p. 212). This, finally, is how we see the form of *The Waves* – as a
splintered mosaic, incomplete pieces of uncompleted lives, bereft
of the organising principles of balance and harmony.

Yet there is a principle of unity at work, one which does not
come from the National Gallery or the concert hall, or from the
pens of a Shakespeare, a Keats or a Woolf. The background of the
sea and the sun remind us of the shared physical world in which
the six personae live; the consistent style and the elaborate cross-
references and echoes of imagery and leitmotifs create a similar
impression through the landscape of the text itself. Just as the six
personae are waves in the eternal sea, so their experiences, with
the individual variations of temperament and experience, draw
on a common pool of deep emotions and symbolic referents. I
should hesitate to say that the speeches come from the Freudain
unconscious, but I should assert that together they seem to
emanate from a Jungian collective unconscious. 'I retrieved them
from formlessness with words' (p. 232), says Bernard of the daily
struggle of life. *The Waves* is a statement not just of his novelistic
power, but of the power in all of us to comprehend experience in
words. Although these six personae never within our hearing
actually speak to each other, they speak, unaware, in a kind of
chorus: that is the message of Woolf's technique.

Art cannot conquer the ravages of time. Paintings and music
have nothing to say directly to the greatest fact of human time
which is our impending deaths. Nor can the artful arrangement of
social functions, which Bernard attempts, stem the tide of dissolution and inward-looking despair. But the linear movement of the
novel can both assert the disruptive effect of time and suggest
methods of combat. This is what Woolf does in *The Waves*.
Bernard's dinner at Hampton Court, unlike Mr Ramsay's trip to
the lighthouse, does nothing to reconcile him or any of the party
with time, in the form of Percival's death. Bernard lives on,
beyond the simple symmetry of the novel, to discuss his life with
strangers at dinner tables. But death must be combated – not by

Bernard's fine phrases, but by a knowledge which Woolf (as distinct from Bernard) has been able to demonstrate in the phrases of *The Waves*. No man is an island, and, although Bernard does not realise it, the other five personae share many of his problems and perceptions, and care for him. Against the inadequacies of art, and the loneliness of the artist himself (Bernard), Woolf sets the solace of community.

Bernard's decision to do battle with death once more is one he almost does not reach. It is made with a sigh, almost reluctantly – not only that, but it is immediately answered and qualified by the fall to the italicised line, reminding us of the remorselessness of time. Bernard himself will eventually lose the battle. Elizabeth Heine is correct to observe that, 'like *A Passage to India*, *The Waves* marks the most complete development of the author's techniques of imparting significance to structure'. [97] Similarly James Hafley says, '*The Waves* is a work of art in which subject justifies form and form intends subject.' [98] We must be careful, however, to resist the strong urge (to which both these critics succumb) to equate Woolf with Bernard and with the triumphant artist. In *The Waves* Woolf uses all her art to show that art is not enough.

A clue to the best analogy for the formal techniques of *The Waves* can be found in Woolf's mention of the Bloomsbury artists and Ethel Sands, the composer, or in her diary entry when she contemplated the conclusion:

> It occurred to me last night while listening to a Beethoven quartet that I would merge all the interjected passages into Bernard's final speech and end with the words O solitude: thus making him absorb all those scenes and having no further break. This is also to show that the theme effort, effort, dominates: not the waves: and personality: and defiance: but I am not sure of the effect artistically; because the proportions may need the intervention of the waves finally so as to make a conclusion. [99]

Here one can detect the tension which existed throughout the composition of *The Waves*, between the domination of the elemental, architectural principle of the sea and the individual (albeit solitary) human being with his moments or 'fins' in the water. But, when she tackled (with neat if unconscious pun) 'the last lap of The Waves' she did indeed keep 'starkly and ascetically to the plan'[100] as she boasted, and the waves remained the frame, not the artist.

The painting-metaphor which I have been using constantly in this book applies well, as I have shown, to the interludes, those nine prologues 'hung', as Mario Praz puts it, 'at intervals throughout the novel like as many impressionist paintings translated into words'.[101] But although the six personae often use oceanic imagery – waves, seabed, seashore – the interludes remain detached from the human world, on the walls; they are not merged at all into Bernard's final speech. In *To the Lighthouse* Woolf was able thoroughly to merge metaphor with 'plot' by focusing on Lily Briscoe, a painter. Here her artist is a writer, and paintings remain, like her sister's canvas, inscrutable on the gallery walls. The 'perpetual solicitation of the eye' avails the reader as little as it does Bernard in the National Gallery.

Rhoda, however, has an epiphany at the concert, and it is the musical mataphor which is most illuminating when considering the form of *The Waves*. Woolf observed that 'this rhythm (I say I am writing *The Waves* to a rhythm and not to a plot) is in harmony with the painters',[102] but in the final analysis rhythm is more usefully seen in the sense in which E. K. Brown developed it in relation to Forster's Indian novel than in the Fryean sense of the rhythm of the line. Beethoven's late quartets provide the most interesting analogies. Bernard's final speech might be described as a cadenza (when a solo performer 'bursts away from his companions to indulge himself in the unrestrained expression of his enthusiasm'[103]), but more rewardingly likened to the *Grosse Fugue* originally ending Beethoven's B flat Major quartet. Bernard, in that speech, does summarise the lives of each of his friends in turn.

The whole novel might indeed be likened to fugal form, where a fixed number of melodic strands or voices 'at the outset enter in turn with a scrap of melody called subject, until at last all are singing'[104] and, considering the framing interludes, 'at the end the piece veers round to the original key'. Or that last line of the novel might be likened to a coda at the end of a work exhibiting the basic musical form of compound binary form: the exposition of the first idea up to the death of Percival, and the change to the dominant (Percival is, after all, the 'dominant' influence in the lives of the six), then the progress of the second idea back to the tonic, as the six personae grow older. The italicising of the interludes is analogous to the daring process of paring away which one notices in Beethoven's last quartets. Consider that final line, in the setting of Charles Rosen's description of Beethoven's process, where 'the structure of tonality is made to appear for a moment naked and immediate, and its presence in the rest of the work as a dynamic and temporal force suddenly becomes radiant'.[105]

Something like that effect is achieved by the last line of *The Waves*, when we appreciate not Bernard's stoical resolution but the 'dynamic, temporal force' of the waves. This effect and the successive structure of the whole novel can again be seen in relation to the great C minor Quartet. Perhaps it was this, Beethoven's own favourite, to which Woolf was listening as she composed her ending. The quartet is in seven movements with scarcely a break, beginning with a fugue. The final movement, like Bernard's speech, is described by a commentator as an allegro with 'a grim, tragic theme'.[106] He goes on to describe the movement: 'The full violence of this affirmation of life through struggle is only revealed in the coda . . . asserting the link with the first movement.' He calls the movement a 'thrashing out of the issue', and no better description could be given of Bernard's speech.

Some such musical analogy as these seems appropriate to a novel which Woolf saw as one saturated with sound but girdered with design, where images bubbled up in endless variation, with the 'sound' of the sea a constant background [Plate 21]. In 1927 she wrote in her diary, 'I shall sketch here, like a grand historical portrait, the outlines of all my friends.'[107] It was left to Vanessa Bell to execute the composite portrait with the brush. Instead Woolf evolved *The Waves*, which capitalises on all the assets of fiction to give us, not the outlines, but the insides of six friends. Through all their lonely arguments and withdrawals we alone see, by the consistent style and by the unifying arch of the interludes, that they share the same basic human predicament and are bound on the same wheel of time. By 1930 Woolf observed in her diary, '[Ethel Sands] says writing music is like writing novels. One thinks of the sea – naturally one gets a phrase for it. Orchestration is colouring.'[108] This was her progression – from people to a musical phrase, the various consciousnesses simply orchestrating the antecedent, elemental picture.

The personae were right to turn away from Bernard and his fine phrases. They were wrong to turn to the man of action Percival, whose whole being was at the mercy of their greatest enemy, time (or death). But they had no Virginia Woolf for friend, no artist[109] who could encompass both the spontaneity of human hope and despair and the eternal rhythms of nature in the beautiful hoop of art. She felt she had placed her statues against the sky; or, in Rhoda's musical terms, she had placed her oblongs on the square – 'The structure is visible. We made a dwelling-place.'

THE YEARS (1937)

> *Neither one thing nor the other* . . . .
> – North of Eleanor (p. 427)

After the renunciation of a simple, spatial, painterly aesthetic purity in the novel in *The Waves*, Woolf spent the next five years working intensely on a novel which many critics, including Forster, have frankly dismissed as a realistic failure. The genesis of *The Years* was an 'essay – novel' called *The Pargiters*, 'and it's to take in everything, sex, education, life etc.: and come, with the most powerful and agile leaps, like a chamois, across precipices from 1880 to here and now'.[110] Gradually the essay part was teased out to form *Three Guineas*, published a year after *The Years*. When the *Times* reviewer called *The Years* 'a creative, a constructive book' Woolf rejoiced that her polemical essay would now 'strike on a hot iron'.[111] But, whether one takes the novel as a kind of Forsyte Saga or as a political tract, it falls well below, say the critics, the complexity which one expects from a Woolf novel. Once again, the clue to Woolf's real intentions is to be found in her diary. In 1933 she was debating the question of form, 'the sense that one thing follows another rightly'.[112] She contrasted the merits of Dostoevsky with his 'inundation' and Turgenev with his paring away to essentials, and her subsequent comments show that she favoured the latter. The most common word in her deliberations over *The Years* is 'compress': 'My idea is to contract the scene; very intense, less so; then drama; then narrative, keeping a kind of swing and rhythm through them all.'[113] This talk of 'agile leaps' and 'swing and rhythm' suggests that Woolf was more concerned here than in previous novels with the unfolding surface structure and how different elements were juxtaposed. This implied not only a more conscious awareness of the reading-experience as cumulative and associational, but a new approach to characterisation itself. Instead of the leisurely hollowing out of character through interior monologue, Woolf intended to keep the psychological level pitched at the surface, at dialogue, visual observation and action:

> What I want to do is to reduce it all so that each sentence, though perfectly natural dialogue, has a great pressure of meaning behind it. And the most careful harmony and contrast of scene. . . . It's obvious that one person sees one thing and another another; and that one has to draw them together. Who was it who said through the unconscious one comes to the conscious, and then again to the unconscious?[114]

With *The Years*, more than any other novel, Woolf was concerned with form. It was partly the result of twisting what was originally a large lump of polemical material into art, but partly a new concern with a more organic concept of form as something growing, within the generations of the novel as well as during the reader's progress through it. At the end of 1935, when she finished the first draft and correctly predicted that it would take a whole year to do the final editing, she was worried about form: 'Does it hang together? Does one part support another? Can I flatter myself that it composes; and is a whole? . . . I must still condense and point: give pauses their effect, and repetitions, and the run on.'[115] Finally, after a long process of what she called 'perpetual compressing and re-writing always at that one book',[116] she was convinced that she had made 'a taut, real, strenuous book'.[117] She had managed to create a shape without losing reality, a danger she always felt and especially with this novel, with its abstract, political background – and a danger she referred to in 1935 when she opened an exhibition of Roger Fry's paintings: 'Is it a good thing that an artist should be also a critic, or does it inhibit his creative power?'[118]

While Woolf was clearly convinced that an artist could be both creative and critical, her critics were not. Edwin Muir complained that *The Years* was 'dead and disappointing',[119] but the following day an astute Maynard Keynes told her it was her best book – 'symbolism not a worry; very beautiful; and no more said than was needed'.[120] This was the kind of criticism Woolf needed, because it identified both the artistry and the message. One is tempted to suppose that Keynes, through his association with Fry, was able to read *The Years* in the way Woolf intended, responding to the rhythms and repetitions and constituting them into a significant form, while Muir, reading for the luminous halo of the moment or for an explicit metaphor, was left with nothing. At any rate, his criticism of what Woolf called 'inhumanity' worried her a great deal.

But it was Edward de Selincourt who pleased her most. He described the novel as a 'kaleidoscope' of tiny, isolated 'cubes' of experience.[121] That word 'kaleidoscope' is a useful description of the novel because it links the spatial and temporal ideas. As a kaleidoscope is made of several pieces of coloured glass reflected, through various mirrors, into a thousand patterns and a thousand pieces, so *The Years* gives us a seeming multitude of tiny scenes, but each one illustrates three or four constant themes: the place of women, the attitude towards England and towards older people, the importance of sexual love. A more precise visual example might be taken from Walter Sickert, one of Woolf's favourite artists, on whom she wrote an essay in 1934. There she actually compares him favourably to Turgenev, both artists composing their scenes carefully and letting the observer do much of the work of locating the meaning. Sickert, she says, 'never goes far from the sound of the human voice, from the mobility and idiosyncrasy of the human figure'.[122] Neither does Woolf in this novel, which seems so uncommonly full of dialogue. Sickert is a biographer and a poet, showing the past in a face and eternity in a background. In the depiction of a music-hall scene, so 'formal, so superficial', he can evoke a powerful emotional reaction which is beyond words. Woolf too lets her scenes do the talking for her, and her final aim, after all the politics, is a beauty beyond words.

What Woolf does in *The Years* is present us with a series of Sickert-like domestic scenes, each unique and therefore reminding us of the changing mores and conditions of the time, but each also irradiated by larger, constant themes. That larger background is most obviously evoked by the *Waves* method of initial natural descriptions. There they were quite programmed in their content and effect, but here the seasons, like the years, seem to occur randomly. The opening lines – 'It was an uncertain spring' – set the tone. At times there is the obvious pathetic analogy with the episode following, as when the sun disappears while the Colonel and Mira make love or it rains when Mrs Pargiter dies. But in general, as in the famous example of 1914, the weather is cruelly out of keeping with the human events: 'It was a brilliant spring; the day was radiant. Even the air seemed to have a burr in it as it touched the tree tops; it vibrated, it rippled' (p. 241). Most of the novel takes place in London, and these opening descriptions, while often finally focusing on the city, concentrate on pastoral, seasonal activities. Again this serves to underline the impression that human affairs have no relation to the grand cycles of nature and the spheres – the background is evoked only to be exposed as irrelevant.

From what has been said already, it is obvious that *The Years* must be read in a complicated way. Because much of the effect comes from sequential juxtapositions (of scenes, not just of the initial natural descriptions with human affairs), I shall first move through the novel commenting on these scenes as they occur, before standing back to apprehend the overall aesthetic shape.

The opening scene puts tradition and sameness against spontaneity and change. The Colonel is a hypocrite and his wife is dying, so we meet the Pargiter family when change is in the air after a long period of security. Outside, Rose has her traumatic confrontation with the man by the pillarbox; inside, Delia is restive and the children are interfering with the process of boiling the kettle to make it happen faster. When Martin runs out to that same pillarbox with a letter for Edward at Oxford, we sense the disparity between an old world trying to insulate itself in a network of civility and scholarship, and a new world of raw desires and horrors.

Kitty's restlessness – her longing for the moors rather than the mediaeval, dressed-up scholars of Oxford (pp. 78–9) – is confirmed by her meeting with the Robsons, which begins the breakdown of social barriers. While her mother cleverly weaves everything that happens into the mechanical pattern of her embroidery (p. 83), Kitty refuses to help her father to embroider a similar pattern out of the history of the college. In a striking image (neatly applicable to the intentions of her own text), Woolf has Kitty with a brush of her arm 'obliterate five generations of Oxford men' (p. 86).

Her aunt Rose's death confirms the destruction of the old order. At the funeral Delia insists that it is all pretence, and we, having witnessed the Colonel's infidelity, know that she is right. Nevertheless the weight of the past will be hard to move: little Rose's bunch of violets is smothered by the bouquets of the official mourners.

The break-up of the old order is felt through deliberately violent changes in point of view within and without the novel. At the end of Kitty's visit to the Robsons we are shocked by Jo's sudden thought, 'She's a stunner' (p. 75), and as readers we must drag ourselves from the elegiac conclusion of the long opening sequence to a change of scene eleven years later, in 1891. The breakdown of the social classes is indicated in a similar, painterly way when we see Eleanor from the perspectives of the windows of the tenants she has come to help (pp. 102–3). Eleanor herself contemplates the picture of the Princess of Wales on a wall and the attitudes of her motley group of social workers towards 'England'. She feels, in her own phrase, 'spun around' (p. 11), and reading Martin's letter from India as she travels to the law court only exacerbates this feeling of things falling apart. Even her attempt to approve of her barrister brother Morris, looking like 'eighteenth century portraits hung upon a wall' (p. 116), disintegrates as she sees the human frailty of the judge. The death of Parnell is the historical event which signals this time of change, and it links Eleanor with her father. But already we have seen old Colonel Pargiter pathetically attempting to establish contact with his grandchildren, and the idea of time sweeping the established order away links father and daughter in the image of falling leaves (pp. 123, 137). This section is a good example of the way Woolf demands agility of her reader, the ability to feel the intensity of the moment as well as the larger point about the corrosive, dissolving effect of time.

In 1907, the philosophical questioning of the two girls Maggie and Sara ('Am I that, or am I this?' – p. 150) is interrupted by their mother's reality in the beauty of her dancing away her era in a silent waltz. By the following year, both their parents are suddenly dead, and we see the Pargiter children recoiling into their childish selves: Rose looks like the portrait of her father's uncle (p. 169); Martin forgets that Miss Pym died twenty years ago. But the impetus towards the future gathers during 1910 when Rose makes the effort to get to know Maggie and Sara. We see

Kitty, now married into aristocratic security and counting the cost of her conservatism. During *Siegfried* at the opera we see her, in the best Forsterian manner, counting the goblins and ruminating on the lives she might have led. This example of the failure of the new generation to respond to the challenge of change is counterpointed by the news of the death of the King (which in turn recalls the death of Parnell).

In 1911 Eleanor visits Morris at Wittering, having returned from abroad to feel that English history was admirably 'near, domestic, friendly' (p. 210). She tries to match this sense of time with a similar patriotic feeling for space (i.e. the English land- scape) but after a long inner debate she concludes, 'It's not the landscape any longer . . . it's people's lives, their changing lives' (p. 227). Even the personal past is as meaningless as the admira- tion of old Dubbin for Eleanor. The orientation of the new age is towards the here and now, and personal relations. But where, asks Eleanor, are we going?

The section '1913' completes the rout of the old order. Now the Pargiters are alone in space and time, just as the reader – having leapt from one arbitrary date to another, from one arbitrary pastoral setting to another – is alone in space and time. Woolf now explores the various responses of her characters to each other and to beauty during the war years. Martin comes as close to Fry's aesthetic emotion as one could imagine, when he exults in the form of St Paul's Cathedral: 'All the weights in his body seem- ed to shift. He had a curious sense of something moving in his body in harmony with the building; it righted itself; it came to a full stop. It was exciting – this change of proportion' (p. 244). With the drop-out Sara, Martin then leads us through war-time London with its deceiving waiters and medley of political haranguers. This section ends with Kitty escaping from her party to make an escape by train to a northern pastoral idyll. She feels that 'past and present became jumbled together' (p. 293), but this epiphanic escape from time is obviously just an escape and no solution – *and* one that requires wealth.

By 1917 and the air raid we encounter new, strange in- dividuals. Faces are lit up by torchlight for an instant, conversa- tion and meals are broken up into fragments. Yet in this modern chaos Eleanor finds a moment of harmony in front of a painting of the south of France (a Cézanne landscape?) when she feels imper- sonal, 'immune' (p. 317).

In the long final section, 'Present Day', which brings together the two younger Pargiter generations, individuals search for friendship and beauty amid the debris. Maggie sees a pattern in the furniture   (p. 376); Eleanor sees the pattern of history repeating itself in the actions of Nicholas (p. 398); and Peggy has a vision of wholeness (p. 420). But North, who becomes the focusing consciousness (like another writer, Bernard, at the end of *The Waves*) has only a nightmarish epiphany when he imagines himself alone and silent (p. 458). Like Peggy he refuses to make a speech, and later, when their incomprehensible song draws the partygoers momentarily together, Eleanor doubts that anyone feels the same as she even as she agrees with Maggie that it is beautiful.

All the characters in the final party are seeking a comprehensive pattern. As for us, the most satisfying would be one which makes sense of the passing of time. The theme of the conflict between the generations is inevitable in a study of three generations, from Abel's interview with Sara and Maggie to Edward's dessicated appreciation of *Antigone*. He once translated it with an exhilarating sense of relevance. Now, quoting a line to his nephew North ('My nature is to share in love, not in hate', says Antigone to Creon – p. 446), he refuses to translate it. North reacts to Hugh Gibbs and his kind with a violent feeling of revolution. Peggy observes Martin and Rose falling into the old childhood patterns, 'the old brother-and-sister turn. Now they could only go back and repeat the same thing over again' (p. 387). Yet she also had listened to Eleanor before the party, observing, 'One thing seemed good to one generation, another to another' (p. 351), and had concluded, 'Old age must have endless avenues, stretching away and away down its darkness, she supposed, and now one door opened and then another' (p. 358).

We have here, then, various perspectives on the achievement of the middle generation of Pargiters, Woolf's own generation. The greatest admiration seems to be reserved for Eleanor. As North observes, 'she was neither one thing nor the other' (p. 427) but has kept pace with time. Yet she has achieved little, and has no family and few friends; and, anyway, praise or blame is not Woolf's object. Rather she gives us Sara's vision of the Pargiter family standing against the window like a family portrait (p. 467), and then her enigmatic conclusion as Eleanor holds out her hands to Morris and asks, 'And now?': 'The sun has risen, and the sky above the houses wore an air of extraordinary beauty, simplicity and peace' (p. 469). The moment, like the photograph of the Pargiter family, is full of Sickert's human interest, but behind it is a background of meaningless change or the repetition of the follies of the past. The uncertainty of the opening lines has been replaced by the certainty of this natural description, which deliberately echoes the opening of *The Waves*. But nothing is certain, and like the younger Pargiters and the enlightened Eleanor we look beyond the frame of the book to the future, 'And now?'

Eleanor's final epiphany, as she looks out the window and sees a couple leaving a cab, is drawn from Woolf's passage in *A Room of One's Own* when she describes the extraordinary sense of unity and satisfaction to be got from looking out a window and seeing a couple getting into a taxi (chapter 6). That is not the end of the resonance of the image. At the opening of *The Years* Delia looks out the window and sees a young man getting out of a hansom cab (p. 18). There the sunset was 'red and fitful'; indeed the light of the whole of the first scene is 'the mixed lights of the lamps and the setting sun'. The opening description ends, 'Slowly wheeling, like the rays of a searchlight, the days, the weeks, the years passed one after another across the sky' (p. 2). Eleanor may have her moment of peace, then, and the day may indeed by purely lit, but the reader is thrown back to the time sixty years before when Eleanor and her sister had a similar moment of beauty when the lights were fading. Just as the years pass by mechanically like the rays of a searchlight, each flash illuminating one of the sections of this novel, so too do the epiphanies of the characters pass, changing nothing. Woolf's ending teases us into wanting to feel completion along with Eleanor, but in reality it directs us to feel the endless progression of time, and the irrelevance of beautiful sunsets. After all, Woolf *was* prophetic in throwing us forward out of the end of the novel into our present day, beyond 1937, which must be 'red and fitful' indeed.

So far I have followed the 'plot' of *The Years*, showing how time bulldozes on over the individual epiphanic moment, how the force of the previous generations, its follies and politics, swamp the aspirations of the young. It seems that in all cases the shaping power of the individual is overwhelmed by the meaningless stumble of the seasons, history, or time. Woolf's artistic devices seem to be wholly at the service of this vision of society, which was the basis of her political stance in *Three Guineas* over the question of how to bring about any social change. As Victoria Middleton observes, 'several types of structural repetition create the impression that the Pargiters are forced to repeat their lives'.[123] Middleton reasons from the deliberate non-framing of the last natural description that 'Woolf wants us to see how she does her magic trick, in order to destroy the illusion.'[124] But I do not think Woolf has totally lost faith in the resources of her art, any more than *The Waves* denies the power of art. There it was a matter of breaking the shell to create an even more complex artifice; here the shell is obviously broken from the outset. Everything about *The Years* – the length of sections, the dates, the style, the moving focus – suggests an anti-novel, 'a deliberate failure' in Middleton's term. But there is a pattern here still in the carpet, not the pattern of analogy with opera, Greek drama and so forth (the list could be endlessly invented) which Jane Marcus offers, but a pattern already there concealed by the numerals of the dates.

A schematisation of *The Years* will help to reveal this pattern. At the outset, it would seem only to confirm the haphazardness of it all:

Year	Season/month	Pages
1880	Spring	93
1891	October	43
1907	Midsummer	18
1908	March	14
1910	Spring	33
1911	August	23
1913	January	10
1914	May	59
1917	Winter	23
1918	November	3
Present Day	Summer	140

But if one considers the tripartite structure of *To the Lighthouse* and many of Forster's novels, and looks for such a division here, one sees a natural pattern with divisions falling after 1907 and after 1918. The three resulting sections have a quantitative symmetry (154, 151, 140 pages) and also define three broad historical phases. The first is a detailed description of a damp Victorian household, and ends with Eugenie and Digby returning from a midsummer ball – 'then the lights went out' (p. 156). That is the end of an age of elegance and ignorance, a world where, despite

the quarrelling of the couple and the Colonel's lechery, real
beauty is possible in the party going on outside Maggie's window
or in Eugénie's haunting dance. The central sequence leads up to
and includes the war, descending to the winters of 1917 and 1918
It moves from those heady pre-war days of optimism so movingly
described by Vanessa Bell, to the Chekhovian inconsequentiality
of Crosby, the displaced servant, cursing her Count and walking
to the grocer's – 'the guns went on booming and the sirens
wailed' (p. 328). Although the war has ended, these last words
effectively presage the mood of the restless inter-war years of 'Present Day'.

These divisions also exemplify Woolf's desire for scenes to
'follow each other rightly', to have 'harmony and contrast'. The
first section ends with the Pargiter children just about to take their
places in the adult world, a world of challenge (Eleanor's town
houses) and personal danger (Rose and the pillarbox). The next
section announces that Eugénie, the one Pargiter adult who seems
to have a rapport across the generations with her children, is
dead. It pivots on the central episode of the novel, both temporally and physically, in 1913. As the snow falls, Eleanor shuts up the
family home, Crosby moves to her rooms, and Martin avoids her
with embarrassment. 'It was a lie', he reflects, consciously turning that sentence into an epitaph for the Victorian age. It is only
now that the Pargiter children, though grown-up for some time
now, make a final, irrevocable break with the past, and look
about for a new social and personal order. The second section
ends with the war's end, a society literally and spiritually blown
apart. Kitty has taken off for the north and the city is filled with
homeless, uprooted people of various sexual persuasions and
ideologies.

The party of the present day which comprises the third section
is a particularly divisive affair. It lacks the centralising hostess of a
Mrs Ramsay or Mrs Dalloway. Through the fresh, objective eyes
of North and Peggy we see the Pargiters for what they are. Their
father Morris began the novel asking Eleanor 'How's Mama?'
but their subsequent conversation revealed the separation of the
sexes which, for Woolf, is the inevitable link between the social
and personal life. Morris has given up explaining the business of
the law court to Eleanor, effectively barring her from control over
her life or the life of the state. Growing up in such a society,
though they share a common background and equal intellect, has

separated brother and sister – 'When they met they never had time to talk as they used to talk – about things in general' (p. 35). At the party Eleanor observes, 'My life's been other people's lives . . . my father's; Morris's; my friends' lives' (p. 396). When she reaches out to him at the end, he is ambiguously quaffing another drink. In the cynical, estranged eyes of his children, he is draining the dregs of his life. The section, then, shows us individual efforts at rapprochement within a society whose conventions force people apart, brother from sister, father from son.

To refer to the kaleidoscope image once again, then: the individual scenes are the various patterns to be seen by shaking the contraption then looking through the aperture; the issues of female equality, family relations, and so forth, are the themes which colour the patterns; and the tripartite division is the arrangement of mirrors against which the patterns are produced (Vanessa Bell's cover – three circles crossed by a vibrant rose – is a perfect graphic representation [Plate 22]). In this structure Woolf, in the words of Mitchell Leaska (who has studied the evolution of *The Years* most closely), 'created that aesthetic tension which is generated from documented vision in union with poeticised truth'.[125]

Painting and the visual sense are also important within this apparently most unaesthetic novel. The opening sequences remind us constantly of the quality of the light, and this is carried within each section, as in the description of the curtains where the balls are taking place, 'semi-transparent and sometimes blowing wide' (p. 138), or in Martin and Sara's pointilliste vision of the world:

> The sun dappled the table and gave her a curious look of transparency, as if she were caught in a net of light; as if she were composed of lozenges of floating colours . . . Sara had walked on. She too was netted with floating lights from between the leaves. A primal innocence seemed to brood over the scene. (p. 260)

But here the visual image is being used to suggest Sara's shattered frame of mind. Typically in the novel, visual effects are subordinated to other themes. A striking example is where Eleanor daydreams about the quality of light: 'The sun was shining fitfully; it was going in and it was going out, lighting up now this, now – ''Eleanor'', Rose interrupted' (p. 16). If the idea of rhythm is mocked here, so much more is the idea of significant form in the description of North and Sara's dessert: 'Here the girl came in with the pudding. It was an ornate pudding, semi-transparent, pink, ornamented with blobs of cream' (p. 345).

Painting also features prominently in the novel, especially during 1880, a time when the household gods were enshrined in family portraits – the past impinges in space. In her mother's room Delia sees her grandfather's portrait and wonders, 'Why had the artist put a dab of white chalk on the tip of his nose?' Later she looks up at her mother's portrait – 'She seemed to simper down at her daughter with smiling malice' (p. 40). By 1908, Martin at least is free from the personal content of the portraits: 'In the course of the past few years it had ceased to be his mother; it had become a work of art. But it was dirty' (p. 160). Eleanor cares for this portrait of their mother and cleans it. Once again, Woolf shows the power of art from another angle than the aesthetic, when Peggy ruefully observes, 'Somebody had told her that she was like her grandmother and she did not want to be like her. She wanted to be dark and aquiline: but in fact she was blue-eyed and round-faced – like her grandmother' (p. 350).

Paintings signify the Victorian world and its power over the present. Mr Robson admires a photograph of his mother, and as he stands there with his hand on his daughter's shoulder Kitty feels 'a sudden rush of self-pity' (p. 77). Here is the virtuous epitome of family life and tradition, mocked by the apparent ancestor-mongering but aridity of the Malone household:

> The pictures seemed to be looking down at the empty chairs, and the empty chairs seemed to be looking up at the pictures. The old gentleman who had ruled the college over a hundred years ago seemed to vanish in the daytime, but he came back when the lamps were lit. The face was placid, solid and smiling, and singularly like Dr Malone, who, had a frame been set around him, might have hung over the fireplace too.   (p. 18)

Kitty tries to fill this vacancy of humanity by marrying Lasswade and filling her house with paintings of the earls and one of herself, 'emerging from a cloud of white muslin' (p. 276). But Martin, on a visit, objects to 'the 'horrid daub of you over the mantelpiece' (p. 283), and Kitty agrees. She feels like scraping away all these portraits with a knife. When Martin leaves Kitty, he observes a Canaletto on the wall – 'a nice picture; but a copy' (p. 286). Kitty, too, has fallen into the trap of keeping up appearances of family and artistic taste. Eleanor is wary of this trap from early on in the novel when, after comforting her sister Rose, she stares at a 'heavy frame' and imagines herself up on the wall with her ancestors. Like Martin, she returns hastily from art to life, Martin to observing the pattern of black and white tiles in Kitty's hall, Eleanor to examining the dog's bowl.

Through the younger characters, Woolf attacks portraiture because it represents an outmoded way of looking at the world. When Sara sees Rose on a charger saying to men 'Damn your eyes', 'as if she had been drawing her picture on the table-cloth', Rose agrees that it is an accurate description, but only partial – 'she had the odd feeling of being two people at the same time' (p. 182). Victorian portraits, like Victorian novels, do not allow people to be mercurial. So at the party Peggy rejects her portrait of Eleanor: 'She's not like that – not like that at all, she said, making a little dash with her hand as if to rub out an outline that she had drawn wrongly' (p. 360). And North rejects the 'little snapshot pictures' that a novelist makes, 'like a fly crawling over a face' (p. 341). Both Peggy and North's vague insistence at the party that people must 'live differently' has to do with a change of actual vision, the way we see people and history. The partygoers play a game of each contributing in ignorance to a composite portrait, and the result is a monstrous hybrid. But Peggy is prompted to a vision of real happiness in a utopia where 'this fractured world was whole; whole, and free' (p. 420). In such a world, complex and contradictory portraits such as the one created at the party, or the portraits of a Picasso, would be comprehended whole as encompassing contradictory aspects of the personality in one whole.

The relevance of this implicit and explicit critique of fine art to the texture of Woolf's novel should be apparent. There is a strong strain of iconoclasm in the form and style of *The Years*, even as it sets up the framework and appearance of a three-volume Victorian novel. At times Woolf seems to emphasise the documentary accuracy of her saga, in the way she reports only dialogue and not inner thoughts, or, like a camera, records only what is going on in front of it. What happens to the Robsons, for example, and why do we not see Edward, Rose or Delia for such long stretches? On the other hand Woolf often reminds the reader of the fabrication of the fiction. There is the playing on the word 'rose' at the beginning of the novel; the way 1891 is filled with the smoke of burning leaves and then concluded with crude obviousness when the Colonel says to himself, 'One must burn one's own smoke' (p. 136); and near the end of 'Present Day' North talks to Edward – 'Not carapaced – the words ''comparison'' and ''carapace'' collided in his mind, and made a new word that was no word' (p. 44). Woolf has already used this 'new' word in the opening to this section, when she describes a dress 'majestically caparisoned'. (p. 329).

Such incidents remind the reader that what he is reading is, like the best portraits, a composition aesthetically arranged out of blocks of reality. During the party when North talks to Sara, he feels over and above her actual words 'the excitement with which she had spoken, due to wine perhaps, had created yet another person; another semblance, which one must solidify into one whole' (p. 368). The reader of *The Years* must accomplish a similar act, solidifying the disparate scenes, impressions and characters into a vision of life. He must do the work of Turgenev's readers and compose a whole. *The Years* attempts to transcend the Victorian portrait of *Mrs Dalloway* and the aesthetic impositions on *The Waves*. Mrs Dalloway looks out of her window across at the old woman and thinks, 'Here is one room; there another'; in *The Years* the key phrase, often repeated, is 'neither one thing nor another'. Woolf encompasses both rooms in a larger, more comprehensive vision.

The Years, then, is 'a book full of symmetries that is at war with shape'.[126] I do not think we have to resort to political theories to explain its aesthetics (as when Margaret Comstock sees an antifascist gesture in the invitation to the reader to enter the work[127]) nor must we imagine an artist who has lost faith in her art. Rather, Woolf is here in supreme control of her art, carving out of sixty years of English history a complex edifice whose building-blocks are spaces and psychological volumes. If we want to retain a painting analogy for the work, we might take a clue from de Selincourt's review and think of the kaleidoscope in time which is Magritte's *Nude Descending a Staircase*. Each section of *The Years* is a self-contained moment, but is related to the events before and after by historical connection and literary cross-references. Woolf refused, to the disappointment of many critics, to make Eleanor into the reader's agent, binding the Pargiter family into a vision of completeness at the end of the party. Woolf was after something much more difficult, the swing and rhythm of a Cubist painting that suspends us, miraculously, between space and time.

BETWEEN THE ACTS (1941)

> *Each of us a free man; plates washed by machinery; not an aeroplane to vex us; all liberated; made whole.* (p. 127)

Although Woolf began writing *Between the Acts* in the form of *Poyntz Hall* early in 1938, it was not until April 1940 that she was asked by the local Women's Institute to write a pageant for the villagers of Rodmell – and, what is more, to produce it. [128] Woolf may not have been in the mood at that late stage in her life and the history of her nation to relish the irony, but there is much of herself in Miss La Trobe. The 'bossy' producer of the pageant in the novel has an acute sense of the multiple relationships between art and life, as she observes the backstage area before the show and thinks, 'It has the makings. . . . For another play always lay behind the play she had just written' (p. 48). She feels this not simply in the sense of the next pageant some time in the future, but she has a vision of the Chinese-box effect when art is placed in the very heart of a society. So her pageant ends with a line of mirrors reflecting the audience to themselves. Mrs Manresa, with her own mirror out to make up her face, may reflect the actors back upon themselves, and so on.

This sense of perspective and the kinds of perspective is surely the theme at the heart of *Between the Acts*, with its central premise of the observer observed. That Woolf intended to break down even further the divisions between the subjective consciousness and the outer world is evident from her 1938 description:

> all literature discussed in connection with real little incongruous living humour: and anything that comes into my head; but 'I' rejected: 'We' substituted: to whom at the end there shall be an invocation? 'we' . . . the composed of many

different things . . . we all life, all art, all waifs and strays – a rambling capricious but somehow unified whole – the present state of my mind? . . . and a perpetual variety and change from intensity to prose, and facts – and notes . . . .[129]

It should be remembered too that Woolf was composing *Between the Acts* alternately with her biography of Roger Fry, and her notes reveal that the one affected the other. In 1938 she wrote to her sister,

> I adore painting's severity; its bareness from impurity. All books now rank with the slimy seaweed of politics; mouldy and mildewed. I wish I could settle to pure fiction; indeed had to rush headlong into a novel as a relief; but am now back to Roger and the compromise of biography again.[130]

Woolf came to refer to her 'P. H. poetry', but this was not the free-flowing lyric poetry of her earlier novels, except in Isa's fabrications. It was rather a deliberately spare, chunky prose, broken up like the Post-Impressionist canvas into elements of light and sound. Her habitual poetic style was confined to the lines of the pageant itself or to particular lyrical moments. Otherwise the prose of the novel, like its overall arrangment, was deliberately brutal and jagged. That she learnt the value of the latter style from Roger Fry is evident from her diary. It was not just the thirty years of tutelage in art criticism, but the fact that all of that was being recalled as she wrote her biography of him:

> I think I have got at a more direct method of summarising rela-tions; and then the poems (in metre) ran off the prose lyric vein, which, as I agree with Roger, I overdo. That was, by the way, the best criticism I've had for a long time – that I poetise my inanimate scenes, stress my personality; don't let the meaning emerge from the matière.[131]

Later she complained that the rhythm of the last chapter of *Between the Acts* was becoming 'obsessive' and she had to write some memoirs to break it up and loosen it. She felt this idea about the possessive effect of prose rhythm was 'profound'.[132]

Various attempts have been made to see thematic unities in the novel, in response to Leavis's challenge that it possessed merely 'extraordinary vacancy and pointlessness'. A. Y. Wilkinson, beginning promisingly with the observation that 'in *Between the Acts* Woolf succeeded in making form part of the statement and statement part of the form', ends with a mystical assertion of the unity of isolation and connection.[133] Don Summerhayes sees here 'a world of total analogy',[134] and Stephen Fox finds a centre in the pond.[135] Such interpretations cannot rest with the gaps in the drama which is the subject and techique of the novel, but must fill in the conflict with meaning. The ending of the novel, however, is surely a clear indication that by this stage Woolf had lost faith in the capacity of her art to 'say' anything meaningful in such a direct way. The 'meaning' of *Between the Acts* remains between the acts and between the lines. Just as in *The Waves* the simple pattern is broken and Bernard achieves no vision, so *Between the Acts* does not present us with life but rather sets up a framework through which we may see life more clearly. Any representation of community in space or time is doomed, like Miss La Trobe's pageant, to end with the real audience being dispersed: ' "Dispersed are we", Isabella followed her, humming. "All is over. The wave has broken. Left us stranded, high and dry. Single, separate, on the shingle. Broken is the three-fold ply..." ' (pp.70–1). Instead of trying to document the wave, Woolf here gives us the chaos of the ever-changing sea, the fragmented shoreline of Arnold's 'Dover Beach'.

As the villagers are set against the pageant of English history, so the whole cast of the novel is set against the backdrop of eternity. Lucy's *Outline of History* reminds her how England was 'populated, she understood, by elephant-bodied, seal-necked, heaving, surging, slowly writhing, and, she supposed, barking monsters; the iguanadon, the mammoth, and the mastodon' (p.10). She returns to her book at the end of the novel, and her history lesson forms one frame. By the end she has reached prehistoric man, half-human, half-ape, but for Lucy Swithin history is so vast that it is virtually non-existent. She does not believe there were such people as the Victorians, only themselves dressed differently (p. 122). She sees the whole world swimming like fish in a pond, and during her excursion with William Dodge sees her own childbed as the cradle of mankind.

It would be nice if we could take Lucy's vision as the vision of the novel, but it is severely challenged instead. Woolf had spent her life documenting the struggle against the Victorian way of life and her last novel had shown the painful transition from that world into this. Here the world of the picnic in the pageant is quite different from the modern world of cars and aeroplanes and gramophones, and, even if the progression of social changes were denied, Lucy's final observation about the caveman ushers in the conflict between Isa and Giles, eternal maybe, but also unique to that couple and that time and place.

One of Woolf's habitual symbols of the Victorian legacy in her novels is the use of portrait-paintings. In *Between the Acts* they feature prominently. In the dining-room hang two pictures, one a conventional painting of an Oliver ancestor with his dog, the other bought because Bart liked it. It is the portrait of a lady, and Woolf describes it in almost cheeky Fryean terms:

> she led the eye up, down, from the curve to the straight, through glades of greenery and shades of silver, dun, and rose into silence. The room was empty.
>
> Empty, empty, empty; silent, silent, silent. The room was a shell, singing of what was before time was; a vase stood in the heart of the house, alabaster, smooth, cold, holding the still, distilled essence of emptiness, silence.   (p. 30)

The impression of this remarkable passage, that the well-wrought urn of art has nothing to say to us in human terms, is reiterated later when the picture is referred to as leading down the green paths of silence (pp. 36, 39).

Lucy Swithin reduces the portrait in the stairwell from the status of both art and history, exclaiming to William that 'we claim her because we've known her' and that she likes her best in moonlight (p. 52). Art for Lucy has the value of familiarity, habit, and nostalgia. Just before this passage, Mrs Manresa had not got much further with landscape: 'Nobody answered her. The flat fields glared green yellow, blue yellow, red yellow, then blue again. The repetition was senseless, hideous, stupefying' (p. 51).

Earlier Bart had asked why the present generation were unresponsive to art, the words 'Reynolds, Constable, Crome!' meaning nothing. Lucy's answer to the powerlessness of painting comes cryptically: 'We haven't the words – behind the eyes; not on the lips; that's all' (p. 43). Like Lucy, Woolf in this novel faces the modern crisis in communication, doubting the ability of her characters to communicate with one another or of herself as writer to communicate to us. There is none of the earlier mastery of phrase in this novel. Indeed, it seems to be almost an anti-novel, words coming in for just as brusque a dismissal as paintings.

Much of the action takes place in the Olivers' library, but books are not read there. When Isabella enters, she looks over the shelves as if looking for a medical cure, and realises that 'for her generation the newspaper was a book' (p. 18). Horrific stories of rape and war are read with the same avidity and lack of real outrage as thrillers. Lucy gestures to the books on the landing to William, and murmurs, 'Here are the poets from whom we descend by way of the mind' (p. 52); but there is no continuity between past eloquence and present silence. Even Isabella's poetry is a medley made up of her own revampings of half-forgotten phrases, and not the real thing.

So too the literature of the pageant itself is lost to the wind, garbled, interrupted or forgotten by the players. Isabella thinks, 'Did the plot matter? She shifted and looked over her right shoulder. The plot was only there to beget emotion. There were only two emotions: love, and hate. There was no need to puzzle out the plot' (p. 67). By the end of the novel, the sensitive soul of Isabella has rebelled against even emotion. Seeing her husband Giles in the evening she thinks, ' "The father of my children, whom I love and hate." Love and hate – how they tore her asunder! Surely it was time someone invented a new plot, or that the author came out from the bushes ...' (p. 150).

Miss La Trobe, hiding in the bushes, presents a pageant whose only plot is the winding trail of British history. Even that is but sketchily drawn, and the most sustained presentation, *Where There's a Will There's a Way*, is itself abridged. The one unifying strand through the whole production itself is the peasantry. This was a stock device of village pageants, as one can see by the way Forster skilfully uses the chorus of the Woodman in his *Abinger Pageant* (1934). But Miss La Trobe is not so skilful, and her peasants far less disciplined and profound. Instead of talking wisely about man's relationship to the countryside, the villagers haphazardly weave through the trees and throughout the performance singing a ragged chorus about digging and delving. It is during the comedy, indeed, that they falter and the whole show grinds to a halt. 'This is death', the producer wails; but then in step the cows:

The whole world was filled with dumb yearning. It was the primeval voice sounding loud in the ear of the present moment. Then the whole herd caught the infection. Lashing their tails, blobbed like pokers, they tossed their heads high, plunged and bellowed, as if Eros had planted his dart in their flanks and goaded them to fury. The cows annihilated the gap; bridged the distance; filled the emptiness and continued the emotion. (p. 99)

It is only Isabella's loathed emotion that is continued, but for the audience and Miss La Trobe *that* constitutes design and plot. The cows are not at all like Forster's orderly sheep which open and close his pageant with a symbolic reminder of the true possessors of the English countryside. The cow episode is a vivid example of what the modern age has come to; its demand for activity and sensation only, in whatever form, while the orderly books and better plays lie unread, inside in the library.

Virginia Woolf, as distinct from Miss La Trobe, has concocted a plot of sorts for her novel. It revolves around Giles and Isabella Oliver, and shows Giles having a fling with the gaudy Mrs Manresa. There is a minor resonance between this plot and the 'Restoration' play, particularly as it comes after the break for tea during which two couples are isolated: Bart and Lucy in the library, and Isa and William in the greenhouse. Both couples hear scales being played on the piano, and identify the sound as 'CAT' or 'DOG'. The younger couple suggest the young lovers Valentine and Florinda, and the older couple the scheming elders Lady Harpy and Sir Spaniel. The animal names suggest the animal basis of human relationships.

But it is an unsatisfactory correlation, and deliberately so. Similarly, the climax of the Giles–Isabella plot is presented unobtrusively, in the manner of Breughel's painting *The Fall of Icarus*. Isa stumbles on Giles and Mrs Manresa coming out of the greenhouse (p. 110), but we have nothing of her reaction; we go on with the show. Lucy's moment upstairs with William disappoints us because nothing is really communicated between them, and even Lucy's feelings are unclear to the reader. Similarly, we await the big scene between the central protagonists Giles and Isa at the end, and do not get it. The book shuts just as the curtain rises.

This refusal by Woolf to capitalise artistically on her creation, at all points, has a deeper motive than sheer perversity or the gloom of her old age and her frightful times. All the way through the novel the characters almost willingly destroy even their own subjective moments of unified vision. Giles Oliver can see not the view before him but the political agitations further afield in Europe. Lucy observes that the sad thing about views is that they will be here when we are not (p. 41). Bart imagines that if he were a painter he would paint that landscape, but returns instantly to the world of telegrams and anger in his newspaper (p. 14).

The whole rhymic movement of the novel is from separateness to unity and apart again. The opening scene shows Mrs Haines being excluded from the emotional circle and responding in a violent way: 'Mrs Haines was aware of the emotion circling them, excluding her . . . she would destroy it, as a thrush pecks the wings off a butterfly' (p. 9). The audience moves away from the stage at each interval, breaking up the green lawn into a motley quilt of colour. Each time they are recalled and recompose themselves. After the first interval

> Music makes us see the hidden, join the broken. Look and listen. See the flowers, how they ray their redness, whiteness, silverness, and blue. And the trees with their many-tongued much syllabling, their green and yellow leaves hustle us and shuffle us, and bid us, like the starlings, and the rooks, come together, crowd together, to chatter and make merry . . . .   (p. 86)

But even the prose is ragged and broken, and in the next paragraph the audience, facing an empty stage, begin talking in 'scraps and fragments'. Music seems to save the day again after the final speech of the pageant:

> Like quicksilver sliding, filings magnetized, the distracted united. The tune began; the first note meant a second; the second a third. . . . Compelled from the ends of the horizon; recalled from the edge of appalling crevasses; they crashed; solved; united.   (p. 132)

But even this remarkable description of music, reminiscent of Forster's handling of the Beethoven concert in *Howards End*, is shattered as the audience looks up to see the 'irrelevant forked stake' of the Rev. G. W. Streatfield, and to remember the 'scraps, orts, and fragments' of the previous voice, which is *our* voice.

That speech, protesting the dignity of mankind and challenging the audience – 'All you can see of yourselves is scraps, orts, and fragments?' (p. 131) – must be the 'invocation' which Woolf talked of ending the novel with. It is an indication of the sophistication of her vision that it is not at all the end of the novel. It is but one more attempt to make the moment and the community cohere, and like the others it is destroyed by time and chaos: *'Dispersed are we.'*

It might be protested that one character is vouchsafed a vision of unity: Lucy Swithin. Certainly she has a strong awareness of history and is at home with the past and the present. She feels 'all is harmony, could we hear it. And we shall' (p. 122), and at the end of the novel she has her vision by the pool when the world contracts and the fish become all humanity – 'seeing in that vision beauty, power, and glory in ourselves' (p. 142). As the passage goes on ('Fish had faith, she reasoned') it makes a series of references to the Mrs Moore of *A Passage to India* (that remarkable lady who made contact with India in the mosque, 'between the acts' of *Cousin Kate*, as she says – p. 32): in Lucy's mysticism, her image of beauty as a sea on which our leaky boats float (cf. 'Temple'), and in Bart's opposition as the torch of reason carried 'till it went out in the darkness of the cave'. But, just as Mrs Moore leaves the stage of Forster's novel for her own enigmatic salvation, so Lucy Swithin, with her cross, has little to say to help the active characters in the novel such as Isa and William. Certainly she has one of the few warm moments of communion in the novel when she goes backstage to Miss La Trobe:

> She gazed at Miss La Trobe with a cloudless old-aged stare. Their eyes met in a common effort to bring a common meaning to birth. They failed; and Mrs Swithin, laying hold desperately of a fraction of her meaning, said: 'What a small part I've had to play! But you've made me feel I could have played ... Cleopatra!' (p. 107)

It is Miss La Trobe's moment of glory, too – the moment when author and reader alike sense limitless opportunities for the imagination.

But that moment is of little help to the actors in the real world of emotions and plots. How is Isa to cope with a husband she hates who uses a pageant to arrange a quick assignation in the shrubbery? Even Mr Streatfield's sermon, 'Each is part of the whole . . . surely, we should unite?' (pp. 133–4) is destroyed first by the mercenary plea for money for electric lighting in the church (though the church may be more and more empty), and second, in the very moment of his appeal, by the flight of twelve aeroplanes. They burst onto the scene and vanish in a few lines, but they leave the audience gaping and their sound is described by Woolf, '*That* was the music.' That indeed is the real music of the world, not the harmonising strains of Miss La Trobe's gramophone but the blare of weapons of war, mocking the call to unity and celebration. The aeroplanes, and not the villagers at one with nature, are the culminating point of British history. The endless cycle of love and hate, aggression and empire, is turning one more cog.

Public and private worlds are deftly interwoven by Woolf at the end of the pageant. Just as Miss La Trobe confronts her audience with mirror images, so Woolf confronts her readers with the political horror of the present moment, tearing them away from the pleasantries of the picnic scene and the depiction of the League of Nations. At the same time, the public world is seen as the private stage writ large. This, effectively, has been the structure of the whole novel, alternating between communal telling of the nation's story and the novelist's account of the relationships between a small group of people in an English country house. So the League of Nations is juxtaposed with a children's nursery rhyme which accounts for its collapse by referring to the timeless, personal motivations of greed and sexual conflict:

> *The King is in his counting house,*
> *Counting out his money,*
> *The Queen is in her parlour . . .* (p. 126)

Between the Acts presents a world of people reacting to the emotions of themselves or the group. 'Reality is too strong' for them, as Miss La Trobe observes during the ten minutes of present time. The moment is saved only by a shower of rain, which people can react to simply by erecting parasols, or emotionally, as Isa does, by indulging in the emotions of the pathetic fallacy – 'O that our human pain could here have ending!' (p. 126). But even Isa is harbouring a secret passion for another man. Only Mrs Manresa lives actively and openly in the world of emotions, which is why she is not thrown by the mirror scene.

Poor Miss La Trobe judges that her pageant was a failure. She had tried to confront her audience with the truth that while they inherit a glorious past they are responsible for the present, here and now. They must not simply react but take charge and act. She had attempted to convey her message with the whole panoply of literary forms; then with silence; then with the audience itself. She judges that the message has not got across, and so she goes off to the pub, rejecting words as shrewd Bart observes: 'What she wanted, like that carp . . . was darkness in the mud; a whisky and soda at the pub; and coarse words descending like maggots through the waters' (p. 141). So we see her at the end of the novel listening to the sounds of 'words without meaning – wonderful words':

> The cheap clock ticked; smoke obscured the pictures. . . . There was the high ground at midnight; there the rock; and two scarcely perceptible figures. Suddenly the tree was pelted with starlings. She set down her glass. She heard the first words.   (p. 147)

Miss La Trobe realises that words are only the sounds of emotion being communicated, from person to person. Like the 'quivering cacophony, a whizz and vibrant rapture, branches, leaves, birds syllabling discordantly life, life, life, without measure, without stop' (p. 145) which she had heard at the house, the words which human beings use may be abstracted as 'love' and 'hate', and set down by a writer or a theatre director. But they are, for the user, simply a way of acting, of existing in the present and creating the future.

Giles, for all his nasty behaviour, has been aware of this truth all day. During coffee he felt,

> 'We remain seated.' – 'We are the audience.' Words this after-noon ceased to lie flat in the sentence. They rose, became menacing, and shook their fists at you. This afternoon he wasn't Giles Oliver come to see the villagers act their annual pageant; manacled to a rock he was, and forced passively to

behold indescribable horror. His face showed it; and Isa, not knowing what to say, abruptly, half purposely, knocked over a coffee cup.   (p. 46)

Like Conrad's Kurtz, Giles has seen the 'horror' – whether it be human depravity in himself, or the political storm clouds in Europe – but in a typically modern way he cannot describe it and Isa can say nothing. Her action of smashing the crockery is echoed later when Giles stamps on the hideous tangle in the grass. This is one of the most grotesque images in all of Woolf's fiction. As the 'planes sum up in a perfectly oblique fashion the whole historical situation, so the snake and toad are perfect objective correlatives for the horror, for the preverbal natural warfare between species (and, perhaps, between the sexes):

There, couched in the grass, curled in an olive green ring, was a snake. Dead? No, choked with a toad in his mouth. The snake was unable to swallow; the toad was unable to die. A spasm made the ribs contract; blood oozed. It was birth the wrong way round – a monstrous inversion. So, raising his foot, he stamped on them. The mass crushed and slithered. The white canvas on his tennis shoes was bloodstained and sticky. But it was action.   (p. 73)

If this was Woolf's vision of her world, it was bleak indeed. Equally bleak, from the evidence of *Between the Acts*, appeared to be her faith in her art. I have shown how painting, books and music all fail to communicate beauty or unity to the cast of the novel. Lily Briscoe succeeded in embodying her vision in an abstract painting, and Woolf too there completed her plan. But the artist in this novel is a theatre director, involved with recalcitrant actors and the drama of human life rather than the 'pure' world of pigment and line. Miss La Trobe curses her audience when they cannot become the play during the silence – 'O to write a play without an audience – *the* play' (p. 125). The impulse to give up her audience must have been very strong in Woolf's mind, too, as she wrote this novel. One feels more than ever an anti-novel, bristling with the self-destructing devices so popular in post-modernist fiction. Like the gramophone it chuff-chuffs along, long passages of inconsequential dialogue interrupted by obscure, unconnected imagery – all in a crabbed, thin style.

But does Woolf commit the mistake of confusing her vehicle with her tenor; of creating scraps, orts and fragments to convey a vision of scraps, orts and fragments? The evidence of her diaries and a close reading of the novel would answer no. The novel, consisting as it does of large chunks of another literary form – the pageant – and examining the place of music, books and paintings in people's lives, is a demonstration of the inability of all art to embody the drama of human confrontation, Isa's 'love and hate', Giles's snake and toad. Near the end of the novel Lucy Swithin stands on the stairs 'by the great picture of Venice – school of Canaletto. Possibly in the hood of the gondola there was a little figure – a woman; veiled; or a man?' (p. 149). Painting can record architecture and light, but not the mysteries of the love story of a man and a woman (even Woolf's favourite Sickert in his famous *Ennui* [Plate 23]). It can provide a setting and a memory, no more. But that is not the only irony of the moment. When Lucy 'returns from her voyage into the picture' she stands in the evening light, looking 'like a tragic figure from another play'. Lucy herself, seen by the reader or the artist, becomes an object to be moved about from this novel (where she is a mild old Christian lady) to a tragic play. With the flick of a switch or an eye, another setting could be arranged. But would we ever really be able to know how Lucy became either a tragic lady or a sweet Christian, through any art?

With the achievements of Mrs Dalloway and Mrs Ramsay behind her, one might expect Woolf to say, 'Yes, through my own rendition of subjective consciousness an audience may learn how a character loved and hated.' Possibly; but in *Between the Acts* Woolf is addressing herself to the interactions of human beings, those constant shiftings and modifications of consciousness which occur in relationship with someone you love or hate. About those, she admits in the last lines, she must keep silent. All she can do is to suggest that how we do behave with those close to us shapes nations and world wars. The connection is direct, profound, and startling. Yesterday's *Times* article uses the usual lying words to assure us that we shall be whole and have no aeroplanes to vex us. *Between the Acts*, through its many pauses and gaps (like the pauses in the modern drama of Pinter and Beckett), points the reader to the disturbing truth. Yet, at the same time as it torpedoes art in the pageant, it is a triumph of artifice in itself. The psychological volumes of Giles and Isa, so carefully built up during the novel, are placed on a rock in the last line and left to history. The whole novel, we now see, is a pause between the acts of love and hate which determine the world but which must remain private to every one of us.

Nancy Bazin argues ingeniously for *Between the Acts* not as a novel which laments its own limitations, but as the supreme achievement in Woolf's lifelong effort to create an art novel. She argues that Woolf is like Miss La Trobe, refusing to explicate, creating instead a pageant of effects to please all the senses:

> Woolf is more silent than she was in her other works. That is, the reader now receives less guidance from her than he previously did (for example, there is no principal spokesman for the author like Bernard or Lily Briscoe); therefore, the reader must seek more actively than before to find out what the novel is about. . . . Thus, the reader can 'see' the pageant much as he would see a 'silent painting', that is, in terms of colors and patterns. [136]

Although this reading would seem a suitable climax to my own approach to Woolf, and a justification of the aesthetic viewpoint, I think it confuses art and reality. *Between the Acts*, in its very title, points beyond itself to what it cannot adequately comprehend and communicate. It provides a setting for human activity in space and time, but does not rest with itself as an abstraction. It is deliberately incomplete, a thing of scraps and fragments not welded into a watertight whole.

Woolf's dissatisfaction with her sister's art, however much she envied the serenity and purity of the painter's way of life, remained right until her death. Indeed, the suicide itself can be seen as a statement that art cannot provide salvation or even an alternative to the business of living. The chuff-chuff of art has nothing to contribute to what Isa and Giles will speak.

Conclusion

The best critics . . . wrote of literature with music and painting in their minds. [1]

It is so tempting, even to those with no aesthetic axe to grind, to see in an artist's oeuvre the beauty and completion which were perhaps denied to their individual productions. *Between the Acts* can be seen as Woolf's swansong, her farewell to an art form which failed her just as the villagers, cows, gramophone and audience failed Miss La Trobe. It is difficult to imagine a successor to that novel; but then, it is just as difficult to imagine successors to Woolf's previous novels. Forster's *A Passage to India* is perhaps more understandably a final novel, not simply from the evidence of the author's subsequent silence.

For one can find the germ of *Between the Acts* almost forty years previously, when Woolf had not yet contemplated her first novel. In a letter of 1902 she imagined 'a man and woman coming nearer and nearer and never meeting'. [2] At this earlier age Woolf demonstrated that acute sense of art's limitations and its necessary reticence which remained with her throughout her life. In 1906 she complained in a similar vein, 'Don't you think the flesh is a cumbersome illustration, and the text is all written or spoken in half a dozen words?' [3] It is no wonder that this recoil from life, the stuff of fiction, to the one symbolic image and pattern prompted Woolf to become 'an artist to the public'. Fortunately for literature, her sister assumed that role and Woolf turned back to words, but always with a nostalgia and at times real envy for the simplicities of painting.

After exploring bravely the intricacies of lived experience in several novels, Woolf returned to her early fascination with structure and the non-human world of shape, colour and sound, in *Between the Acts*. It is a turning-away from the human activity of *The Voyage Out*, *To the Lighthouse* and *The Years*, to the sensuous patterns which form the setting for action in *Jacob's Room*, *Mrs Dalloway*, and the interludes in *The Waves*. Between the activities

217

of people, even those activities which take place between the acts of a pageant – between these activities fall the shadows and silences, sights and sounds out of which we weave our human worlds. And the novelist cannot hope to weave this unravelled sleeve back into a work of art.

Whatever one's imaginings might be about the future development of Woolf's art beyond *Between the Acts*, it is essential to recognise that by this point her command of form, rhythm, pattern in the novel had reached such a sophisticated point that she was able to 'play' with the possibility of form itself. All great artists reach this point in their art, as do all the media. (Film, being an immediate and comparatively crude art form, did not take long to reach the point where film-makers were making films about people making films, exposing the artifice of celluloid, and so on.) We must not apply the principles of aesthetic unity, which worked so well with *To the Lighthouse*, to this last novel. Critics such as Mary Shanahan, who talk about 'kinetic harmony' in the novel, weave an uplifting unity which has nothing to do with Woolf's creation:

> The ultimate end of Woolf's little 'entertainment' projects a pattern expansive enough, as it subsumes history and art, to comprehend, if not to reconcile, the chaos and the violence of the world around her – for Miss La Trobe's play (and, thus, Virginia Woolf's novel) has emerged at once the product and the mirror of civilization.[4]

As I have argued, the crucial difference between Woolf's last novel and Forster's is that Woolf seems consciously to use the limitations of her craft to open up further, more profound vistas. *A Passage to India* starts out to build up a fairly obvious aesthetic shape, a triad, but then abandons the endeavour in the last section with a vehemence which undermines the whole artistic process. In my discussion of the novel I did not go over the many and varied accounts of the triadic unity of the novel, from Forster's own 'cold weather – hot weather – rains' to Hegelian dialectic and sonata form, because I do not believe tht these familiar conceptions take us very far into the heart of the novel's meaning. Even R. Cammarota, skilfully applying the sonata or 'ternary form' pattern *within* each of the three sections, fails to illuminate the developing emotional climate of the novel.[5] This is because all these aesthetic formulae presuppose a 'rage for order' and demand a musical resolution for satisfaction; and *A Passage to India* resolutely refuses to close any doors or set any minds at rest.

I have dwelt on the end points in the development of these two novelists because I think Woolf and Forster exemplify two artistic responses to the Moorean vision of early Bloomsbury, which in later years have become incorporated into two large camps of fiction criticism. Moore, you will remember, posited two things good in themselves: friendship, and the appreciation of beautiful objects. Together these goods went towards the establishment of civilisation. Now, to put it crudely, Forster's novels are studies of friendship, and the essential element in the business of fiction for him is the friendship between writer and reader; Woolf's novels are studies of how to contemplate (aesthetically) the world, and the essential element in the business of fiction for her is the novel as a beautiful object. Of course this is a crude division, because both writers agreed on the importance of art and civilisation, and the constituents of that civilisation. But there is a fundamental difference in their conceptions of what a novel is and what the reading-process is, which divides them as surely as this book falls into two halves.

This distinction may be put neatly in a painterly way with reference to Clive Bell's essay on Duncan Grant. 'There is something Greek about him,' says Bell, 'that romantic, sensuous Hellenism of the English literary tradition.'[6] This sounds very much like Forster, as does Bell's sense of 'something fantastic and whimsical and at the same time intensely lyrical'. But the 'artistic integrity' which Grant also possesses, and which takes him from the front rank of English painters to the company of Cézanne, Matisse and Picasso, reminds one of Woolf:

An artist must be able to convert his inspiration into significant form; for in art it is not from a word to a blow, but from a tremulous, excited vision to an orderly mental conception, and from that conception, by means of the problem and with the help of technique, to externalisation in form.[7]

I have shown the slow evolution of Woolf's technical expertise in converting inspiration into significant form, through the two early novels to the frame of *Jacob's Room* and the luminous halo which is *Mrs Dalloway*. In the very image of that famous manifesto, Woolf suggests that life, while it may not be symmetrically arranged, does compose itself for each of us in a circular shape or halo. But, even in that novel which has for its title the name of the central character, Woolf was aware of two other areas which must be given shape by herself as novelist: the social world around Clarissa, and the reader's aesthetic reaction to the novel. So she gathered the novel together at the end not into Clarissa alone but into a party, about which she noted in her diary,

> A general view of the world.
> The different groups:
> All sketched in.[8]

This artistic approach to the social gathering extends also to her consciousness of the reader working his way through the disparate elements of the story. In the introduction to the American edition of *Mrs Dalloway* Woolf talked about 'the effect of the book as a whole', and surrendered to the aesthetic appreciation of the reader – spectator – 'Given time and liberty to *frame* his own opinion he is eventually an infallible judge' (italics added).

As her novels widen to take in not just central characters but also communities, the onus on the reader to respond to the 'whole' novel and compose it into some aesthetic order becomes more demanding. Even in *To the Lighthouse*, her novel with the strongest sense of a simple plot – 'will James get to the lighthouse?' – we never limit ourselves to that question, but are directed to share with Lily the problem of composing the Ramsay family, alive and dead, into a whole. And even *The Years*, that most unwieldy of aesthetic wholes, was described by Woolf in a letter to Stephen Spender in 1937 almost totally in spatial, painterly terms:

> to give a picture of society as a whole; to give characters from every side; turn them towards society, not private life; exhibit the effect of ceremonies; keep one toe on the ground by means of dates, facts; evvelop the whole in a changing temporal atmosphere; compose into one vast many-sided group at the end; and then shift the stress from present to future.[9]

She did lament that she had 'altogether muffed the proportions', but I have found there a pattern which reverberates richly with the apparent progress of time. Such a sophisticated aesthetic response is necessary to Woolf's novels, otherwise one falls into the kind of trap which Ortega y Gasset finds himself in when he complains that *The Years* seems hopelessly stranded between genres: 'The author falsifies the historical facts by bringing them too near to us and weakens the novel by removing it too far away from us toward the abstract plane of historical truth.'[10] We cannot approach a Woolf novel in such an 'either – or' frame of mind, just as we cannot approach a Post-Impressionist canvas looking for either design or representation.

Woolf's novels become increasingly ambitious in scope – both in breadth of history and cast of characters – as her focus moves from the epiphanic moments of her characters to the possibility of the reader having an epiphanic moment upon completion of the novel. This is why one must always distinguish the reader's journey from the discoveries of the characters. These two aspects of the novel have often been confused, resulting in, for example, an unwarranted emphasis on the element of time and the influence of Bergson in Woolf. D. S. Savage goes so far as to condemn the later novels for their 'disintegration of form expressing a surrender of all significance to the accidental process of time'.[11] But time is significant in her novels only in so far as it relates to the reader's progression from the beginning of the novel to the end, and even that is more properly imaged as a development of the painting in space. Clive Bell wrote of Proust bringing the past into the present and 'creating a shape not in space but in time . . . situations unfold themselves not like flowers even but like tunes'.[12] Such a description might well apply not to the world of Woolf's novels, but to the experience of reading them. Similarly, Leonard Woolf is reported as saying that the human personality is like a thread with our various selves hanging on it like beads.[13] Those beads would constitute Woolf's characters as we see them, moment by moment, but our privilege as readers is to see the complete thread, and in relation to other threads composing a completed tapestry.

Indeed, the experience of time rendered subjectively was of little interest to Woolf. She would eagerly devote herself to a section called 'Time Passes', but that section has no people in it. The new novel as she saw it would be dramatic, juxtaposing rather than suggesting the sequential stream: 'Instead of enumerating details he [the new novelist] will mould blocks.'[14] Woolf even looked ahead to film when she wrote with prescience of the cinematic devices of cutting and collage: 'The gulfs which dislocate novels . . . could by the sameness of the background, by the repetition of some scene, be smoothed away.'[15] Even when it came to the analysis of individual moments, she favoured the precision of a spatial rather than a temporal exploration: 'Roger Fry's criticism has something of the enthralment of a novel . . . as exciting as the analysis by a master novelist of the human passions – the analysis of our sensations. It is as if a great magnifying glass were laid over the picture.'[16]

Woolf constantly referred to the novel as an object which one could examine at leisure. In *A Room of One's Own* she talked about the 'spider web' of fiction, lightly attached at four corners to life. The novel holds things together and holds scenes up to the light so one can see them translucently; even sentences individually build 'into arcades or domes'.[17] One of her most vivid images for the novel as a thing of structure is her description of the reality which the novel conjures up – 'this: what remains over when the skin of the day has been cast into the hedge'.[18] She relished the spatiality of the novel exactly because she felt so acutely the transitoriness of life:

> Now is life very solid or very shifting? I am haunted by the two contradictions. This has gone on for ever: will last for ever; goes down to the bottom of the world – this moment I stand on. Also it is transitory, flying, diaphanous. I shall pass like a cloud on the waves. Perhaps it may be that though we change; one flying after another so quick so quick, yet we are somehow successive, and continuous – we human beings; and show the light through. But what is the light? I am impressed by the transitoriness of human life to such an extent that I am often saying a farewell – after dining with Roger for instance; or reckoning how many more times I shall see Nessa.[19]

'What remains over' is now a different order of reality, and the mention here of Fry and Bell reminds us of Woolf's envy of the painters and their medium (cf. Vanessa Bell's easy reconciliation of life – the flowers – and pattern in the dust-jacket for *A Writer's Diary* [Plate 24]). Space has not permitted a close examination of Woolf's language, but my conclusion is that her language is not as transparent as some critics would lead us to believe. I rarely feel when reading a piece of so-called 'stream of consciousness' writing in Woolf the kind of shock of shared experience that one gets in Joyce's *Ulysses*, for example. Her style is uniformly (and most markedly in *The Waves*) elegant, often complicated in syntax, precise. In 1913 Fry wrote to Dickinson, 'In proportion as poetry becomes more intense the content is entirely remade by the form and has no separate value at all. You see the sense of poetry is analogous to the things represented in painting.'[20] Woolf followed Fry's ideal of poetic language and avoided what he called that 'hybrid art' of sense and illustration which refers to the everyday world. *The Mark on the Wall* was her first successful experiment in this style, and Fry was one of the first to congratulate her:

> You're the only one now Henry James is gone who uses language as a medium of art, who makes the very texture of the words have a meaning and quality really almost apart from what you are talking about. Nearly all the other good writers have something of rhetoric however hidden beneath reserve and good taste.[21]

Woolf uses language as a painter uses paint, then, having a relationship primarily with the colours or words next to it and in the canvas as a whole. Whether one can go far with any real illumination in analysing Woolf's prose from this perspective is debatable. Certainly I find the following example, excellent of its kind, only minimally helpful:

> Woolf's flat surfaces of juxtaposed touches open onto space and we see a scooped-out space, which calls to mind Seurat's own definition of his art as hollowing out the canvas. Woolf also combines effects of closeness, flatness, volume, and distance: this corresponds in her world to the impressionists' recreation of the moment, the post-impressionists' depth of characterization, and a reduction to contours. As Woolf's characters recede in the distance and become reduced to points, linear patterns of relationship emerge. This latter aspect is most characteristic of Woolf's later work.[22]

The danger of such a description, as with those which see novels musically, is that it reduces one art into the grossest elements of another. Woolf may have been able to write of her great-aunt, the pioneer photographer Julia Margaret Cameron, 'Painters praised her art; writers marvelled at the characters her portraits revealed';[23] but such an approach to her own novels splits them in an unsatisfactory dichotomy. This is why my analyses have remained general, referring to structure and theme rather than to style.

Woolf described Fry's painterly approach to fiction in her biography with admiration and just a touch of criticism:

> As a critic of literature . . . he looked at the carpet from the wrong side; but he made it for that very reason display unexpected patterns. And many of his theories held good for both arts. Design, rhythm, texture, there they were again – in Flaubert as in Cézanne. And he would hold up a book to the light as if it were a picture and show where in his view – it was a painter's of course – it fell short.[24]

E. M. Forster's approach as a critic was always to hold a book up to life, not the light. Of a Beresford novel he complained that the symbolism was too neat and should be turned upside down – 'It happens quite often in life, and might lead to clearness of vision in art.'[25] A bad novel 'may have the coherence of logic, it will never have the coherence of life'.[26] When he was able to respond to the beauty of a work, as with Chekhov's stories, there remained a sense of dissatisfaction at the segment of life selected for treatment; the Russian was too sad for Forster.

As I have shown in my analysis of Forster's novels, art itself is, as Alan Wilde puts it, 'a force for the bad'.[27] Painting is especially destructive, suggesting as it does detachment and distance; but music is the least objectionable art since it at least involves performance by one individual and appreciation by another. Even in the later essays, when, in the face of Fascism, Forster was busy defending art and artists, it is not so much the art object as the act of creation itself which is valued. The reader of a novel has the supreme experience when he relives the creative act of the novelist. Always for Forster it is life or people first, and art second.

Because the characters in the novels themselves are always seeking enlightenment (the heroes and heroines at any rate), their epiphanies and successes may be seen as artistic achievements:

His novels imply but never catagorically assert a connection between the transfiguring acts of consciousness enjoyed by some of the characters, as they struggle to harmonise the disparate elements of their experience, and the unifying process of the literary imagination. [28]

But we are never taken through these experiences of Forster's heroes from the inside; Forster's literary genius did not take him in that direction. Instead, those experiences gain extra significance for the reader because he can place them in a temporal context. This, however, makes for a different kind of experience altogether. The 'eternal moment' batters and changes a Forsterian character, but reading a Forster novel will not overwhelm a reader in the same way. It might give him a theoretical appreciation of what is needed to live a full life, and he might be better prepared to accept such a moment if it comes to him. But the two experiences are radically different, and it is this difference which is slurred over in Glen Cavaliero's otherwise thoughtful summation:

> Although what Forster specifically deals with is 'the eternal moment', in doing so he organises his novels in a pattern of symbolism that implies a whole series of 'living moments' related to an overall design that, as art, has a permanent significance. The visionary moment or epiphany is for him a call to life, not merely an object of static contemplation; and his characters have to learn to realise it as such. [29]

That phrase 'permanent significance' is dangerously vague, because there can be no doubt that the reader is intended to be changed by a Forster novel. And having changed he will no longer need the message of that novel. Forster's readers, like his characters, have to learn to realise his novels as calls to life. At their worst, his novels are like those Victorian tomes which Woolf talks about, requiring one to *do* something – write a cheque, for example – in order to complete them. At their best they are parables whose shape almost approximates a work of art.

Critics talk about the balance in Forster's novels. Austin Warren observes that for Forster 'the novel has its own function, that of a persuasive equilibrium: it must balance the claims of the existence and the essence, of personalities and ideas'. [30] And the

elusive Forsterian tone has often been noted: 'Forster expands
and shrinks the aesthetic distance in a tantalising movement of involvement and disengagement, of love and scorn.' But a better
word than 'balance' would be 'non-commitment', serving to
underline Forster's self-doubt as an artist and his concentration
always on the reader rather than on the thing read. It is paradoxical that a writer whose novels are so clearly spatialised in terms of
patterns, rhythms and triple divisions, and who is so much in control of his point of view and tone, should write such unartistic
books. But it is inevitable when one considers his suspicion of all
the arts and his love of friendship, which is seen in one of its most
beautiful, intense versions in the relationship of writer to reader.
Hence the world of *Howards End* is almost crudely joined together,
'but it is badly soldered'.[31] The most moving thing about that
novel is not in the text at all, but in the author's appeal to the
reader in the epigraph, 'Only connect ...'.

It is perhaps ironic that in Forster's last novel, *A Passage to
India*, where the theme of non-connection would not at all be
undermined by the formal completion of the three parts, he still
instinctively destroys the aesthetic object. Recognising this unnecessary strategy he said in hindsight, 'I needed a lump. . . .
But there ought to be more after it.'[32] Those words of the sculptor
are reminiscent of Forster's obvious antipathy to the non-
symmetrical, plot elements of fiction when he made his famous
remark, 'Yes – oh dear yes – the novel must tell a story.' But
together these comments also point to Forster's (perhaps
deliberate) simplistic understanding when it came to the possible
aesthetic dimensions of the arts. He admitted his feelings of inadequacy in the presence of Roger Fry. One can imagine what he
would think of such sophisticated elaborations of aesthetic theory
as Mauron's psychological volumes. It is really not surprising that
he should consider Woolf's aesthetic triumphs as a row of little
silver cups.

It might be objected that Forster did indeed write artistic
novels, but that they were modelled on music rather than on painting. The musical approach to Forster has been encouraged by his
own espousal of both arts. John Rosselli, for example, says,
'Forster's secret is that he is at once moralist and musician. In a
literal sense he loved music, played it, and wrote about it keenly.
His novels must mean little to those who have no sense of musical
structure in writing.'[33] But it seems to me that the musical
analogies exist only in the crudest sense of movements and

repeated imagery, spatial ideas which could be equally well arrived at from the fine-art analogy. The main sense of temporal development in a Forster novel is never in the transcendent musical realm of modulation, variation and recapitulation, but in the very human realm of the parable or morality play. It is the story which carries the meaning, the desserts meted out to the representatives of various moralities, and the patterns of rhythm and imagery merely reinforce this. Forster's idea of music in his novels is in terms of clearly programmed goblins. Real music, the kind of musical shape the critics would like to see in his novels, remains outside them, to be sung by characters to themselves during their most exalted moments or to exist beyond everyone but the singer – like the song of the Bedouin who sings tunes to his camel 'that he can only sing to the camel, because in his mind the tune and the camel are the same thing'.[34]

In *Aspects of the Novel*, of course, Forster does argue that music 'does offer in its final expression a type of beauty which fiction might achieve in its own way'.[35] The example he uses is the symphony of *War and Peace*, and the final effect is one of 'expansion'. But this expansion does not occur within the work. It is not resonance which he has in mind but a kind of spilling-over. The elements of the novel are 'liberated' from their aesthetic place; the chords which begin to sound behind us as we read are important because they are affecting us in our own lives; and the items which 'lead a larger existence than was possible at the time' lead an existence beyond the work of art in the more important world of the reader's ongoing personal experience. Even when Forster does refer to symphonic form, it is to show that the form of the novel may break the barrier between art and life and cast us back into life illuminated. That final return is all-important for Forster. As F. McDowell concludes an analysis of his theory of literature, 'Though art matters, it is not all that matters.'[36]

Since what Forster most objects to in painting is the square frame which divides off that world from this, a final comparison might be made between him and Woolf in terms of the endings of novels, for it is there that the frame completes its ringing around, or is deliberately shattered.

In 'How Should One Read a Book?' Woolf argues that there are two distinct phases in the reading-process: first, the receiving of impressions; secondly, the judging of those impressions – 'we must make of these fleeting shapes one that is hard and lasting'.[37]

The imagery of Roger Fry, painter or art critic, abounds in the essay as Woolf goes on to describe how 'we see the shape from start to finish. . . . There they hang in the mind, the shapes of the books we have read solidified by the judgements we have passed on them . . . we shall give books names and thus *frame* a rule that brings order into our perceptions' (italics added). Now, when Forster comes to summarise Woolf's essay, he typically reduces her aesthetic concern to a question of relationship with the creator: 'The first time she abandoned herself to the author unreservedly. The second time she treated him with severity and allowed him to get away with nothing he could not justify.'[38]

Forster goes on to say that 'we ought to look at the book in two ways at once', a feat that is more easily achieved in listening to music. There one can unite 'architecture and sequence'. But it is just this crude split which separates Woolf from Forster. Her account does *not* involve two readings, but rather one reading and then a time of gestation before the novel returns 'without our willing it' as a whole. She does indeed acknowledge that 'we hate and we love' the novelist, but through wide reading certain aesthetic preferences will emerge independent of personalities. Forster, on the other hand, ends his essay 'The Raison d'Être of Criticism in the Arts', 'we must come back to love. That alone raises us to the cooperation with the artist which is the sole reason for our aesthetic pilgrimage.'

Forster can conceive of architecture and sequence being truly united only in music. When it comes to fiction, he finds the gulf too wide between the structure of, say, three large sections, and the ongoing relationship between author and reader as the author builds up a sequence of value judgements about what is happening, and asks the reader to agree with him. Having to choose one side to stand on, he chooses the side of love, the conversation with the reader. As a result we have a novelist whose novels *appear* to be paradigms of significant form, with patterns of imagery, rhythms and broad structures, but whose very texture undermines those patterns and is indeed at war with them. We have such a novel as *A Room with a View*, with two books and a happy ending, but its author is prepared in 1958 to tell us what has since happened to all the principal characters.

That sense of ongoing life spilling out of the novel in the form of real characters or a real author who goes on living and changing, is totally remote from Woolf's fiction. When she finishes *Between the Acts* with Giles and Isa about to speak, it is not for us to write our own postscript or to curse her for stopping too soon. We must see that gesture as the completion of the frame, the last piece in the jigsaw which is what has gone before. Her characters do not live beyond her books. Indeed, the very distinctions between flat and round characters and life and art are inappropriate within her fictions. Nor is Woolf present in her novels as fellow sufferer; the issues the narrative voice occasionally raises are to find resonance within the frame of that novel, not to be taken outside it into the common room.

Forster's antipathy to pictorial art probably need not be laboured. In 1959 he readily admitted, 'I am weak on pictorial art.'[39] But I hope the context of this discussion of his achievement has not therefore denigrated it. His novels are as fascinating for their rhetorical use of paintings, the possibilities of significant form and the final denial of it, as Woolf's are for their triumphant assertion of its power. Together Forster and Woolf show that awareness of the reading-process that underpins so much contemporary fiction theory and practice. My approach to their novels may have seemed at times limited to a particular thesis, but I hope I have shown that the work of their contemporaries in aesthetic theory affected both novelists profoundly. I also hope that my sequential study of their novels reminds us, once again, that both Forster and Woolf followed the example of Roger Fry in attempting new solutions and fresh equations in each new novel. In her biography Woolf admired Fry's avoidance of repetition, 'the fate that attends so many artists, both in paint and in life'.[40]

Of Woolf's critical writing Mark Goldman has said, 'Her criticism involves a basic counterpoint of form and feeling, art and emotion – saving her from a critical nihilism on the one hand and a rigid, systematic aesthetic on the other.'[41] I have tried to avoid the same traps and achieve the same counterpoint in my analysis of Woolf's and Forster's novels, but the task is not an easy one. The translation of words to pictures and vice versa is fraught with difficulties, as Woolf pointed out in her 1925 essay 'Pictures'. There she admits that the modern age has certainly seen a close dialogue between literature and painting: 'Were all modern paintings to be destroyed, a critic of the twenty-fifth century would be able to deduce from the works of Proust alone the existence of Matisse, Cézanne, Derain, and Picasso . . . .'[42] But the modern writer, besides using his outward eye to 'fertilise' his thought, employs a third eye which penetrates below the surface into the 'cave of darkness'[43] which is the subconscious. This is a different vision from the painter's, this effort to make sense of the human soul, and words alone can do it. The best painters, such as Cézanne and Sickert, are silent, and 'make fools of us [writers] as often as they choose'.[44]

Woolf employs the image of the mackerel in the aquarium to depict the painter who lives in a medium quite alien to our verbal one. Occasionally the mackerel may tap on the dividing glass wall – 'Matisse taps, Derain taps, Mr Grant taps; Picasso, Sickert, Mrs Bell, on the other hand, are all mute as mackerel'.[45] Here Woolf adroitly displays her aesthetic acumen, well learnt from her master, Roger Fry, exalting the exponents of pure form and ranking with them her sister, leaving the whimsical illustrator Duncan Grant with the 'tappers'. Although she ends the essay with a rueful reference to Fry and the 'exquisite torture' of standing before a painting with such a lecturer, Woolf's sympathy is clearly with him and with the clearsighted division between artistic genres. The tappers may appeal to the literary, but the image is so grotesquely crude that the author's sympathies are clear.

One can turn this image around and apply it to writers, too, and produce a neat image with which to summarise the findings of this study. Forster the novelist, no matter how cleverly he arranges his world, is not content to let his characters and the narrative persona swim about in the imaginative medium; he must tap on the glass and catch the viewer's attention, addressing himself to the ear as well as to the eye. Woolf, on the other hand, particularly in the novels which followed in the fifteen years after the 'Pictures' essay, lets her characters swim mutely. Every so often there is a vertical movement: a fin will break the waste of waters, but only to signify the uncertainty of a character's 'level' of existence and his relationship with the other fish in the tank. If any pattern of movement is to be seen, it is in the occasional orchestrated movement as if the fish come together momentarily as a school (Forster's patterning would be the equally occasional minuet of two fish alone). For the most part, Woolf's characters drift mutely about before our eyes. The artistry in all this comes not in the synchronised grace of the swimming, but in the beautiful shape of the containing bowl which gives its own pattern to the contents, however obliquely. In counterpoint to the struggling lives, her bowls – her novels – are not golden, but semi-transparent, bestowing a momentary meaning to the viewer not in words, but in the significant form of a halo.

This halo effect is produced in Woolf's novels by the texture of words, phrases and paragraphs, as well as by the over-arching design. Fry's description of poetic language (which I quoted in chapter 1) as 'emotion aroused by rhythmic changes of states of mind due to the meanings of the words' applies perfectly to her mature style. To return to the two figures at the end of her last novel: we recognise the 'inevitable sequences' (Fry's term again) of Giles and Isa's marriage, and what is more, we recognise their pattern as common to all human life in some general way of connection and separation. Compare this with the situation of Forster's two characters at the end of his last novel: Aziz and Fielding are also dear friends estranged, but we cannot predict their future. Their separation, while caused by political and national differences in turn based on the most profound religious differences, does not in itself touch (in Fry's phrase) 'the substratum of all the emotional colours of life'. We cannot predict what will happen to them, just as there seems no inevitability within the novel of their estrangement. The rocks and hills, those physical surroundings with which Woolf's characters are in constant interaction, are for Forster only divisive. His early heroes tried to merge with the physical environment, his later ones with each other. Like his artistic point of view, the aspirations of Forster's main characters are extreme and dialectical: 'I am here, you are there; we are here, the world is there; I the author am here, you the reader are there – if we could but connect!' So Forster's novels tap out at us, convinced (as Clive Bell put it) that there is 'some more ultimate harmony' out there, some 'all-pervading rhythm'. We must search for it out there, says Forster, not satisfied with the idea that the glass itself and the convolutions of his characters might simply mirror perfectly the age-old workings of the human soul. Yet different as they were in intention and technique, both Forster and Woolf found in the aesthetics of Bloomsbury, in the resonance between significance and form, the perfect frame for their activity. The ancient definition of poetry as a 'speaking picture' was refined through the efforts of Fry, Bell and Mauron, and the examples of James and Proust. Manipulation of the element of time, both in the lives of the characters and in the reading-process, became the key.

Forster began with Italian novels which cross-examine aesthetics and find it wanting. The simple binary frame of *Where Angels Fear to Tread* is abandoned for the ongoing parable of *A Room with a View*. *The Longest Journey*, *Howards End* and *Maurice* all convey a message on the scaffolding of design; but the more Forster wants us to believe his realism, the less believable (even in the carefully submerged quartet of movements in *Howards End*) his stories become. The narrative voice mocks the very aesthetic shapes he is erecting. Only in *A Passage to India* do his contradictory impulses coincide perfectly, where the authorial message of non-communication and shapelessness is echoed by the experiences of the characters and by the land itself. Forster's earlier novels exhort the reader only to connect the moral with his own life, even though the goal seems very similar to Bell's transcendent 'ultimate reality'. In his last novel Forster sees that reality not as aesthetic ecstasy, nor as pastoral friendship; but at last he is like Bell's artist who 'does not want to act, but to understand'.

Woolf came more slowly to the idea of shaping her novels. More interested than Forster in the varieties of perception itself, she used her first two novels to explore the ways people picture themselves. In *Jacob's Room* she reached the existential chasms of *A Passage to India*, but turned her doubts into a protest and lament as moving as some of Forster's later essays. In *Mrs Dalloway* she used art and artifice (*Cymbeline* and Big Ben) to picture a society in a way which fits the psychological volume of the eponymous hostess. Lily and the reader together work through time to create what Fry would call 'a single perfectly organic aesthetic whole' in the masterpiece *To the Lighthouse*; but from this high point (including the other celebration of androgynous literary imagination, *Orlando*) Woolf turned her attention to the reading-process and the postmodernist resistance to closure: the statues of *The Waves* are washed away by Bernard's final speech; the reader wars with dissolution and the tantalising shadow of shape in her last two novels. At the ends of their careers then, the two writers are together with Fry in their recognition of the effort of artist and reader to 'express an idea' from 'intractable material'; the significance of their final forms lies in the momentary therefore illusory yet glorious sense of the understanding's triumph over time.

Notes

The following abbreviations have been used for works cited in the notes to more than one chapter:

AH	E. M. Forster, *Abinger Harvest* (Harmondsworth: Penguin, 1967).
Aspects	E. M. Forster, *Aspects of the Novel* (Harmondsworth: Penguin, 1974).
Bell	Quentin Bell, *Virginia Woolf: A Biography* (New York: Harcourt Brace Jovanovich, 1972) 2 vols in 1.
Bloomsbury Group	*The Bloomsbury Group*, ed. S. P. Rosenbaum (Toronto: University of Toronto Press, 1975).
CE	*Collected Essays of Virginia Woolf* (London: Hogarth, 1966–7) 4 vols.
Cézanne	Roger Fry, *Cézanne* (New York: Noonday, 1960).
Colmer	John Colmer, *E. M. Forster: The Personal Voice* (London: Routledge & Kegan Paul, 1975).
D	*The Diaries of Virginia Woolf*, ed. A. O. Bell (London: Hogarth, 1977–80) 3 vols.
Dehumanization of Art	J. Ortega y Gasset, *The Dehumanization of Art* (New York: Doubleday Anchor, 1956).
Fur	P. N. Furbank, *E. M. Forster: A Life* (London: Secker & Warburg, 1978) 2 vols.
Heine	Elizabeth Heine, 'The Significance of Structure in the Novels of E. M. Forster and Virginia Woolf', *English Literature in Transition*, 16 (1973).
LF	*Letters of Roger Fry*, ed. Denys Sutton (London: Chatto & Windus, 1972) 2 vols.
LW	*The Letters of Virginia Woolf*, ed. N. Nicolson and J. Trautmann (London: Hogarth, 1975–80) 6 vols.
Mallarmé	Stéphen Mallarmé, *Poems*, trs. Roger Fry, ed. Charles Mauron and Julian Bell (New York: New Directions, 1951).
Meyers	Jeffrey Meyers, *Painting and the Novel* (Manchester University Press, 1975).
Nature of Beauty	Charles Mauron, *The Nature of Beauty in Art and Literature* (London: Hogarth, 1927).
Proust	Clive Bell, *Proust* (London: Hogarth, 1928).
Roger Fry	Virginia Woolf, *Roger Fry: A Biography* (London: Hogarth, 1940).

Spalding   Frances Spalding, *Roger Fry: Art and Life* (London: Granada, 1980).
Stone   Wilfred Stone, *The Cave and the Mountain: A Study of E. M. Forster* (Stanford, Calif.: Stanford University Press, 1966; London: Oxford University Press, 1966).
Three Guineas   Virginia Woolf, *Three Guineas* (London: Hogarth, 1952).
Transformations Roger Fry, *Transformations* (New York: Brentano's, 1926).
Two Cheers   E. M. Forster, *Two Cheers for Democracy* (Harmondsworth: Penguin, 1965).
WD   Virginia Woolf, *A Writer's Diary*, ed. Leonard Woolf (London: Hogarth, 1953).

INTRODUCTION: PAINTING AND WRITING

1. Gauguin, quoted in *Impressionism and Post-Impressionism: Sources and Documents*, ed. Linda Nochlin (Englewood Cliffs, NJ: Prentice-Hall, 1966) p. 163.
2. Meyers, p. 1.
3. G. E. Lessing, *Laocoön* (London: J. M. Dent, 1930) p. 67.
4. Friedrich Schiller, *On the Aesthetic Education of Man*, ed. and trs. E. M. Wilkinson and L. A. Willoughby (Oxford: Clarendon Press, 1967) p. 156.
5. *Impressionism and Post-Impressionism*, p. 14.
6. R. Arnheim, *Art and Visual Perception* (Berkeley, Calif.: University of California Press, 1974) p. 15.
7. Ibid., p. 302.
8. Ibid., p. 378.
9. E. H. Gombrich, *Meditations on a Hobby Horse and Other Essays* (London: Phaidon, 1963) p. 153.
10. Ibid., p. 159.
11. E. H. Gombrich, *Art and Illusion* (New York: Pantheon, 1960) p. 389.
12. *Dehumanization of Art*, p. 9.
13. Solomon Fishman, *The Interpretation of Art* (Berkeley, Calif.: University of California Press, 1963) p. 98.
14. Wassily Kandinsky, 'Reminiscences', in *Modern Artists on Art*, ed. R. L. Herbert (Englewood Cliffs, NJ: Prentice-Hall, 1964) p. 39.
15. Ibid., p. 35.
16. Carol Dornell-Kotrozo, 'Cézanne and Cubism', *Journal of Aesthetic Education*, 13 (1979) 100.
17. *Impressionism and Post-Impressionism*, p. 163.
18. *Cézanne*, pp. 58–9.
19. M. Merleau-Ponty, *Sense and Non-Sense*, trs. H. L. Dreyfus and P. A. Dreyfus (Evanston: Illinois University Press, 1964) p. 14.
20. Edith Wharton, 'The Writing of Fiction', quoted in Suzanne Langer, *Feeling and Form* (London: Routledge & Kegan Paul, 1953) p. 293.
21. Larry McCaffery, 'Meaning and Non-Meaning in Barthelme's Fictions', *Journal of Aesthetic Education*, 13 (1979) 76.

22. Quoted in Jo-Ana Isaak, 'Joyce and Cubism', *Mosaic*, XIV (Winter 1981) 82.
23. René Wellek, 'Henry James's Literary Theory and Criticism', *American Literature*, XXX (1958) 312.
24. Georges Poulet, *Studies in Human Time* (Baltimore: Johns Hopkins University Press, 1956) p. 261.
25. Marcel Proust, *Time Regained*, trs. Stephen Hudson (London: Chatto & Windus, 1957) p. 247.
26. Roger Shattuck, *Proust's Binoculars* (New York: Random House, 1963) p. 51.
27. Henri Bergson, *Matter and Memory* (London: George Allen, 1913) p. 194.
28. Henri Bergson, *The Creative Mind*, trs. M. L. Andison (Westport, Conn.: Greenwood Press, 1968) p. 219.
29. Wolfgang Iser, *The Implied Reader* (Baltimore: Johns Hopkins University Press, 1974) pp. 276–88.

CHAPTER ONE: BLOOMSBURY AESTHETICS

1. Clive Bell, *Art* (New York: Capricorn, 1958) p. 17.
2. Cf. Quentin Bell, *Bloomsbury* (London: Weidenfeld & Nicolson, 1968); *Bloomsbury Group*, ed. Rosenbaum; Richard Shone, *Bloomsbury Portraits* (London: Phaidon, 1976).
3. *Bloomsbury Group*, p. 26.
4. Ibid., p. 25.
5. Clive Bell, *Art*, p. 8.
6. Ibid., p. 19.
7. Ibid., p. 28.
8. Ibid., p. 54.
9. Ibid., p. 141.
10. Ibid., pp. 30–2.
11. Ibid., p. 110.
12. Ibid., p. 68.
13. Roger Fry, *Vision and Design* (Harmondsworth: Pelican, 1937) p. 39.
14. Ibid., p. 231.
15. Clive Bell, *Art*, p. 28.
16. Fry, *Vision and Design*, p. 236.
17. *Cézanne*, p. 51.
18. Ibid., p. 79.
19. Roger Fry, *The Artist and Psychoanalysis* (London: Hogarth, 1924) p. 19.
20. Roger Fry, *The Arts of Painting and Sculpture* (London: Gollancz, 1932) pp. 20–1.
21. Roger Fry, *French, Flemish and British Art* (London: Chatto & Windus, 1951) p. 37.
22. *LF*, I, p. 189.
23. *LF*, II, p. 369.
24. Ibid., p. 501.
25. Mallarmé, p. 297.
26. *LF*, II, p. 594.

27. Ibid., p. 629.
28. Ibid., p. 524.
29. *Transformations*, p. 6.
30. A. C. Bradley, *Oxford Lectures on Poetry* (London: Macmillan, 1959) p. 19.
31. Fry, *French, Flemish and British Art*, p. 149.
32. *LF*, II, p. 534. (*Stimmung* = mood, atmosphere.)
33. *LW*, III, p. 69.
34. *LF*, II, p. 543.
35. Roger Fry, *A Sampler of Castile* (London: Hogarth, 1923) p. 39.
36. Ibid., p. v.
37. *LF*, II, p. 632.
38. Fry, *Sampler*, p. 16.
39. Clive Bell, *An Account of French Painting* (London: Chatto & Windus, 1931) p. 185.
40. *Proust*, pp. 11, 45.
41. Clive Bell, *Pot-Boilers* (London: Chatto & Windus, 1918) p. 206.
42. *Bloomsbury Group*, p. 228.
43. *LF*, I, p. 351.
44. Roger Fry, *Duncan Grant* (Harmondsworth: Penguin, 1944) pp. 13–14.
45. Roger Fry, 'Vanessa Bell and Othon Friesz', *New Statesman*, 3 June 1922, pp. 237–8.
46. Clive Bell, *Pot-Boilers*, p. 207.
47. Quoted in Shone, *Bloomsbury Portraits*, p. 230.
48. Fry, *The Arts of Painting and Sculpture*, pp. 154–5.
49. Ibid., p. 121.
50. *LF*, II, p. 515.
51. Clive Bell, *Essays, Poems and Letters* (London: Hogarth, 1938) p. 282.
52. Ibid., pp. 293–4.
53. Clive Bell, *Art*, p. 47.
54. Ibid., pp. 47–8.
55. Ibid., p. 54.
56. Fry, *Vision and Design*, p. 236.
57. Ibid., p. 236.
58. Fry, *The Artist and Psychoanalysis*, p. 12.
59. Virginia Woolf, *The Common Reader* (first series) (New York: Harcourt Brace Jovanovich, 1925) p. 155.
60. Fry, *The Artist and Psychoanalysis*, p. 19.
61. Ibid., p. 12.
62. *Transformations*, p. 10.
63. Roger Fry, 'Mr. Walter Sickert's Pictures at the Stafford Gallery', *The Nation*, 8 July 1911, p. 536.
64. Clive Bell, *Since Cézanne* (London: Chatto & Windus, 1929) pp. 111–12.
65. Clive Bell, *Civilisation and Old Friends* (Chicago and London: University of Chicago Press, 1973) p. 76.
66. Roger Fry, 'A New Theory of Art', *The Nation*, 7 March 1914, p. 938.
67. *Transformations*, p. 5.

CHAPTER TWO: TWO CONNECTIONS

1. *Nature of Beauty*, p. 63.
2. Stone, p. 56.
3. Spalding, p. 251.
4. *Roger Fry*, p. 284.
5. Ibid., p. 268.
6. *LF*, I, pp. 75–6. (*État d'âme* = state of soul.)
7. *Nature of Beauty*, pp. 66–7.
8. Ibid., p. 82.
9. *Transformations*, p. 9.
10. Ibid., p. 11.
11. *LW*, III, p. 316.
12. *LW*, IV, p. 49.
13. Ibid., p. 57.
14. *LW*, V, p. 85.
15. Charles Mauron, *Aesthetics and Psychology*, trs. Roger Fry and Katherine John (London: Hogarth, 1935) p. 22.
16. Ibid., p. 79.
17. Mallarmé, p. 290.
18. *Julian Bell: Essays, Poems and Letters*, ed. Quentin Bell (London: Hogarth, 1938) p. 253.
19. Ibid., p. 240.
20. Fur, II, p. 252.
21. Spalding, p. 27.
22. *Roger Fry*, p. 287.
23. E. M. Forster, *Goldsworthy Lowes Dickinson* (London: Edward Arnold, 1962) p. iv.
24. Ibid., p. 101.
25. *Roger Fry*, pp. 51–2. E. F. Benson described a party in Oscar Browning's rooms.
26. *Aspects*, p. 125.
27. Forster, *Dickinson*, p. 109.
28. Ibid., p. 111.
29. Ibid., p. 193.
30. Ibid., p. 216.
31. Introduction to *A Passage to India*, ed. Oliver Stallybrass (London: Edward Arnold, 1978) p. xvi.
32. Ibid., p. xxvi.

CHAPTER THREE: FORSTER AND THE ARTS

1. *Two Cheers*, p. 134.
2. Lionel Trilling, *E. M. Forster* (Norfolk, Conn.: New Directions, 1943) p. 184.
3. Introduction to the *Aeneid*, trs. Michael Oakley (London: J. M. Dent, 1957) pp. ix–x.
4. *LF*, II, p. 486.
5. Ibid., p. 555.

6. Ibid., p. 573.
7. *AH*, p. 49.
8. *Two Cheers*, p. 114.
9. Ibid., p. 137.
10. *AH*, p. 46.
11. *Two Cheers*, p. 17.
12. Ibid., p. 47.
13. Ibid., p. 68.
14. Ibid., p. 99.
15. Ibid., p. 284.
16. E. M. Forster, *Alexandria: A History and a Guide* (Gloucester, Mass.: Peter Smith, 1968) p. 115.
17. *Listener*, 19 Jan 1956, p. 111.
18. *Listener*, 26 Mar 1959, p. 551.
19. Oliver Stallybrass, *Aspects of E. M. Forster* (London: Edward Arnold, 1969) p. 81.
20. *Aspects*, p. 151.
21. Stallybrass, *Aspects of Forster*, pp. 82, 85.
22. *Two Cheers*, pp. 135–6.
23. *Aspects*, p. 154.
24. Ibid., p. 169.
25. Ibid., p. 103.
26. Ibid., p. 147.
27. Ibid., p. 76.
28. Ibid., p. 49.
29. Stone, p. 102.
30. Ibid., p. 121.
31. Colmer, p. 212.

CHAPTER FOUR: FORSTER'S NOVELS

1. Heine, p. 293.
2. Meyers, pp. 31–45.
3. *AH*, p. 25.
4. Meyers, p. 35. Philip seems to be responding correctly, however, in terms of Ghirlandaio's art as judged by Roger Fry in 1909: 'Ghirlandajo lacked not only all fervour of poetic conception but all sense of the significant movement and rhythm of the figure. He was almost as incapable of creating a real figure as he was of imagining an ''ideal'' head' (review of *Ghirlandajo* by G. S. Davies, *Burlington Magazine*, 14 March 1909, p. 370).
5. E. M. Forster, 'Anniversary Postscript', *Observer*, 27 July 1958, p. 15.
6. Ibid.
7. F. C. Crews, *'A Passage to India'*, in *Twentieth Century Interpretations of 'A Passage to India'*, ed. A. Rutherford (Englewood Cliffs, NJ: Prentice-Hall, 1970) p. 88.
8. Meyers, p. 44.
9. Forster, in *Observer*, 27 July 1958.
10. E. M. Forster, interview with David Jones, *Listener*, 1 Jan 1959.

11. S. P. Rosenbaum, '*The Longest Journey:* E. M. Forster's Refutation of Idealism', in *E. M. Forster: A Human Exploration*, ed. G. K. Das and John Beer (New York: New York University Press, 1979) pp. 52–3.
12. Virginia Woolf, in *CE*, I, p. 348.
13. Introduction to the Abinger edition of *Howards End* (London: Edward Arnold, 1973), p. xvii.
14. Ibid., p. xiii.
15. *CE*, I, p. 349.
16. R. N. Parkinson, 'The Inheritors; or a Single Ticket for Howards End', in *Forster: A Human Exploration*, p. 57.
17. E. M. Forster in a letter to Forrest Reid, quoted by P. N. Furbank in introduction to *Maurice* (Toronto: Macmillan, 1971) p. viii.
18. E. M. Forster, *The Hill of Devi* (London: Edward Arnold, 1953) p. 73.
19. *CE*, I, p. 351.
20. Stone, p. 345.
21. Ibid., pp. 343, 346.
22. Heine, p. 296.
23. Forster, *The Hill of Devi*, p. 155.
24. Ibid., p. 77.
25. Ibid., p. 108.
26. Ibid., p. 87.
27. Ibid., p. 116.
28. *Listener*, 10 Sep 1953, p. 420.
29. *Daily News and Leader*, 30 Apr 1915, p. 7.
30. John Beer, Foreword to G. K. Das, *E. M. Forster's India* (London: Macmillan, 1977) p. xi.
31. Benita Parry, '*A Passage to India:* Epitaph or Manifesto?', in *Forster: A Human Exploration*, p. 137.
32. Ibid.
33. Edwin Thumboo, 'E. M. Forster's *A Passage to India:* from Caves to Court', *Southern Review*, 9–10 (1976–7) 141.
34. Avrom Fleishman, 'Being and Nothing in *A Passage to India*', *Criticism*, 15 (1973) 125.
35. John Colmer, 'Promise and Withdrawal in *A Passage to India*', in *Forster: A Human Exploration*.
36. Michael Orange, 'Language and Silence in *A Passage to India*', ibid.
37. Interview with David Jones, *Listener*, 1 Jan 1959.

CHAPTER FIVE: FORSTER AND WOOLF

1. *D*, III, p. 24.
2. Fur, II, p. 143.
3. Fur, II, p. 18.
4. Bell, I, p. 171.
5. Bell, II, p. 133.
6. *D*, I, p. 295.
7. *D*, II, p. 96.
8. *LW*, III, p. 266.

9. Fur, II, p. 18.
10. Bell, II, p. 133.
11. *D*, II, p. 171.
12. Leonard Woolf, *An Autobiography* (London: Oxford University Press, 1980) II, pp. 423–4.
13. *LW*, IV, p. 218.
14. Fur, II, p. 18.
15. *AH*, p. 121.
16. *Aspects*, p. 27.
17. *CE*, II, pp. 51–2.
18. Bell, II, p. 134.
19. *CE*, I, p. 342.
20. *Two Cheers*, p. 252.
21. *LW*, III, p. 189.
22. *Two Cheers*, p. 254.
23. *CE*, IV, p. 210.
24. *AH*, pp. 39–40.

CHAPTER SIX: WOOLF AND PAINTING

1. *Three Guineas*, p. 158.
2. *LW*, I, p. 41.
3. Ibid., p. 170.
4. *LW*, II, p. 15.
5. *D*, I, p. 168.
6. *LW*, II, p. 377.
7. Ibid., p. 382.
8. *LW*, III, pp. 405–6.
9. *LW*, II, p. 592.
10. *LW*, V, p. 285.
11. *New Statesman and Nation*, 10 Aug 1940, p. 141.
12. *LW*, II, p. 385.
13. *LW*, V, p. 59.
14. *LW*, II, p. 46.
15. *LW*, V, p. 20.
16. *D*, I, p. 140.
17. *LW*, II, p. 197.
18. Ibid., pp. 77–8.
19. *D*, I, p. 80.
20. *D*, I, p. 225.
21. *LW*, II, p. 356.
22. *LW*, I, p. 475.
23. *LW*, II, p. 197.
24. Ibid., p. 257.
25. Ibid., p. 259.
26. Ibid., p. 428.
27. *LW*, III, p. 270.
28. Ibid., pp. 340–1.

29. *Bloomsbury Group*, pp. 169–73.
30. *LW*, V, p. 236.
31. *D*, I, p. 72.
32. *LW*, V, p. 354.
33. *CE*, III, p. 242. Here is Wendy Baron's account of Woolf's connection
with Sickert:

> On the few occasions when Virginia Woolf and Sickert met, each
> recognised the other as a kindred spirit. Virginia Woolf, talking to
> Sickert at a Bloomsbury party in 1923 where he had acted Hamlet,
> discovered that his extrovert gusto masked a workmanlike and totally
> committed artist with values the same as her own – and therefore right!
> She met him only once during the following ten years, again at a party,
> and found him rather toothless and set. Then, in 1933, a loan exhibi-
> tion of his work was held at Agnew's. Sickert . . . pressed Virginia
> Woolf to write about it. He may have divined that she was capable of
> refuting the approach to his art dictated by Roger Fry's assertion that
> things for Sickert 'have only their visual values, they are not symbols,
> they contain no key to unlock the secrets of the heart and spirit'. At first
> Virginia Woolf demurred, but Sickert dismissed her excuse – that
> being a writer painting was an alien art – as a Bloomsbury cliché: 'I am
> not a baker but I enjoy a good loaf', he retorted. She went to the
> exhibition armed with Sickert's written instruction that she should
> '*saute pardessus* all paint-box technical twaddle about art which has
> bored and will always bore everybody stiff. Write about it, the
> "humour and drama" you find in it. You would be the first to do so. *I
> have always been a literary painter*, thank goodness, like all the decent
> painters.' . . .
> By relating their respective crafts, by suggesting that just as the
> writer paints pictures with words so the painter describes words with
> paint, and by implying the sterility of criticism which concentrates
> exclusively on the formal components of a painting, she did exactly
> what Sickert had demanded. Was Sickert satisfied? He made no
> response. Virginia Woolf was neither surprised nor hurt. At the Clive
> Bell dinner she already suspected that he was changeable, forgetful,
> and as she later told Miss Ethel Sands, 'No doubt, now I've done his
> will, he'll commit me to the flames – that's what artists are –
> ungrateful, exacting, morbid, impossible. But I like his pictures.'
>
>   (*Duncan Grant and Bloomsbury* catalogue, Fine Art Society, 1975)

34. *LW*, II, p. 284.
35. Ibid., p. 429.
36. *LW*, V, p. 243.
37. *LW*, II, p. 368.
38. Virginia Woolf, *Moments of Being*, ed. J. Schulkind (Brighton: Sussex
University Press, 1976) p. 113.
39. Ibid., p. 122.
40. Ibid., p. 71.
41. Ibid., pp. 114–15.

42. Ibid., p. 66.
43. Ibid., p. 98.
44. Ibid., p. 75.
45. Ibid., p. 42.
46. Ibid., pp. 40, 85.
47. *LW*, I, p. 356.
48. *CE*, III, p. 241.
49. *LW*, III, p. 135.
50. *LW*, III, p. 133.
51. *CE*, III, pp. 129–30.
52. *CE*, II, p. 2.
53. Ibid., p. 9.
54. Ibid., p. 25.
55. Ibid., p. 68.
56. Virginia Woolf, *Books and Portraits*, ed. Mary Lyon (London: Hogarth, 1977) p. 164.
57. *CE*, I, p. 75.
58. Ibid., p. 169.
59. Ibid., p. 305.
60. Ibid., p. 354.
61. Ibid., p. 55.
62. *CE*, III, p. 228.
63. *CE*, I, p. 346.
64. Patricia Stubbs, *Women and Fiction* (Brighton, Sussex: Harvester Press, 1979) p. 233.

CHAPTER SEVEN: WOOLF'S NOVELS

1. Bell, I, p. 209 (letter of Clive Bell to Woolf, 1909).
2. L. A. De Salvo, *Virginia Woolf's First Voyage* (Totowa, NJ: Rowman & Littlefield, 1980) p. 158.
3. *WD*, p. 24.
4. Bell, I, Appendix D, p. 208.
5. Ibid., p. 209.
6. Ibid., II, p. 28.
7. *AH*, p. 121.
8. *D*, I, p. 240.
9. *LW*, II, p. 82.
10. Katherine Mansfield, *Novels and Novelists* (London: Constable, 1930) p. 111.
11. *WD*, p. 10.
12. *AH*, p. 122.
13. *WD*, pp. 20–1.
14. *WD*, p. 19.
15. *LW*, II, pp. 394, 400.
16. E. M. Forster, in *AH*, p. 123.
17. *D*, II, p. 214.
18. Allen McLaurin, *Virginia Woolf* (Cambridge University Press, 1973) p. 127.

19. Alice van Buren Kelly, *The Novels of Virginia Woolf* (Chicago: University of Chicago Press, 1973) p. 79.
20. Hermione Lee, *The Novels of Virginia Woolf* (London: Methuen, 1977) pp. 89–90.
21. *Virginia Woolf*, ed. Ralph Freedman (Berkeley, Calif.: University of California Press, 1980) p. 131.
22. *WD*, p. 13.
23. David Daiches, *Virginia Woolf* (New York: New Directions, 1942) p. 61.
24. *English Literature and British Philosophy*, ed. S. P. Rosenbaum (University of Chicago Press, 1971) p. 326.
25. Woolf, *Books and Portraits*, p. 207.
26. *D*, II, p. 14.
27. Quoted in *English Literature and British Philosophy*, p. 327.
28. Quoted in ibid., p. 331.
29. *Cézanne*, p. 42.
30. Lee, *Novels of Virginia Woolf*, p. 87.
31. *D*, II, p. 92.
32. Ibid., p. 14.
33. *Cézanne*, p. 61.
34. *Transformations*, p. 7.
35. *WD*, p. 78.
36. *WD*, p. 77.
37. *WD*, p. 52.
38. *WD*, pp. 54, 58, 60, 61, 66.
39. *WD*, p. 69.
40. Seymour Chatman, 'The Structure of Narrative Transmission', in *Style and Structure in Literature*, ed. Roger Fowler (Oxford: Blackwell, 1975) p. 254.
41. Avrom Fleishman, *Virginia Woolf: A Critical Reading* (Baltimore: Johns Hopkins University Press, 1975) pp. 70–3.
42. Ibid., p. 81.
43. H. Marder, *Feminism and Art* (University of Chicago Press, 1968), argues that Woolf's doctrinaire attitude caused her to look away from life itself (p. 50).
44. Fleishman, *Woolf: A Critical Reading*, p. 80.
45. O. P. Sharma, 'Feminism as Aesthetic Vision: A Study of Virginia Woolf's *Mrs Dalloway*', *Women's Studies*, 3 (1975) 68.
46. Quoted in C. G. Hoffmann, 'From Short Story to Novel: The Manuscript Revisions of Virginia Woolf's *Mrs Dalloway*', *Modern Fiction Studies*, 14, no. 2 (Summer 1968) 174.
47. Quoted ibid., p. 183.
48. *Two Cheers*, p. 254 ('Virginia Woolf' [1941]).
49. Ibid., p. 254.
50. *D*, III, pp. 18–19.
51. Ibid., p. 208.
52. Keith May, 'The Symbol of Painting in Virginia Woolf's *To the Lighthouse*', *Research in English Literature*, 8 (1967) 98.
53. *D*, III, p. 34.
54. Ibid., p. 36.
55. Ibid., p. 38.

56. Ibid., p. 132.
57. *Cézanne*, p. 73.
58. Allen McLaurin, 'A Note on Lily Briscoe's Painting in *To the Lighthouse*', *Notes & Queries*, 26 (1979) 338–40.
59. E. M. Forster, *Pharos and Pharillon* (1923; rpt. Hogarth, 1967) p. 20.
60. Ibid., p. 18.
61. *D*, III, p. 106.
62. John Roberts, 'Vision and Design in Virginia Woolf', *PMLA*, LXI (1946) 847.
63. *CE*, IV, p. 229.
64. Ibid., p. 231.
65. Ibid., p. 234.
66. *LW*, III, p. 429.
67. *D*, III, p. 157.
68. Ibid., pp. 167–8.
69. *WD*, p. 136.
70. Clifton Snider, 'A Single Self: a Jungian Interpretation of Virginia Woolf's *Orlando*', *Modern Fiction Studies*, 25 (1979–80) 266.
71. James Naremore, *The World Without a Self* (New Haven, Conn.: Yale University Press, 1973) pp. 202, 216.
72. *CE*, IV, pp. 224–5.
73. Ibid., pp. 225–6.
74. Herbert Marder, *Feminism and Art* (Chicago: University of Chicago Press, 1968) p. 114.
75. *Nature of Beauty*, pp. 66–7.
76. Daiches, *Virginia Woolf*, p. 111.
77. *D*, III, p. 139.
78. *WD*, p. 143.
79. Ibid., p. 142.
80. Ibid., p. 139.
81. Ibid., p. 143.
82. Ibid., p. 147.
83. *D*, III, p. 285.
84. *WD*, p. 156.
85. *D*, III, p. 300.
86. *WD*, p. 175.
87. Ibid., p. 159.
88. Ibid., p. 163.
89. Ibid., p. 169.
90. Ibid., p. 173.
91. Daiches, *Virginia Woolf*, p. 108.
92. *WD*, p. 137.
93. *WD*, p. 162.
94. *Cézanne*, p. 43.
95. Winifred Holtby, *Virginia Woolf* (London, 1932) p. 195.
96. *WD*, p. 137.
97. Heine, p. 299. She goes on quite wrongly to assert, 'It is Bernard, an artist, who reaches the final understanding. Having done this, he welcomes death' (p. 300).

98. James Hafley, *The Glass Roof* (Berkeley, Calif.: University of California Press, 1954) p. 127.
99. *WD*, p. 162.
100. Ibid., p. 158.
101. Mario Praz, *Mnemosyne* (Princeton, NJ: Princeton University Press, 1970) p. 188.
102. *D*, III, p. 316.
103. *Oxford Companion to Music*, ed. Percy Scholes (Oxford: Clarendon Press, 1970) p. 146.
104. Ibid., p. 376.
105. *New Grove Dictionary of Music*, ed. Stanley Sadie (London: Macmillan, 1980) II, p. 389.
106. Martin Cooper, *Beethoven: The Last Decade* (London: Oxford University Press, 1970) p. 401.
107. *D*, III, pp. 156–7.
108. *D*, III, pp. 291–2.
109. Mary Shanahan, in 'The Artist and the Resolution of *The Waves*', *Modern Language Quarterly*, 36 (1975), works hard to fit Bernard's final speech into a more profound pattern than the one of the eight sections or the seven-sided flower. She argues that Bernard finally joins into the 'contrapuntal' rhythm of the waves: 'as the images he incorporates emphasize the motion of the waves, they further reinforce the larger structural design of the novel and so suggest that in the end *The Waves* as art piece belongs to the storyteller, not to his creator' (pp. 71–2). But such a reading distorts the effect of Bernard's speech, which is one of disruption, bewilderment, exhaustion and a loss of pattern.
110. *WD*, p. 189.
111. *WD*, p. 278. The most obvious textual connection between the two books is the reference to *Antigone*. In her footnote in *Three Guineas*, Woolf argues that Sophocles was a great artist because he sympathised even with Creon. Art which serves propaganda, she suggests, is like a mule compared to a horse (p. 302). In *The Years* Woolf treats the issue of feminism with the impartiality of a Sophocles.

    Other literary echoes include the mention of Crosby the servant (p. 234); the photographs from the Spanish Civil War; the procession of learned men; and the request for the correspondent to see the world from the threshold of a private house (p. 34), which reminds us of the front door of Abercorn Terrace. But there is also the tripartite division of *Three Guineas*, and the description of the ideal poet making 'unity out of multiplicity' (p. 260), which could apply to the writer of *The Years*.
112. *WD*, p. 210.
113. *WD*, p. 234.
114. *WD*, p. 239.
115. *WD*, p. 261.
116. *WD*, p. 266.
117. *WD*, p. 273.
118. 'Roger Fry', in *CE*, IV, p. 92.
119. *WD*, p. 280.
120. *WD*, p. 281.

121. Quoted in Victoria Middleton, *'The Years:* "A Deliberate Failure"',
      Bulletin of the New York Public Library, 80 (Winter 1977) 160.
122. 'Walter Sickert', in *CE*, II, p. 240.
123. Middleton, in *Bulletin of the New York Public Library*, 80, p. 165.
124. Ibid., p. 169.
125. Mitchell Leaska, 'Virginia Woolf, the Pargeter', ibid., p. 176.
126. Joanna Lipking, 'Looking at the Monuments: Woolf's Satiric Eye', ibid.,
      p. 142.
127. Margaret Comstock, 'The Loudspeaker and the Human Voice: Politics
      and the Form of *The Years*', ibid., p. 252.
128. *LW*, VI, p. 391.
129. *WD*, pp. 289–90.
130. *LW*, VI, p. 294.
131. *WD*, p. 311.
132. Ibid., p. 359.
133. A. Y. Wilkinson, 'A Principle of Unity in *Between the Acts*', *Criticism*, 8
      (1966) 53.
134. Don Summerhayes, 'Society, Meaning, Analogy: Virginia Woolf's World
      Between the Acts', *Modern Fiction Studies*, 9 (1963–4).
135. Stephen Fox, 'The Fish Pond as Symbolic Centre in *Between the Acts*',
      ibid., 18 (1972).
136. Nancy Bazin, *Virginia Woolf and the Androgynous Vision* (New Brunswick,
      NJ: Rutgers University Press, 1973) pp. 220–1.

CONCLUSION

  1. *CE*, II, p. 242.
  2. *LW*, I, p. 60.
  3. Ibid., p. 274.
  4. M. S. Shanahan, *'Between the Acts:* Virginia Woolf's Final Endeavour in
      Art', *Texas Studies in Literature and Language*, 14 (Spring 1972) 138.
  5. R. S. Cammarota, 'Musical Analogy and Internal Design in *A Passage to
      India*', *English Literature in Transition*, 18 (1975) 39–46.
  6. Clive Bell, *Since Cézanne* (London: Chatto & Windus, 1929) p. 106.
  7. Ibid., pp. 109–10.
  8. Quoted by Hoffman, in *Modern Fiction Studies*, 14, no. 2, p. 183.
  9. *LW*, V, p. 116.
 10. *Dehumanization of Art*, p. 86.
 11. D. S. Savage, *The Withered Branch* (London: Eyre & Spottiswoode, 1950)
      p. 71.
 12. *Proust*, p. 45.
 13. Ibid., p. 53.
 14. *CE*, II, p. 228.
 15. Ibid., p. 272.
 16. *Roger Fry*, p. 227.
 17. Virginia Woolf, *A Room of One's Own* (Harmondsworth: Penguin, 1945)
      pp. 43, 72, 77.
 18. Ibid., p. 108.

19. *D*, III, p. 218.
20. *Roger Fry*, p. 227.
21. Spalding, p. 212.
22. Jacqueline Thayer, 'Virginia Woolf: From Impressionism to Abstract Art' (unpublished dissertation, University of Tulsa, 1977) p. 22.
23. *Victorian Photographers*, ed. Tristram Powell (London: Hogarth, 1973) p. 18.
24. *Roger Fry*, p. 240.
25. *Daily News*, 19 Mar 1919.
26. *Daily News*, 23 Apr 1919.
27. Alan Wilde, *Art and Life* (New York: New York University Press, 1964) p. 159.
28. Colmer, *Forster: The Personal Voice*, p. 212.
29. Glen Cavaliero, *A Reading of E. M. Forster* (London: Macmillan, 1979) p. 37.
30. Austin Warren, *Rage for Order* (Ann Arbor: University of Michigan Press, 1959) p. 122.
31. Wilde, *Art and Life*, p. 13.
32. *Writers at Work*, ed. Malcom Cowley (New York: Viking, 1958) p. 28.
33. *Guardian Weekly*, 20 June 1970, p. 16.
34. E. M. Forster, *Pharos and Pharillon* (London: Hogarth, 1923) p. 83.
35. *Aspects*, p. 170.
36. F. P. W. McDowell, 'E. M. Forster's Theory of Literature', *Criticism*, 8 (1966) 21.
37. *CE*, II, p. 8.
38. *Two Cheers*, p. 126.
39. Interview with David Jones, *Listener*, 1 Jan 1959, pp. 11–12.
40. *Roger Fry*, pp. 295–6.
41. Mark Golding, 'Virginia Woolf and the Critic as Reader', in *Virginia Woolf*, ed. Claire Sprague (Englewood Cliffs, NJ: Prentice-Hall, 1971) p. 161.
42. Virginia Woolf, *The Moment and Other Essays* (New York: Harcourt Brace Jovanovich, 1974) p. 173.
43. Ibid., p. 175.
44. Ibid., p. 176.
45. Ibid., p. 178.

Index